ADVANCE PRAISE FOR
THE BAD CATHOLIC'S GUIDE TO GOOD LIVING

If I had not been given a free copy of this book, I would have bought it, but I would have done it online or in disguise at a bookstore. I certainly will give it to many friends, but anonymously. Unfortunately, I still have remnants of a respectable reputation to preserve. This book is outrageous. . . . What rescues it is that it is not based on a sophomoric parody of Catholic exaggeration, but on a clear love for the sheer facticity of Catholicism. Their contribution to the "new evangelization" may not be exactly what the Holy Father and the bishops have in mind, but it is certainly based on the same point of departure: Christianity as a wondrous event and not a discourse.

> —**Msgr. Lorenzo Albacete,** theologian and author, former president of the Pontifical Catholic University of Puerto Rico, and professor at the John Paul II Institute for Studies in Marriage and Family

Truth is often hard to distill from the thousands of self help and life style books available today, but I am happy to say that I have found my mantra in *The Bad Catholic's Guide to Good Living*. Silly some of the time, respectful most of the time and hilarious all of the time, even the squirrel recipes sound delicious and will have me driving slower through the red states on the two lane road all the way to Mardi Gras.

> —**Mario Batali,** chef, host of "Molto Mario," "Mario Eats Italy," and "Ciao America" on the Food Network, author, *The Babbo Cookbook*

All saints suffer one way or another but there are no sad saints. As this book makes clear, some more than others had the gift of "laetitia" or earthly gladness which, by not being lived as an end in itself, points the way to "beatitude" or heavenly joy.

> —**Rev. George Rutler,** author theologian, host, Eternal Word Television Network

It isn't often that a book comes along that forces you to laugh as hard as it makes you believe—Mr. Zmirak and Miss Matychowiak have produced such a book. Its irreverence is not toward Catholicism. Instead, it is a book that laughs its head off at the crazy world around us that denies the Faith. Because they believe in the Catholic religion, the authors feel no need to pretend belief in anything else—and everything comes in for a skewering, from modern notions of respectability to sheer bad taste. But mixed in with the banter are solid Church teaching, history, and custom. Oh, yes—and the food and drink recipes are delicious. This book brings home Belloc's dictum that "wherever the Catholic sun doth shine, there's laughter and music and good red wine."

> —**Charles A. Coulombe, KCStS,** Author of *Vicars of Christ: A History of the Popes*, former contributing editor, *National Catholic Register*

For thirty years, heavy-handed works of "humor" by lapsed-Catholic writers have been a dime a dozen. Thanks to Zmirak and Matychowiak's uproarious cornucopia of Catholic fun, now we can laugh ourselves up and out of that literary purgatory. Their sharp-witted irreverence seldom fails to amuse—because they know the Church so well, and love her so dearly.

> —**Thomas McArdle,** White House speechwriter, former communications director, the Catholic League for Civil and Religious Rights

I have long thought it significant that Our Lord's first public miracle was turning water, a dull liquid in which fish fornicate, into glorious wine. That's my kind of Christianity. John and Denise understand that an authentic Catholic life is one of fasting and feasting, to the point of cheerfulness, in anticipation of the great wedding banquet in heaven.

> —**Rod Dreher,** editorial writer, *The Dallas Morning News*

It is important that Catholics insist upon how orthodox this book is, so as to chase non-Catholics away from reading it. For the non-Catholic there are too many calories, and too many trade secrets.

> —**Richard Cowden Guido,** veteran Catholic journalist, author of *John Paul II & the Battle for Vatican II*

Imagine Mel Gibson crossed with Monty Python—a hilarious, in your face, *Late-Nite Latin Mass.*

> —**Angelo Matera,** Publisher, Godspy.com, former CEO of the *National Catholic Register*

Bad Catholics beware, Zmirak and Matychowiak have a hidden agenda: to make you better Catholics. Beneath the puns, ribaldry, and hilariously apt (and no doubt delicious) feast-day recipes lie a profound reverence for—and knowledge of—the Church, her saints, her teachings, and her traditions. Whether you're the 'lapsed' kind of bad Catholic, or just the sinful kind like me, this guide will put you back on the straight and narrow.

> —**Jeffrey Rubin,** editor, Conservative Book Club; former editor, the *Latin Mass* and *Susum Corda* magazines

The ideas outlined here for food and fun are zany, sophisticated, and delightful! How many guides to seasonal cooking urge their readers to flambé chickens, smother squirrels, put antidepressants in the punch bowl and sell indulgences? Not nearly enough, if you ask me.

> —**Georges Briguet,** proprietor, Le Perigord, NYC, which opened April 1, 1964.

This ingenious guide will leave you educated and entertained. A comical yet dignified must-read.

> —**Erik Blauberg,** chef, *(www.erikblauberg.com),* former Executive Chef, The 21 Club.

The *Bad*
Catholic's
Guide to
Good Living

The Bad
Catholic's
Guide to
Good Living

A Loving Look at
the Lighter Side of the Catholic Faith,
with Recipes for Feasts and Fun

JOHN ZMIRAK
&
DENISE MATYCHOWIAK

A Crossroad Book
The Crossroad Publishing Company
New York

The Crossroad Publishing Company
16 Penn Plaza, Suite 1550, New York, NY 10001

Printed in the United States of America

Library of Congress Cataloging-in-Publication Data

Zmirak, John.
  The bad Catholic's guide to good living / John Zmirak and Denise Matychowiak.
    p. cm.
    ISBN 0-8245-2300-8 (alk. paper)
  1. Christian saints--Biography. 2. Fasts and feasts--Catholic Church--Humor. I. Matychowiak, Denise.
II. Title.

  BX4655.3.Z55 2005
  248.4'82'0207--dc22

2005016088

  3   4   5   6   7   8   9   10   10   09   08   07   06   05

God has given us the papacy:
Let us enjoy it.

—Pope Leo X—

Contents

Pope John Paul II (1920–2005): A Tribute to His Humor   xiii

Introduction by Pope Alexander VI   xv

Acknowledgments and Dedication   xvii

January

The Holy Name of Jesus Fish   1

     RECIPE: Jasmine-Scented Tilapia   2

Elizabeth Ann Seton (1774–1821): Shush . . . Don't Attract God's Attention   2

John Neumann (1811–1860): Not Just President of the Relic Club—
   He's a Member   4

Epiphany and Carnival: The Work Ethic Be Damned   6

     RECIPES: Smothered Squirrel, King Cake, Sazeracs   10

Marguerite Bourgeous (1620–1700): Be Careful What You Wish For   12

Sacramental Executive Summary #1: Baptism   13

     RECIPE: Pesto with Gnocchi   14

February

Brigid of Ireland (453–523): A Nun Gets a Makeover   15

The Purification of Mary and Presentation of Jesus: Holy Groundhogs!   16

Agatha: A Feast of Breasts   18

     RECIPES: St. Agatha Popovers, Minni di Virgini   19

Bonus Saint: Pius IX (1792–1878): Just Say "Nono."   21

Clare of Rimini (1282–1346): Bite Your Tongue   22

Julian the Hospitaller (Dates Unknown): Fiddlers, Murderers, and
   Circus Clowns   23

Valentine: If It Feels Good . . . Stop It!   24

March

Cunegundes (+1040): A Holy Hot-Foot   30

Katherine Drexel: What You Get for Pestering the Pope   31

Frances of Rome (1384–1440): Exorcise that Gremlin!   32

John Ogilvie (1579–1615): Death before Haggis   33

Serafina (+1253): Bring Yapping Dogs to the Housebound   33

Patrick: Bobbing for Potatoes   34

    RECIPES: Salt Roasted Shrimp in the Shells, Apple Oatmeal Crumble   37

Joseph: He Couldn't Get No Respect   38

    RECIPE: St. Joseph's Day Fava Beans   39

Sibyllina Biscossi (1287–1367): Patroness of Church Ladies   39

The Annunciation: Salvation is from a J.A.P.   40

A Bowl of Mary, with Virgin Oil   41

    RECIPE: Virgin Petal Salad   42

Season of Lent   42

Shrove Tuesday: Pancakes and Proxy Penance   42

    RECIPES: Crepes with Strawberries in Orange Sauce,
        Blueberry Pomegranate Sauce   44

Ash Wednesday: Catholic Mating Identification Day   46

Top Ten Catholic Pick-Up Lines   47

    RECIPE: "Here's My Number, I Think You're Kind of Hot"
        Cross Buns   48

Not Particularly Penitential Recipes for Lent   49

    RECIPES: Mussels in White Wine, Spinach with Raisins and
        Pine Nuts, Potatoes Aoli, Shrimp in Garlic Sauce, Manchego
        Cheese and Quince Paste, Cuban Style Black Bean and
        Rice Soup, Soft Olive Oil Bread, Provençal Bouillabaisse   49

April

Isidore of Seville (560–636): Urban Legendary   53

Lidwina of Schiedam (1380–1433): Let's Go Skating, Kids!   54

Bernadette of Lourdes (1844–1879): Kitsch and Miracles   54

Expeditus (dates unknown): Saint Overnight of Delivery   56

Agnes of Montepulciano (1268–1317): The Flying Nun   56

Bonus Saint: John Payne (1574–1582): So Long and Thanks for the Martyrs   57

Catherine of Siena (1347–1380): Grabbing the Pope by the Collar   58

Holy Week and Easter   59

Holy Thursday: Sangria in the Streets   59

    RECIPE: Holy Thursday Sangria   60

Good Friday: No Laughing, No Talking, No Showing Your Teeth   61

Jesus's Reproaches from the Cross   62

Celebrate the Resurrection: Roasting the Easter Bunny   63

      RECIPES: Tangy Plum Soup, Beet Salad, Eggplant Salad,
          Spring Potato Salad, Resurrection Cheese Cake, Cheese Pascha,
          Easter Bunny Fricassee   65

Sacramental Executive Summary #2: The Eucharist   69

      RECIPE: Baby Jesus Cookies   71

May

Filling the May Hole   72

Athanasius (295–373): But Don't Quote Him on That . . .   73

The Feast of the Holy Shroud: Property of J. Arimathea Funeral Home,
   Inc.—Do Not Remove   74

Damien of Molokai (1840–1889): Father Damien and Mr. Hyde   75

      RECIPE: Pineapple and Torrontes Compote   76

Ascension Thursday: Did Christ Fly Standby?   77

Fatima: Our Lady in the Sky with Diamonds   77

Dymphna (dates unknown): A Halfway House Party   79

      RECIPES: Shrimp in Crazy Water, Lunatic Cookies, Coco-"Nut"
          Sorbet   83

Simon Stock (1165–1265): Eternal Life Insurance   84

Madron (+540): The Saint of Lost Socks   84

Simeon Stylites the Younger (521–597): A Treehouse for Dad   85

Martyrs of Mexico (+1926): Trash for the Temple   86

June

Kevin (498–618): Milking the Wolf   88

Boniface (680–754): St. Paul Bunyan   88

Onuphrius (+440): Hermits at Houlihan's   89

Anthony of Padua (1195–1231): The Celestial Lost and Found   90

Cyriacus of Iconium (+304): Baby Got Boar   91

      RECIPE: Roast Pork   91

Sacramental Executive Summary #3: Confession   92

Hypatius (+450): Boycott the Olympics   93

Juliana Falconieri (1270–1341): Little Miss Perfect   94

      RECIPE: Nun's Farts   95

The Birth of John the Baptist: Charging Bulls and Naked Sambas   96
        RECIPE: Red Wine Tapioca Pudding   97
The Feast of Pentecost: Flaming Punch and Speaking in Tongues   98
        RECIPES: Flaming Spinach Salad, Saganaki (Greek Flaming Cheese)   102

July

Independence Day: Dress Your Kids as Kennedys   103
Benedict of Nursia (480–547): Enjoy a Dominican with Your Benedictine   105
Bastille Day: Vive le Roi!   106
        RECIPES: Bay Scallops with Cherry Tomatoes, Cheesecake with
            Chèvre and Nectarines   109
Margaret of Antioch (fourth century) and Wilgefortis (dates unknown):
    The Dragon Lady and the Bearded Nun   110
Mary Magdalene (first century): Toot-toot, hey, beep-beep!   111
Christina of Bolsena (+250), Christina of Tyre (dates unknown),
    and Christina the Astonishing (1150–1224): The Terminator Saints   112
Sacramental Executive Summary #4: Confirmation   112
Anne (first century): God's Grandma, the Yenta   114

August

Jean Baptiste Marie Vianney (1786–1859): The Penance Express   115
The Transfiguration: Trinkets on Mt. Tabor   116
Dominic (1170–1221): Hound of Heaven   117
        RECIPE: Quatres Mendiants   118
Lawrence (+258): Sanctity, Slow-Cooked   119
Feast of the Assumption: The Vatican Space Program   120
        RECIPES: Yiouvetsi Lamb with Orzo Pasta, Simnel Cake   124
Sarah (Old Testament): The Power of Laughter   125
Rose of Lima (1586–1617) and Ebbe the Abbess (+879): Eternal Makeovers   126
Genesius (+286): Roman Snuff   127
Monica (322–387) and Phanourios (dates unknown): Saintly Spam   128
        RECIPE: St. Phanourios Bread (Phanouropita)   128
Raymond Nonnatus (1204–1240): Seen but Not Heard   129
Sacramental Executive Summary #5: Matrimony   130

September

Giles (eighth century): Gather the Rams   134

Marinus (fifth century): The Saint of Restraining Orders   134

Magnus of Füssen (700–750): Bear-Claws for the Bears' Claws   135

     RECIPE: German Honey-Cakes for Bears   136

Exaltation of the Holy Cross: Sacred Splinters   137

Hildegard of Bingen (1098–1179): Polyphony for Bikers   138

Joseph of Cupertino (1603–1663): The Flying Piñata   139

Gennaro (+305): Take His Head to the Volcano   141

Andrew Kim Taegon (+1846): Of Martyrs and Rotting Cabbage   142

Martyrs of the Spanish Civil War (1936): Homage to Valencia   144

     RECIPE: Arroz Negre   145

Padre Pio (1887–1968): Warning—Soul Reader!   146

Vincent de Paul (1580–1660): "Godfather of the Soul"   147

Bernardine of Feltre (1439–1494): Holy Pawnshop!   148

The Holy Archangels: Flying Two-Year Olds   150

     RECIPE: Devil's Food Cake   152

October

Therese of Lisieux (1873–1897): Carmel-Covered Corn   153

The Guardian Angels: Avon Calling!   154

Francis of Assisi (1181–1226): Flogging "Brother Ass"   156

Bartholomew Longo (1841–1926): Highway to Hell   158

Lepanto Bowl Upset: "Hail Mary" Helps BVM Pulverize Saracens 72–6   160

Kenny (Canice) (515–600): Sacred Pest Control   161

Bertrand of Comminges (+1123): Imposing Celibacy on the French   162

North American Martyrs (+1642–1649): Typhoid Mary and Jesus   163

     RECIPE: Warm Indian Pudding with Ice Cream   165

Sacramental Executive Summary #6: Holy Orders   165

Karl I of Austria (1887–1922): Vote Habsburg!   167

Bonus Saint: Ursula (dates unknown): The Saint of Slasher Movies   168

John of Capistrano (1386–1456): Homeland Security   170

British Martyrs (1535–1679): Atrocities? We've Got Atrocities. . . .   171

Jude (first century): A Saint for Your Brother-in-Law   172

All Hallows' Eve: The Seven Deadly Courses   174

     RECIPES: Flaming Purgatory Punch, Stuffed Dates   177

Bonus Celebration: Sell Indulgences   178

November

All Saints' Day: Tomb of the Unknown Saint   181

The Feast of All Souls: A Black-Letter Day   182

Sacramental Executive Summary #7 Sacrament of the Sick   183

RECIPE: Lengthy Wake Rice Krispies Treats   184

Hubert (656–728): Bring Out Your Beagles   184

Bonus Saint: Martin de Porres (1579–1639): A Friend to Vermin   185

Guy Fawkes Day: Go Out with a Bang   186

Viennese Carnival: Pretzel Crowns and Explosives   188

RECIPE: Fastnachts   189

Bonus Saint: Martin of Tours (316–397): Goose-Strangling in the Suburbs   190

RECIPE: Garlic Soup   191

Livinus (+633): Speaking in Tongue   192

Cecilia (+117): Cleaning Out the Choir Stalls   192

Thanksgiving: Thank God for Mediocrity   194

The First Sunday of Advent: Scrooge You   195

December

Francis Xavier (1506–1552): A Piece of the Saint   197

Barbara (+235): Death from Above!   199

Nicholas (+346): Kids in a Barrel   199

Feast of the Immaculate Conception: The Addams Family Chapel   201

RECIPE: Dead Men's Bones   202

Our Lady of Guadalupe (1531): Bleeding Hearts, Liberated   202

RECIPE: Aztec Truffle Fondue   204

Lucy of Syracuse (+269): Blind Man's Buffet   205

John of the Cross (1542–1591): The Saint of OCD   206

Adam and Eve: Schmucks!   207

The Twelve Days of Christmas: One Fibber Fibbing   209

The Nativity: Christmas on the West Bank   210

RECIPES: Feta Cheese Cigarettes, Chicken with Apricots   212

The Circumcision of Christ (Vigil): No Skin Off His Nose   213

About the Authors   216

Pope John Paul II (1920–2005)

A Tribute to His Humor

As you might have noticed, on the cover of this book is a famous picture of the late Pope John Paul, horsing around with photographers early in his pontificate. In the picture, he is young, cheerful, playful—clearly having a ball. To those of us who came of age in the 1970s and 1980s, this is how we will forever think of this pope. For us, he will always be the man in white skiing and climbing in the Italian Alps, traipsing gleefully through adoring crowds in Communist Poland, and bending over to kiss the tarmac in places like New York, New Guinea, even New Jersey. We recall his vigor and his humor—how he joked with crowds of us teenagers at Madison Square Garden, responding to our cheers with his own playful cry of "Woo, woo, woo!" how he lapsed into Roman "street" dialect during a speech to tease the local clergy, how he stole Bono's sunglasses (relic hunting?).

We also think of this pope as the great advocate of the lay Catholic—the ordinary churchgoer. He gave us better bishops, a clear new Catechism, and a voice for peace in times of war. He also spoke up—frequently and eloquently—for the sanctity of married sexuality, creating a whole new theological movement devoted to exploring the graces that the Church teaches come to couples *through* (not despite) their acts of mutual love.

And yes, of course, Pope John Paul helped create the movement that brought down the Iron Curtain. It's easy to take that for granted—unless you think back to what it felt like to live your whole life under the atomic gun. From childhood on, we remember always assuming that we knew how we would die: along with the whole human race, in a thermonuclear war. Dreams came and went, of falling missiles, blinding flashes, and radioactive rubble. It was not until 1989, the great year made possible by Solidarity and this pope, that these visions began to fade.

This man who resisted the Nazis and the Communists also spoke out against the new threats to the sanctity of life and the human person, from terrorism and extremism to euthanasia and human cloning. Having made impossible Orwell's nightmare of *1984*, the pope did his best to save us from the advent of Huxley's *Brave New World*. It will remain to his successors and to us to carry on this fight—a subtler battle against the tyranny not of the Soviets but of the self.

We never sent this book to the pope to read; in his heroic struggle with the illness brought on by an assassination attempt, we thought he had more important things to do than peruse a humorous cookbook of the saints. (No, we don't have recipes for sautéed saint.) But we feel confident that if he'd been granted the time to read it, he would have given that old Slavic grin we remember so fondly from his younger, stronger days and said, infallibly, "Woo, woo, woo."

Introduction

by Pope Alexander VI

When the authors presented me with this book, I was delighted. There aren't enough believing Catholics nowadays who are willing to laugh at themselves. Sometimes it seems that those who laugh don't believe, and those who believe, don't laugh. We need more writers who can do both—who can chew gum and pray, at the same time. In other words, where is the Catholic Jackie Mason?

The writers are strange birds indeed: postmodern New Yorkers who watch *The Simpsons*—then cook elaborate French meals on Bastille Day in honor of Marie Antoinette. Well-read, faithful lay Catholics who see the lives of most saints as "cautionary tales." People who go to Confession regularly—but shop around for priests who don't speak English. We haven't seen many Catholics like this since the good old days of Erasmus and Rabelais. Though Chesterton comes to mind. And Walker Percy—one of whose heroes confesses, "I love bourbon and women best, God next, and my neighbor least of all." As they say in any number of those admirable recovery groups meeting in church basements around the world even as you read this, *the first step is admitting it*. One of the greatest problems in the Church over the centuries has been what we theologians call Pelagianism. It's the idea that God has established a set of perfectly reasonable rules, which are entirely within our power to obey—and if we don't, it's just because we're weaklings. We don't belong in the Church—which is a club for saints. On this model, the Church is like a gourmet health spa for Olympic athletes—or the gym run by Ben Stiller[1] in the recent, wonderful movie *Dodgeball.* A place of rippling muscles, cardiovascular efficiency, and a great deal of sweating and grunting.

Any priest who has spent time hearing confessions knows better, of course. So should every self-reflective believer. In fact, the Church is less like a gymnasium than a trauma ward for gut-shot sinners. The gurneys and chairs are full of patients with varying levels of injury, while the doctors are spattered with blood. And Christ is less like an elite surgeon than the ultimate organ donor. So Catholic humor, while perfectly possible, ought to resemble the dark humor surgeons employ at the operating

---

1. I should caution you here that the esteemed authors of this book regard Stiller's *Zoolander* as the "perfect film" and judge all others from 1 to 10 on the "*Zoolander*" scale."

table—for instance, when they make a kidney they've just removed into a little talking puppet. . . .

The authors seem to understand this. The "rules" laid out for man are completely impossible for him to obey in his fallen condition. Even with constant help from God, he does a pretty lousy job. The sacraments help, of course—in fact, they're absolutely necessary—but people screw up all the time nevertheless, even priests. (Imagine that.) As for Catholic countries: think of Italy. As Pope Benedict XVI once said, "It's a good thing the Church is not run from Germany, but Rome." In the back of ancient Roman temples converted to exquisite Renaissance churches, you will find men smoking cigarettes and old women selling shoes. One confessor at the Vatican regularly tells men who confess to masturbation, "You are making like a monkey. In his cage, all day long—wank, wank, wank!" So some parishioners call him "the monkey priest." Romans *understand.*

We are most of us walking wounded, morally speaking. How do we deal with this fact? Pretend that it's normal, diluting the Gospel so that we can keep a good conscience? Or pretend it isn't true, and clench our fists till our knuckles turn white? Ideally, ortho-doxy (correct belief) ought to lead to ortho-praxy (correct behavior). To which I say, "If only." The authors of this book seem to have come to another solution, which I might call "ortho-laxy." Believe it all, do what you can, admit that you're basically a bastard, and turn to the font of infinite Mercy as humbly and as often as you can. If there's one thing that's incompatible with Christianity, it's pride, or what we today would call "healthy self-esteem" and a "clear conscience."

In this book you will find any number of things that would have earned you a rap on the knuckles from the good old Sisters of Mercy (from the Irish Christian Brothers . . . perhaps a black eye): for the eve of All Saints' instead—a purgatory party. Explanation of the Eucharist in terms of movie tickets. A fête for the Feast of the Circumcision featuring sausages and Bloody Marys. What's wrong with these people?

The answer: the same thing that's wrong with all of us. The thing is that they're admitting it. Sometimes it helps to read the work of people who were seemingly born without the chromosome for shame. Once you've worked your way through this book—made breast-shaped pastries on St. Agatha's Day, dressed your kids up as Kennedys for July 4, sold indulgences on Halloween—you'll never look at the Church and its holidays or saints in quite the same way. Whether that's a good or a bad thing, it's certainly an entertaining ride.

Feast of the Assumption of Our Lady, 2005
Pope Alexander VI
Seventh Terrace of Purgatory

P.S. If some of you charitable souls wouldn't mind saying a few extra intercessory prayers for the dead (see the Feast of All Souls, November 2, below), several of the popes in here would certainly appreciate it. Just asking. . . .

Acknowledgments and Dedication

The authors would like to acknowledge their indebtedness to the deceased editors of the 1917 Catholic Encyclopedia and the kind souls at *www.newadvent.org* who typed it up and posted its contents online, to the editors of the splendid site *www.catholic-forum.com,* which provided source material for many of our saints' stories, and to many talented illustrators who crafted the images used herein and who, most importantly, allowed them to fall out of copyright.

We'd also like to thank the various theologians, philosophers, chancery officials, and, of course, psychologists whom we consulted in the course of our research, to make sure that every jot and tittle of the text was doctrinally orthodox (albeit, not particularly edifying). We would gladly list them, had they not demanded to remain anonymous.

We also thank the Department of the Vendee for permission to reproduce the image of Henri de La Rochejaquelein for July 14, and icon artist Maida Vale for use of her image of St. John of the Cross.

This book is dedicated to our mentors: +Fr. John Hardon, S.J., Prof. John R. May, of Louisiana State University, and Agnes Bellet, chief executive chef at Louis XVI French Restaurant in New Orleans.

Cover photo by Rene Leveque (Corbis); cover design by Bryan McCay.

January 3

The Holy Name of Jesus Fish

Jesus received His name on the day of His circumcision (see December 31 below for the relevant party), marking His identity as a faithful Jew. Artists of the Renaissance disagreed, clearly considering Christ either Flemish or Florentine, with blue eyes and sandy hair. The artist of the Shrine of the Immaculate Conception in Washington, D.C., pictured Jesus as a blond Super-Celt. Afrocentrists have insisted that Jesus was a black man. And modern skeptics have asked, "If Jesus was Jewish, how come he had a Puerto Rican name?"

An excellent question.[1] Which brings us to the importance of Jesus's personal name, which the Church has marked with a feast since the fifteenth century. In the form that has come down to us, "Jesus" is a Greek version of the Hebrew "Joshua," which is no doubt how His friends knew Him before they began to call Him "rabbi" (or "teacher). In later centuries, Jesus's name was no longer written, but was replaced by a coded symbol—the fish, which now adorns Republican minivans across the country. Why a fish? The Greek word for fish is ichthus (ΙΧΘΥΣ) which Christians used as an acronym for "Jesus Christ, the Son of God, Savior," when the Church began to be persecuted.[2]

St. Paul said of Christ's name that at it "every knee should bow, in heaven and on earth and under the earth." It was long customary for Catholics to bow their heads at every mention of the Divine Name. This meant that at Mass the more pious altar boys sometimes resembled those bobble-head dogs that sit in the back windows of cars—a few feet above the Jesus fish on the bumper, to which they are bowing. After Vatican II the tradition was largely abandoned.

But Catholics are still supposed to venerate Jesus's name. Some do so through the pious organization called the Holy Name Society. A men's organization popular in many American parishes, the group exists to promote "the honor and glory of our divine God, the personal sanctification of the members . . . devotion to the

---

1. It is indeed interesting that Hispanic Catholics feel comfortable naming their sons "Jesus." As squeamish, Taco-Bell-eating Anglos we find this unusual—and squirm at the thought of punching Jesus in the face in schoolyard fights, fooling around with a teenage Jesus, much less of consummating a terrestrial marriage with him.
2. This usage was mirrored in modern times by The Artist Formerly Known as Prince (acronym: TAFKAP) who used a symbol as his name when he felt persecuted by his record company.

Most Holy Name of Jesus. . . . faith in the Catholic Church and the magisterium, loyalty to one's country and respect for all lawful authority, both civil and religious." If memory serves, this was done largely by reading the minutes from previous meetings and planning future meetings. But the group always found time to recite the Divine Praises, a beautiful litany of devotion to the Trinity, the sacraments, the Blessed Virgin, and the saints. Then they'd raffle off bottles of whiskey.

CELEBRATE: Throw a dinner tonight for family and friends that marks the feast. Serve up the very fish that Jesus helped St. Peter and the other apostles catch in Galilee, tilapia (St. Peter's Fish). Bake it whole, and on each fish spell out Jesus's name in Greek, ΙΧΘΥΣ, in letters made of tasty puff pastry.

Jasmine-Scented Tilapia

3 tablespoons sesame oil	4 tilapia filets
2 cups strongly brewed jasmine tea, cooled	3 tablespoons sugar
3 tablespoons soy sauce	Toasted sesame seeds
4 scallions, finely sliced	Napa cabbage
	1 package puff pastry

Defrost puff pastry. Roll out to 1/4 inch thickness. Prick all over with fork and cut out the letters to form Jesus' name in Greek, ΙΧΘΥΣ. Chill 15 minutes. Heat oven to 350. Bake 10–15 minutes until golden. Set aside.

Prepare the marinade. Combine half of the sesame oil, half of the tea, soy sauce, and scallions. Marinate fillets 20–30 minutes.

Remove from marinade and dry thoroughly. Reserve 1/4 cup marinade. Heat remaining sesame oil in large sauté pan. Cook filets 4–5 minutes on each side. Remove to a platter serving dish. Sprinkle sugar in pan. Allow to caramelize before adding reserved marinade. Reduce to a medium-bodied syrup. Garnish with Napa cabbage and apply letters of Jesus' name just before serving.

Makes 4 servings

January 4

Elizabeth Ann Seton (1774–1821): Shush . . . Don't Attract God's Attention

This remarkable woman, the first American to be canonized, is patroness of people ridiculed for their faith. Reading her life, you can see that she's also the right saint for middle-class people whose fortunes head south. Elizabeth Bayley was born into the social elite; her father was the first professor of anatomy at Columbia, a doctor so eminent that he was forgiven his loyalty to King George III. Although her mother died young, Elizabeth's stepmother wasn't especially wicked, and she received a fine education, going on to make a happy marriage to a successful businessman, William Seton. It was conducted in the upper-class parish of St. Paul's by the Episcopalian bishop of New York in 1794. Within three years, her husband played host of a gala ball for the nation's first president, George Washington. With another prosperous lady friend, Elizabeth embarked on charitable missions to New York's less fortunate, earning the nickname the "Protestant Sisters of Charity." Elizabeth had every reason to expect a life of comfort and respectability. But God had other plans; glimpsing the seeds of holiness in Elizabeth, He decided, as He so often does, to start hitting the "Smite!" button.

First William's business started to fail and then his health. Within a few years his company was bankrupt, and Elizabeth had to fend off debt collectors. William developed tuberculosis, which grew so serious that doctors urged him to travel to warmer climes. With what little money they had left—they could afford to take along only one of their children—Elizabeth and William sailed to Livorno, Italy, to stay with his business associates, the Filicchi family. But as their ship drew near the harbor, news arrived at Livorno that deadly yellow fever was raging through New York, and the Setons were dumped with the other passengers on a quarantine island and locked in the "Lepers Tower." There they stayed for a month, exposed to the elements, as William's health collapsed. They entered Livorno at last, but he died within eight days.

Elizabeth took her bereaved daughter to stay for more than six months with the Filicchis—a warm and devoutly Catholic family, who sparked in her an attraction to their Church. She found herself jealous of Catholics' strong faith in the Eucharist—and returned to New York full of doubts about her religion. For an impoverished widow in need of powerful friends, this was social suicide.

Lobbied and harassed by her family friends not to embrace "papistry," Elizabeth soon found herself frankly sick of religion and ready to stick to practical matters—such as feeding her numerous children. But God wouldn't let her alone. One holy day as she sat at home, boycotting church, she came upon this passage written by the French preacher Bourdaloue[3]: "It is necessary that our faith be tried, and how?

---

3. This beloved French priest was known for sermons so captivating—and so very, very long—that pious women took to bringing little portable porcelain urinals to his Masses, so they wouldn't have to miss a word. In France, such porta-pissies are still named for Fr. Bourdaloue. Makes you proud to be a Catholic, somehow.

By those abandonments and those privations so common to the souls of the just. . . . We must be mindful of the lights with which we have been favored when it shall please God to deprive us of them." Elizabeth made up her mind. Within two months she joined the Catholic Church at St. Peter's parish on Barclay Street.

Her family and friends wrote her off as lost forever, and Elizabeth had to scramble to make ends meet. She tried to join some Catholics opening a boarding school, but local Protestants suspected it was a scheme for making more papists and forced it to close. A few months later, Elizabeth's sister-in-law, inspired by her example, also became a Catholic. This sent the New York State legislature into action; it threatened to expel her from the state. In search of religious freedom, she considered fleeing to Canada, but eventually Elizabeth found friendlier shores in Maryland. There she opened a school for the poor, staffing it with the religious order she founded, now called the Sisters of Charity. God still wasn't finished with Elizabeth; she had to endure the premature deaths of several of her children and long periods of spiritual despair, before she died in 1821. But her religious order lives on, staffing schools around the United States.

So when that Wal-Mart moves in and drives your family business into Chapter 11, or your computer job is outsourced to Mali, and you have to raffle off your SUV to buy some dried pasta and take a job at the dollar store, don't be discouraged. It might just mean that God has big plans for you.

> **CELEBRATE:** If you are currently engaged in any noticeable acts of charity or piety, tone them down a little, so as not attract the kind of special "attention" shown to St. Elizabeth. Keep a low profile, try to fly under the divine radar, and your life might turn out to be pleasantly mediocre rather than famously heroic.

January 5

John Neumann (1811–1860): Not Just President of the Relic Club—He's a Member

This energetic and learned apostle was the first male American saint and our first canonized bishop. As a youth, he trained for ordination but was turned away because his native Bohemia had too many priests. This was not a problem, he was informed, in the United States—which was still profoundly Protestant and broadly anti-Catholic. So John made his way to France on foot, prudently switching to a ship for his journey to New York. He arrived in 1836. There he was welcomed and ordained, and sent to serve the isolated faithful of rural upstate New York—living for some time in a hut he built himself, and ministering in the twelve languages he had mastered. He joined the Redemptorist order, famous for its stirring parish "missions," and was eventually promoted to bishop of Philadelphia in 1852. Only eight years before, this diocese had been attacked by "antipapist" mobs, which burned down three churches and dozens of Catholic homes.

As a church leader, Neumann faced the challenge of helping to assimilate the hundreds of thousands of new Catholic immigrants who arrived each year on America's East Coast, principally from Ireland and Germany. They faced native hostility, grinding poverty, public schools that taught Protestant doctrine, and well-meaning upper-class Episcopalian women who wished to adopt the children of destitute Irish families and raise them "as Christians." Different sectors of the Catholic immigrant community offered a variety of responses. Most U.S. bishops, themselves "lace-curtain" Irish, advocated enrolling Catholic children in public schools. Neumann and his fellow German bishops suggested founding a system of parochial schools. Leaders of Irish street gangs proposed burning down Protestant neighborhoods.[4] After much debate and a few well-publicized fires, Neumann's plan was deemed the most practical. So every child who ever had to line up in height order, attend First Monday novenas, and practice the Palmer Method of penmanship after reciting *The Baltimore Catechism,* has St. John Neumann to thank.

Neumann was known for his devotion to holy relics—a pious practice that horrified non-Catholics at the time and still creeps out teenagers today. It entails collecting the personal effects, the bones, even the hair and nail clippings of the saints, and using them as aids to prayer. Dating back to the days when the Church survived in catacombs and held its liturgies on the tombs of martyrs, the practice of venerating holy relics reflects our belief that human beings were never meant to be angels—that even in heaven, a saint is somehow incomplete without his body, since man is an amalgam of soul and flesh. At the Resurrection, we believe, our bodies will be restored to us in perfected form, as Jesus's was to Him. So in holding the tibia of St. Lydia, we gain a grip on the New Jerusalem. Anyway, that's the theory, and John Neumann practiced it fervently, gathering so many relics that he eventually became one: his body, miraculously incorrupt after almost 150 years, lies in a glass case in downtown Philadelphia, surrounded by his collection of holy relics, of which he is the most impressive.

---

4. Bishop "Dagger John" Hughes of New York organized the Ancient Order of Hibernians to defend churches from attack, and warned that the entire city would burn if his cathedral was destroyed.

January 6

Epiphany and Carnival: The Work Ethic Be Damned

The visit by the wise men to the infant Jesus is one of the most beloved moments in the Gospels. In much of the Catholic world, this day ("Three Kings Day") has traditionally been celebrated more enthusiastically than Christmas itself. In Latin countries people give gifts on this day, commemorating the presents brought to Christ by the Magi. Since they were the first gentiles to honor Jesus, these alien astrologers are seen as a sign of the Church's universality, her mission to all nations. Their feast day, particularly in Louisiana, is seen as an excuse to switch from celebrating Christmas to celebrating Carnival.

In New Orleans, Carnival is more than a day—it's a whole season, stretching from Epiphany to the very brink of Ash Wednesday. Carnival conveniently consumes the grayest, dullest months of the year—at winter's depths, offering a glint of sunshine and festivity amid the short, dark days.

Efficiency has always run a distant second to fun among Catholics. During the Middle Ages, almost one-fourth of the days on the calendar could plausibly be taken as major feasts, encouraging the masses to stop working and start carousing. An Italian friend chalks up the greater wealth of places such as Sweden, compared to say, Sicily, to the sterner habits acquired along with the "Protestant work ethic." Maybe he's right. But is it really worth it? Where would you rather live? (Swedes have one of the highest suicide rates on earth.)

Of course, if you're reading this book in English, you probably live in one of the countries dominated by the stricter, northern, Protestant worldview. You work five days every week and throw only a limited number of *soirées*. We're here to change all that—to dig into the Catholic past and unearth an unending supply of pretexts for parties.

That's where Carnival comes in. This term means, literally, "Bye-Bye

Carne, Vale!

This traditional Lenten lament was penned in ecclesiastical Latin by St. Hildegard of Bingen and originally sung polyphonically as part of the Office of Vespers on the Vigil of Ash Wednesday by the contemplative nuns of her convent in Rupertsberg, Germany. It later formed the basis for a popular romantic ballad.[5]

"Bye Bye, Meat"

Bye bye, meat
Bye bye, beef and pork
Hello, tofu spork
I think I'm gonna hurl . . .
Bye bye, goose
Bye bye, lamb and veal
Hello, veggie meal
That tastes like chamomile.
Farewell, Chateaubriand.

Meat." The festival, like nearly everything else we enjoy, has pagan roots and was rationalized by early Christians to mark the time separating the glory of Christmas from the austerities of Lent. To pagans, the season was a time to drive the evil spirits of winter out of the fields and make room for the crops to grow. Of course, human sacrifice was another pre-Christian custom. . . .

---

5. Okay, strictly speaking, none of this is true.

LOUISIANA CARNIVAL: DRAG QUEENS, ABSINTHE, AND SMOTHERED SQUIRREL

You've heard about Mardi Gras in the Mudbug State, maybe even watched on MTV as the hordes of drag queens and sozzled Midwesterners snaked their way down Bourbon Street. Doesn't look like much fun, does it? The truth is, natives of New Orleans try to clear out of town by the time Fat Tuesday rolls around; you'll find the rich ones skiing in Aspen. Unless they're part of one of the elite Carnival "krewes" that stage elaborate costume balls and man the parades, New Orleanians throw their best parties around Epiphany and hit the highway before the tourists arrive to throw up all over the city.

The French ways of feasting in Louisiana were filtered through two different groups:

- ☺ Snooty French émigrés from Paris who settled New Orleans in the eighteenth century brought with them elaborate culinary traditions that they adapted to the New World's edible fauna, such as crawfish, snapping turtle, pompano, and catfish, and new crops such as corn, okra, and tomatoes. These French settlers—known as Creoles—looked down their Gallic noses at the Americans who took over in 1803 and kept to their own area of town, which is still known as the French Quarter. Specialties of the Creoles include *Pompano en papillote,* Barbecued Shrimp, Bananas Foster, and, of course, the *roi de gallette,* or King Cake.
- ☺ Acadians (or "Cajuns" as they're now known) are the people of mixed, mostly French descent who settled in the rural areas of southwestern and south central Louisiana—after the British threw them out of Acadia, Canada, because they were Catholics and therefore untrustworthy. After much suffering and years of wandering, the Acadians found their way to the Mississippi valley and spread out in search of good fishing, big dopey edible turtles, and patches of swamp where someday oil would be discovered. Cajun cuisine relies less on elaborate sauces and more on zesty spices and fresh ingredients—such as the last furry thing that ran across the yard.

Celebrations of Mardi Gras in Cajun country are lower-key and much more bizarre than the courtly rituals prevailing in New Orleans. Sure, the cityfolk may be satisfied by a simple parade of half-naked transvestites cheered on by puzzled Baptists from Mississippi. But Cajuns like to *party*. In small towns such as Mamou and Abbeville, they do Mardi Gras the old-fashioned way: with hooded men on horseback riding up to strangers' houses making demands. These riders wear masks and peaked caps, but don't worry—they aren't Klansmen. (In fact, the Klan persecuted Cajuns.) But these riders do have an agenda: they want chicken, and they want it now. Also okra, garlic, celery, andouille sausage, and every other item that goes into a Cajun gumbo. The idea is to ride from door to door collecting ingredients—all the while consuming as much Busch beer as humanly possible and then sharing some with the horse—and then to bring them back to a common pot, where the wives and girls stew up an enormous dinner for all to enjoy. This welter of drinking, riding, pilfering, and eating is accompanied by raucous traditional songs such as "Hey Old Widow, Give Me a Chicken," and "I'm Drunk Enough—You'll Do."

The official colors of Louisiana Mardi Gras are purple, green, and gold. Three colors were chosen for the Three Kings who arrived at Bethlehem on Epiphany, and each has a symbolic meaning: supposedly, *purple* stands for justice, *green* for faith, and *gold* for power. If you've ever lived in New Orleans, you'll realize that they really stand for *wine, money,* and *jewelry*—the city fathers' favorite aphrodisiacs.

It's easy enough to order premade Mardi Gras supplies from specialty Web sites such as *www.mardigrasoutlet.com:* shiny strings of beads, streamers, balloons, and party favors in the three official colors, along with doubloons, feather masks, and even a ready-made King Cake, complete with plastic baby inside, representing the infant Christ. Traditionally, the guest who bites down on the baked-in baby is called upon to throw the next Carnival party. Such events can cost hundreds of dollars and leave your furniture broken to matchsticks. So watch what you're eating.

If you are the host, it is important to serve unfamiliar food that will present your guests with a test of nerve. Louisiana cuisine offers plenty of opportunities; our cookbooks list real, time-tested recipes for cooking turtles, alligators, nutria, muskrats, larks, partridges, pigeons, orlotans, robins, snipe, woodcock, frogs, hare, rabbits, Guinea fowl, mutton, raccoons, possums, and Bambi. Should you live in a snobby suburb where it would be considered socially awkward to shoot, trap, skin, gut, and dismember any of these creatures, this needn't stand in your way. Chances are good that you're within driving distance of a rural area that offers one or more of these treats for sale from truck stops by the side of the road.

So go ahead—invite your boss, your wife's parents, your friends, and serve up a hot, steaming helping of smothered squirrel, or truly delicious Creole turtle soup—a rich, savory broth with a slight "wild" undertaste counterbalanced by fresh lemons and generous helpings of sherry. As they gnaw one of those spindly little legs or move the chunks of turtle dispiritedly around the bowl, they'll learn to see you in a new light. You're not the same tame, manageable person they thought. You're a wild game hunter, a trapper who cruises the bayous scavenging for meat, an adventurer who should not be lightly screwed with. This can only strengthen your hand when you have to deal with them in future.

Smothered Squirrel

A rustic treat your guests will never forget.

Flour	1 sprig thyme
4–6 squirrels, cleaned	1 bay leaf
Salt and freshly ground black pepper	2 strips lemon peel
3 tablespoons butter	1/4 cup heavy cream
2 yellow onions, sliced	1/2 cup sour cream
1 cup chicken stock	1 bunch scallions, sliced
1 pound white mushrooms, halved	Fleur de Sel

Preheat oven to 350 degrees.

Cut squirrels into serving-sized pieces. Season flour with salt and pepper and dredge meat in it. Heat butter to foam stage in Dutch oven. Brown squirrel on all sides, add onions, and sauté until browned on all sides. Add mushrooms and stir to coat with butter. Pour in stock and herbs. Simmer a few minutes. Add cream.

Important: Do not look down while cooking squirrels. They resemble rats in the pot, and you may become dispirited.

Cover and transfer to oven. Cook about 1 hour, until meat is tender. Season with Fleur de Sel and pepper to taste. Stir in sour cream and return to oven 5 minutes. Serve over egg noodles, garnished with green onions. And yes, they taste like chicken. Whenever we serve chicken, we say "Hmmm! This tastes just like squirrel."

Makes 8 servings

King Cake

1/2 cup warm water
2 packages yeast
1/2 cup plus 1 teaspoon sugar
3-1/2 to 4-1/2 cups flour
Several grindings nutmeg
2 teaspoons fine sea salt
1 teaspoon lemon zest
1 teaspoon orange zest
1–2 teaspoons orange blossom water

1/2 cup warm milk
6 egg yolks room temperature
6 ounces butter, soft but still cool
1 egg beaten with a tablespoon of
  milk
1 teaspoon cinnamon
1 plastic doll or 1 kidney bean
Green, yellow, and purple colored
  sugars

Pour warm water into a small bowl or glass measuring cup. Sprinkle in yeast and 2 teaspoons sugar. Mix lightly, making sure each grain of yeast is moistened. Place in a warm draft-free place for about 10 minutes. Yeast will activate, and bubble and foam, as the room fills up with a pleasant, yeasty smell.

Combine 3-1/2 cups flour, remaining sugar, nutmeg, salt, and zest in a large mixing bowl. Whisk to thoroughly distribute ingredients.

Make a well in the center of mixture, and add yeast mixture, milk, and egg yolks. Stir with wooden spoon to combine dry ingredients with liquid. Continue stirring briskly until mixture is smooth and begins to form into a ball. It should be fairly elastic.

Add butter, 1 tablespoon at a time. Dough will start to fall apart. Continue beating until it forms into a medium soft ball. It may be necessary to sprinkle a tablespoon or so of flour to bring the dough together.

Place dough on lightly floured surface and knead, adding a little flour at a time as needed (not more than cup). Knead until it is no longer sticky but smooth, shiny, and elastic.

Lightly butter a large bowl. Place dough in bowl and rotate so top and bottom are buttered. Cover bowl with a towel and allow dough to rise in a warm, draft-free place for 1-1/2 hours or until it has doubled in volume.

Butter a large baking sheet and set aside. Punch down dough with your fist and remove to a lightly floured counter. Sprinkle with cinnamon. Gently pat and shape into a long cylinder. Form an oval by pinching ends together.

Form into a ring by twisting ends together and place on a lightly buttered baking pan. Cover lightly with a towel. Allow to rise another 45 minutes until doubled in volume. Meanwhile, preheat oven to 375 degrees.

Brush top and sides of dough with milk and egg mixture, and place in over for 25–35 minutes, or until golden. Secrete baby or bean in cake, and allow to cool on a wire rack.

Makes 10–12 servings

Poured Icing

3/4 cup confectioners sugar   1/4 cup lemon juice   4 tablespoons water

Combine ingredients until smooth, adding water as needed. Drizzle icing over cake. Then sprinkle on colored sugars, alternating gold, green, and purple. Serve in slices 2–3 inches wide.

January 12

Marguerite Bourgeous (1620–1700): Be Careful What You Wish For

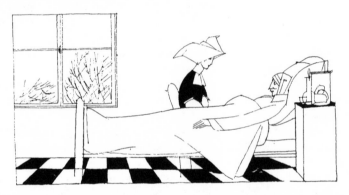

This holy Frenchwoman left a life of middle class, dare we say *bourgeois*, comfort in Troyes, to serve as a missionary in the wilds of New France (now Quebec). With her fellow sisters, Marguerite opened schools and taught basic skills to impoverished French residents and native Indians. She was the first to accept Indian women as sisters in her Congregation of Notre Dame. She set up schools and missions in the newly founded town of Montreal, where she is considered cofounder of the city. In her eightieth year, Marguerite learned that a young sister was dying of a midwinter infection. She piously offered her own life in exchange—and God took her up on it. By the next day, the young sister was cured and Marguerite was dead. We like to think that the pious sister's last words of advice to the nun she'd saved were well-intentioned and practical: "Be careful what you wish for."

---

6. Yes, of course it's illegal. But they sell it in Prague. . . .

Sacramental Executive Summary #1: Baptism

The sacrament that rings in the Christian life began in the early Church as the full immersion of an adult—a messy and complex procedure that entailed converting and catechizing a pagan, dunking him in a river, and hoping that the Romans didn't catch on. As she grew in numbers, wisdom, and institutional efficiency, the Church found it was easier to explain her doctrines to compliant infants, drizzle them with a little holy water while relatives ran video cameras, and then trundle them off to brunch. To be sure, adults are still admitted to Baptism, but only after a lengthy, tedious procedure called RCIA . . . *

But the baptism of infants raised certain theological questions. What happened to infants who died before baptism—still tainted by Original Sin? St. Augustine declared that they went to hell. Bereaved parents found this unsatisfying and lobbied for centuries until Augustine's position was condemned. Medieval thinkers suggested a middle state called "Limbo," a place of perfect natural happiness, lacking only the presence of God. This theory was widely accepted by learned Catholics for almost a thousand years. However, after Vatican II, Limbo began to fall out of fashion (like men's hats). Hadn't the Church always taught that God desired the heavenly company of every human soul? Most Catholics came to believe that innocent children who die unbaptized are sent to heaven, somehow. (The details have yet to be worked out, but they probably entail baptism of desire.)

---

* This stands for "Repelling Converts In-Advertently"

Of course baptized children who die before the age of reason (generally pegged at seven) go straight to heaven. To bury these little saints, the Church would forego the black vestments customarily used for funerals and garb the priest in festive white. Since Vatican II, pure white vestments are used at funerals for just about anyone—from Amway salesmen to Mafia dons. Some complain that this suggests universal salvation. We'd like to suggest, more charitably, that fewer people ever reach the age of reason than you might think.

CELEBRATE: For the next baptism in your family, dramatize the saving powers of the sacramental waters by making potato gnocchi—little lumps of inedible dough, which, once immersed in the roiling waters heated by flaming spirits, float to the top renewed, remade, and ready for sauce.

Pesto with Gnocchi

PESTO:

2 cloves garlic, peeled
1/4 cup pine nuts
3 cups basil leaves
Pinch of salt

1/2 cup extra virgin olive oil
1/2 cup parmigiano-reggiano, finely
  grated
1 package prepared gnocchi

Combine garlic, pine nuts, basil, and salt in blender. Add oil and process. Transfer to a bowl and stir in cheese.

Boil gnocchi until they float to the top, reserving some of the water. Toss with pesto, adding a tablespoon or so of reserved water. Garnish with additional cheese.

Makes 2 servings

February 1

Brigid of Ireland (453–523): A Nun Gets a Makeover

According to chroniclers, Brigid was born to a pagan father and Christian mother and raised in the faith. As was the heathen custom, her father, Dubtach, owned both Brigid and her mother as slaves. Inspired by her own reading of the Gospels, she began to give away much of her father's wealth to the poor. No warnings or punishments squelched Brigid's charity.[1] Dubtach was too fond of his lovely daughter to kill her as a sacrifice to the banshees, so he decided to auction her off. Dubtach tried unloading Brigid on local druids and pagan kings. But Irishmen aren't that easy to fool. Dubtach never found a husband for Brigid, although one king was so impressed by her kindness that he bought her freedom. With an eye to his treasury, he declined to take the girl home.

Once she was free, Brigid resolved upon life as a nun—but was soon deluged by eager suitors. Brigid begged God to make her ugly so men would stop pestering her. (She could have just told them about her philosophy of money management.) God granted her prayer and gave Brigid a face like a badger's behind. That worked and allowed Brigid to pursue her vocation in peace. But on the day she took her final vows her beauty was restored.

CELEBRATE: If you have a teenage daughter, pass along this inspiring story that so perfectly encapsulates the complex, interrelated neuroses connected to sexuality, religion, money, and self-esteem that it seems like Freud must have made it up. Better yet, pass on to your young ones this lovely vision of the kingdom of heaven attributed to St. Brigid, "The Heavenly Banquet":

> *I would like to have the men of Heaven*
> *In my own house;*
> *With vats of good cheer*
> *Laid out for them.*

---

1. For this reason, Brigid is a fitting patron both for high-maintenance women and the men who try to maintain them.

I would like to have the three Marys,
Their fame is so great.
I would like people
From every corner of Heaven.

I would like them to be cheerful
In their drinking.
I would like to have Jesus, too,
Here amongst them.

I would like a great lake of beer
For the King of Kings.
I would like to be watching Heaven's family
Drinking it through all eternity.

February 2

The Purification of Mary and Presentation of Jesus: Holy Groundhogs!

On this feast day the Church has traditionally blessed candles—made of pure wax from virgin bees—and distributed them to the congregation to mark the entry of Christ, light of the world, into His father's Temple. From this custom, the day took the name Candlemas. Set on the fortieth day after Christmas, this feast marks the day when Mary and Joseph took Jesus to Jerusalem in obedience to the law. As a new mother, Mary came to the Temple herself for ritual "purification"; since the birth of a child, like menstruation, involves the spilling of human blood, each rendered a woman temporarily ineligible for worship at the Temple. Of course, as smart-aleck kids in catechism class have been pointing out since the first century, Mary herself was free of sin and perfectly pure. To this, the Church replies that Mary, like Christ, made herself obedient to the law— citing Mary's own words in one of the apocryphal gospels,[2] "Who am I that I should make trouble . . . ?"

The day also marks the Presentation of Christ. Since every child born carries the legacy of Adam and Eve's rebellion, each son or daughter had to be presented to God and then "ransomed" back with a lamb or some birds, which were sacrificed in the Temple. As each Jewish mother took back her daughter or son from the priests, she offered prayers for his or her health, fertility, and acceptance into medical school.

Church fathers have pointed out that the child Jesus carried no taint of sin and did not really need to be redeemed back. Jesus would go on to become *the* sacrificial Lamb, the ransom paid to God for all the sins of men; so the Presentation of Christ in the Temple serves as a little prefigurement of Calvary. This makes it a fitting time to finally take down all those Christmas decorations.

Because it marks one of the transitional moments in the calendar, the weather on this feast of lights was chosen to forecast the coming of spring. As the old poem goes:

> *"If Candlemas be fair and bright,*
> *Winter has another flight.*
> *If Candlemas brings clouds and rain,*
> *Winter will not come again."*

German immigrants who came to America in the eighteenth century recalled this ancient tradition but felt uncomfortable with its Catholic associations. So in good Protestant fashion they replaced Our Lady with a groundhog. That's why Americans think of the Feast of the Purification of Mary and the Presentation of Christ as the day on which Bill Murray romances Andie MacDowell, over and over again, under the benevolent patronage of Punxatawney Phil.

---

2. Okay, not really.

February 5

Agatha: A Feast of Breasts

The Christian faith could fairly be described as a theological system for recycling the worst things in life and turning them into the best. It calls the day when Christ was sacrificed "Good" Friday. The gruesome deaths of persecuted Christians are dubbed their "feast" days. It's in this spirit that medieval Christians began to mark the Feast of St. Agatha, a noble third-century girl from Palermo or Catania whose legend became very popular in that region and spread through Europe.

This beloved Roman martyr could be called the patroness of breast-reduction surgery. Before the Christian notion of marriage as a free sacrament won over the Roman world, the father of a family had the absolute right to marry his young daughters to anyone he chose. Many early martyrs were women who refused an arranged marriage. To keep a private vow of virginity, the spunky Agatha spurned a proposal made by a senator, Quintianus. Roman oligarchs were not used to hearing "No," particularly from young women, so Quintianus pulled some strings and had Agatha arrested for being a Christian—still then punishable by death. Agatha was tortured horribly; Roman soldiers cut off her breasts and left her to die. It's said that no less a personage than St. Peter, the very first pope, appeared to the suffering girl with her breasts on a platter and miraculously restored them to her so she could die intact.

To celebrate this wonder—and let's face it, to satisfy some pretty obscure psychological urges—medieval artists began to depict St. Agatha standing with her breasts on a plate. (They look like little bells.) To mark her feast day, Christians throughout Europe solemnly blessed church bells, and bakers in Sicily began to make pert little desserts called *Minni di virgini,* or "virgin's nipples," which a husband can prepare as a special treat for his spouse, honoring the saint, his wife, and two of her most delightful assets.

CELEBRATE: Husbands, this is a nice day to get your wife a particularly glamorous brassiere at your local lingerie shop. Don't buy something trashy that you would like but rather something elegant that you know would appeal to her. To make this even more special, you really ought to get the bra blessed. Swing by your local rectory and ask to see the pastor. Remind him that this is St. Agatha's day. Ask him to bless the brassiere with holy water. It's worth it just to see the look on his face.

While your wife takes the well-deserved bubble bath you drew for her, whip up a tasty boob-shaped treat—either the British classic popovers, or a few pairs of succulent *Minni di Virgini*.

St. Agatha Popovers

These light, airy, breast-shaped rolls are delicious served with sweet butter or a strong French cheese—or just eaten straight out of the oven.

1 cup all-purpose flour	1 tablespoon butter, melted
1/4 teaspoon salt	1 teaspoon fennel seeds, lightly
1 cup milk, room temperature	crushed
3 large eggs, room temperature	Freshly ground white pepper

Preheat oven to 450 degrees. Spray tins with nonstick spray. Whisk together flour and salt.

In a separate bowl, lightly whisk together milk, eggs, and butter. Pour liquid ingredients into dry and whisk thoroughly, removing all lumps. Add spices and blend until just combined.

Pour batter into tins about half full, place on lowest rack of oven.

Bake 15 minutes, reduce oven to 350 degrees, and bake another 15 minutes. Resist the temptation to open the oven until you remove the popovers. Serve piping hot.

Makes 12 in a standard muffin tin or 10 in a popover pan

Minni di Virgini (Nipples of the Virgin)

Adapted from *Sweet Sicily* by Victoria Granof.

1 recipe Pasta Frolla	1/4 cup tiny bittersweet chocolate
1 recipe pastry cream, cooled	chips
1/4 cup candied pumpkin (succatta),	1 recipe sugar icing
available at specialty shops	16 candied cherries

Preheat oven to 375 degrees.

Roll out dough to about 1/8 inch thick. Cut out 16 2-inch circles and 16 3-inch circles.

Combine pastry cream, pumpkin, and chocolate. Top a mound of this mixture on top of each smaller circle. Top with larger circle and press to seal.

Place on baking sheets and bake 15-20 minutes until light golden.

Cool on rack. Top with icing and a cherry.

Makes 16 pastries.

Pasta Frolla

1/2 pound butter, softened
3/4 cup sugar
2 egg yolks

1 teaspoon lemon zest
1/4 teaspoon fine sea salt
5 cups all purpose flour

In a large mixing bowl or stand mixer combine butter and sugar. Beat in yolks one at a time. Add remaining ingredients, combine until a soft dough forms. Wrap tightly and chill at least 30 minutes.

Crema Pasticciera

2 egg yolks
2/3 cup sugar
6 tablespoons corn starch

2 cups milk
Grated zest of 1/2 orange
Pinch of saffron

Whisk together yolks and sugar in a heavy saucepan or double boiler. Dissolve the cornstarch in a half cup of milk and then gradually add rest of milk and mix well. Slowly pour mixture into yolks, whisking until well blended. Place over lower heat and cook for about 10 minutes, stirring constantly until shiny and thick like a pudding (20 to 25 minutes in a double boiler). Add orange zest. Pour into a bowl and cover with plastic wrap *directly* on cream. Cool. Refrigerate up to three days.

Sugar Icing

6 cups powdered sugar
1/4 cup lemon juice
1/4 cup water

Combine ingredients until smooth. Add up to a tablespoon of water as needed.

Bonus Saint: Pius IX (1792–1878): Just Say "Nono."

One of the longest-reigning and most important popes in history, Blessed Pius IX was responsible for convening the First Vatican Council, which defined at last the extent of papal infallibility, and for declaring the dogma of Mary's Immaculate Conception. But Pius IX spent much of his reign struggling not with theology, but the aftermath of the French Revolution. Catholics who'd lived through the persecutions launched by the French Republic were divided about how to judge its legacy. Some thinkers such as Joseph de Maistre considered the revolution a divine punishment sent to drown Europe's sins in blood. Others, such as Lammenais, argued that Liberty, Equality, and Fraternity were simply secularized versions of Christian principles, which Catholics should embrace.

Pius IX began his reign over the Church and the Papal States as an optimistic liberal. A few years of involvement in Italian politics were enough to cure him of that—as bands of radical nationalists roamed his territories trying to stir rebellions against the pope and seize his lands for a united Italy. Pius IX considered the existence of the Papal States one of the papacy's greatest historical achievements, a guarantee that pontiffs would never again be elected and deposed by Roman mobs or foreign kings. He feared that without a state of its own, the papacy would quickly become a puppet of secular governments. So when secret Masonic lodges began stockpiling guns and ammunition to lead a revolution and hand his lands over to the kingdom of Piedmont—well, Pius IX took that sort of thing personally.

The pope watched with dismay as other churches experimented with romantic, emotion-driven Christianity, neglecting the factual and doctrinal claims made by the Church while invoking the Christian heritage as a vague source of lofty sentiments. He soon changed his mind about embracing modernity, gaining a reputation as the most reactionary pope—perhaps the most reactionary *person*—in history. In a series of starkly written documents like his "Syllabus of Errors," Pius IX condemned the separation of Church and State, secular education, civil marriage, legal divorce, and, most famously, "progress, liberalism, and modern civilization." (He wasn't called "Pio No-No for nothing.) This document scandalized Catholic liberals, encouraged conservatives, and, most importantly, directly inspired the beloved song belted out by Rufus T. Firefly, who ruled the Republic of Freedonia in *Duck Soup:*

"I don't know what they have to say
It makes no difference anyway
Whatever it is, I'm against it.
No matter what it is or who commenced it, I'm against it!
Your proposition may be good
But let's have one thing understood:
Whatever it is, I'm against it.
And even when you've changed it or condensed it, I'm against it!
For months before my son was born
I used to yell from night till morn:
Whatever it is, I'm against it!
And I've kept yelling since I've first commenced it, I'm against it."

Can somebody say "Amen"?

....

February 10

Clare of Rimini (1282–1346): Bite Your Tongue

Here's a saintly woman who started out life like Paris Hilton—rich, gorgeous, and eagerly . . . *affectionate* toward the young bucks of Rimini. (Mercifully, the Internet had not yet been developed, so Bl. Clare's video footage hasn't been widely circulated.) Eventually she married—only to see her husband and later her son executed after a particularly boisterous Italian election. In her second marriage, Clare cheered up her husband by engaging in an escalating series of penances: she replaced her jewelry with kinky-looking iron rings and collars, and she slept on a splintery wooden board (talk about the simple life!). Clare joined the Third Order of the Franciscans, but outdid most of them in charity—once selling herself into slavery to pay a strangers' debts. It is said she punished herself for gossiping by lopping off a piece of her tongue with a scissors.

February 12

Julian the Hospitaller (Dates Unknown): Fiddlers, Murderers, and Circus Clowns

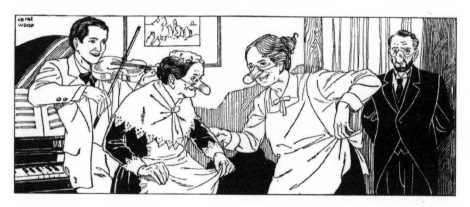

This saint's legendary tale raises all sorts of exciting anxieties, resembling as it does the story of Oedipus. A young nobleman was out hunting deer when he came across a stag with a human face. Instead of capturing the hybrid and bringing it back for scientists or the circus, he nailed it with an arrow. The dying buck cursed Julian with an ugly prophecy: that he was fated to murder his own parents. Julian scoffed that this was impossible—but then so was a talking deer. He fled the area, moving hundreds of miles away. He found a nice apartment and settled down with a beautiful wife. But one day he came home to find a strange man in his bed on top of a woman, and in a rage, he hacked up the offending couple with his sword. At which point his wife walked in, announcing: "Honey, your parents dropped by to surprise us, so I gave them the master bedroom!" As a penance, Julian and his wife journeyed to Rome as pilgrims. Instead of returning, Julian decided to make good for his crime against hospitality by opening a hospital. He set up a shelter and clinic for weary pilgrims traveling to Rome and spent the rest of his life providing free meals, maps, cots, and entertainment for lonely travelers. (It's said Julian played a mean fiddle and welcomed traveling circuses, asking them only to perform for his guests.)

One winter night, late in his life, Julian gave up his own bed to the most unattractive of visitors—a pilgrim with leprosy whose afflicted limbs were freezing off. Julian tucked the man in himself, only to see him turn into an angel. The heavenly messenger told Julian that he had pleased God with his life of penitence and then disappeared. Because of his various adventures, the Church named Julian the patron of fiddlers, murderers, and circus clowns.

....

February 14

Valentine: If It Feels Good . . . Stop It!

This feast named for a Roman martyr is probably associated with romantic love because in medieval England it was around this date "whan every foul[3] cometh ther to choose his mate" (Chaucer). But why do fools fall in love? Because it is what we were made for. Not all love is sexual, of course—although we learn from the Song of Songs and Catholic mystics that a divine eros pervades the cosmos. So this feast makes a fine day to recall the Church's theology of love.

The early Church faced a pagan world that considered sexuality too base to be worth philosophizing about. The Romans left sex as the realm of freedom and fun—by which they meant that rich men were "free" to have "fun" with slave girls and slave boys, regardless of age or consent. The word pornography derives from *pornē*—which is Greek for prostitute or sexual slave. In contrast, some ascetic thinkers such as the Manicheans held that the body itself was evil, and so was sexuality, since it gave rise to—you guessed it—more human bodies. So they encouraged their clergy to practice celibacy, while encouraging their laity to practice "safe" (that is, sterile) sex.

---

3. Native speakers of Middle English may insist that "foul" really means "bird." To them we answer: "You've been dead for hundreds of years. Lighten up already."

The Church took another view. From reading Genesis, it knew that sex was fundamentally good; Jesus himself thought it sacred enough to perform His first miracle at a wedding and to elevate the marital bond to a stubbornly indissoluble sacrament, one of only seven ordinary channels for God's grace. But the sexual instinct is disordered like all the others, and much more powerful. Unlike, say, the hunger for food, the sex craving has as its object another human being; a Church that lost many martyrs to gladiatorial shows that included elaborate, live sex orgies was keenly attuned to sexuality's darker side.

Maybe too keenly attuned. Because of this awareness—and perhaps because the Church has since the Apostles been governed and mostly staffed by celibates, who've made their wedding vows to Christ Himself—all but our greatest[4] theologians and preachers neglected the Church's positive doctrine of sexuality. Some early Church fathers, who fasted and flogged themselves to subdue "the flesh," looked upon marital sex like embittered Atkins dieters staring through a bakery window. Their attitudes carried down through the centuries, particularly through the preaching of Jansenist[5] clergy, all the way down to the present. Young Catholics were taught about sexual morality through a simple, elegant formula: *Sexual intercourse, like killing, is almost always wrong—except in special circumstances, such as self-defense and marriage.* For premarital activities, we found an easy guide in the popular R&B song: "If It Feels Good, Stop It!"

This suspicion toward even marital whoopie was manifested in moral manuals that warned couples repeatedly against the danger of "pollution," in the custom of "Irish foreplay" (five Guinnesses and then the Sorrowful Mysteries), and in the lives of the saints. Up until the twentieth century, very few married folks were canonized—and of those who were, an astounding percentage had renounced sex altogether or left their marital beds to become monks and nuns. This renunciation was typically presented not as grounds for entering marriage counseling, but as proof of heroic virtue. Well, maybe. But it seems to most Catholics today that there was something a little strange going on.[6]

Meanwhile, over in the secular world, people have adopted the sexual ideology

---

4. Aquinas, for instance, was attuned to the goodness of sex, holding that marital bliss would have been much more pleasurable in the Garden of Eden—that God had intended it to be *even more fun* than it is.

5. The heresy of Jansenism, put briefly, holds that God is an angry hostage-taker who (to quote a like-minded thinker, Jonathan Edwards) "holds you over the pit of hell, much as one holds a spider, or some loathsome insect over the fire." It's hard to love this God, but since He's the one with the box-cutter, we're better off placating Him. This view became enormously popular in France and Ireland.

6. To be fair, we should cite the explanation given by Susan Lloyd, author of the delightfully witty *Please Don't Drink the Holy Water* (Manchester, N.H.: Sophia Institute Press, 2004): "The reason we have far more religious than married saints canonized up to recent years is because religious orders had the means to oversee the cause and families generally didn't—not because of sex hangups. In the case of Thomas More we have a high profile martyr, so his cause went through. And he was far from celibate—two wives, lots of kids." So martyrdom really helps.

of the Marquis de Sade—who reasserted the horny Roman aristocrat's privilege of unlimited sexual expression, without regard to partner or progeny. In the early twentieth century, this old creed gained respectability, through the likes of Havelock Ellis and Margaret Sanger, and a birth control movement which made itself presentable by promising to eugenically produce "more children from the fit, and fewer from the unfit." The work of the energetic pervert Alfred Kinsey moved things along, breaking down every barrier of modesty (and massively faking statistics) to "prove" that inside each American lurked a secret de Sade, who hungered to try every imaginable variation of sexual act—if only a prudish society would let him. The result, today, is that we rear children who mature sexually at the age of ten or eleven, and psychologically at forty, who are ready to rut in junior high, but emotionally retarded, unable to contract enduring marriages, unwilling to procreate.

Pope John Paul II, aware of these trends, has labored mightily throughout his pontificate to reinvigorate Church teaching and preaching about marriage. For instance, he has canonized married couples who were really, you know, *married*. John Paul has added innumerable such laymen and laywomen to the ranks of the saints.

The pope has striven, in the words of theologian Johnny Mercer, "to accentuate the positive, eliminate the negative," and "latch on to the affirmative." As he served as Archbishop of Cracow in the 1950s, Karol Wotyjla wrote the seminal study *Love and Responsibility* (1960). Instead of presenting sex primarily as an act of reproduction, with affection as a positive and pleasure as a dubious side effect, the pope emphasized the human love between the spouses as a mirror of the divine love in the Trinity, and a hearkening back to the primordial unity of Adam and Eve.

In fact, the pope urged spouses, especially men, to attend to each other's enjoyment. Indeed, fifteen years before the miserable *Joy of Sex,* the pope was writing about the importance of female orgasm and the duty of a Catholic husband to make sure his wife attains it "by any means necessary."[7] So as long as the seed eventually hits the soil, there's no moral limit as to how you mow the grass. The pope urged men to slow down the rhythm of their own arousal, to more closely match their wives', so that "the subjective happiness which they then share . . . [reflects] the joy which flows from harmony between one's own actions and the objective order of nature." Ways for men to follow the pope's advice and "slow" their "rhythm" include counting to very high prime numbers, thinking about auto repair, and conceiving of ridiculous names for the child you may well be conceiving. (How about Hortensius, Theobald, or Medea?)

The pope continued to develop his "personalist" theology of sexual self-giving

7. Malcolm X picked up this phrase from his early reading of Wotyjla—a fact which has gone unreported by the anti-Catholic American media, simply because it happens to be manifestly untrue.

and mutual love in a series of talks and documents called *The Theology of the Body*. Other writers who follow in the pope's footsteps include Christopher West, author of *Good News about Sex and Marriage,* Gregory Popcak, author of *For Better—Forever!, A Catholic Guide to Lifelong Marriage,* Mary Rousseau, author of *Sex Is Holy,* and Naura Hayden, author of *How to Satisfy a Woman Every Time and Have Her Beg for More.*[8]

CONTRACEPTION, BULIMIA, AND FRANKENFOODS

Most Catholics in the West aren't fond of the teaching, but the Church still condemns all forms of artificial contraception. Just because your local pastor has tactfully avoided mention of this annoying doctrine—say, for the past forty

years—doesn't mean it has gone away. It has a very long pedigree, and between Pope Pius XI and Pope John Paul II, recent popes have piled up a fair-sized bookshelf full of increasingly infallible declarations on the subject. They've left just about no wiggle room for future pontiffs to change the Church's mind.

In the old days, the Church's teaching wasn't much of a problem, since farm families needed all the milkmaids and pig-stickers they could raise, few kids required education beyond the seventh grade, and the problem of too many mouths to feed was solved the old-fashioned way—through infant mortality. The circumstances of child-bearing have changed radically in less than a century, so it shouldn't be surprising that the Church has felt some growing pains. Okay, sometimes they seem more like death pangs; Catholics on either side of the divide over this doctrine barely speak to one another. They read different magazines, attend different liturgies, and quietly hope that the other side will die off or go away. They'll be waiting quite a while, we expect.

Does Church teaching mean that married people are obliged, on pain of mortal sin, to have a houseful of children? Happily, no. All Catholics[9] admit that changing times have demanded development in the Church's doctrine. As early as 1930, a pope taught that parents could limit their families, using the then still-primitive "rhythm method" of skipping sex on fertile days. Since then, techniques for

---

8. Okay, we're kidding about that last one. Women should never have to beg.
9. Except those on the radical right, who regarded Pope John Paul II as a treacherous liberal. Don't ask.

determining fertility have become ever more effective; the reliability of Natural Family Planning approached 98 percent, as the World Health Organization (reluctantly) admits. What NFP amounts to is finding out when you're fertile, and sending hubby to sleep in the doghouse on those days.

Since 1930, the Church has expanded its understanding of when one may choose to postpone pregnancy. As Paul VI wrote in *Humanae Vitae,* and as the recent *Catechism of the Catholic Church* repeated, a couple may choose to delay or avoid pregnancy for "just reasons." That is, not for frivolous motives—but in accordance with prudence,[10] which governs every other virtue, including generosity to the poor and the proper times to preach the Gospel.

Good news: this means that many Catholics who choose to have smaller families are acting in accord with the Church's teaching—except when they use chemical or mechanical methods that change the nature of the sexual act. To utilitarian Americans, this seems like a pointless distinction: the end justifies the means. When we want to lose weight, we get liposuction. When we want the kids to sit still, we give them Ritalin. When we want more milk from a cow, we genetically engineer it using alien DNA from a grasshopper. Descartes taught us long ago that the point of science was to become the "master and possessor of nature." But the Church sees Creation as covered with big, greasy divine fingerprints, which we're not supposed to wipe away in our rage to tidy things up. And because sexuality is even more sacred than eating, we must treat it with more reverence than we do, say veal cattle. The best way to explain the Church's official theology is to compare spacing children to losing weight. You can achieve that through dieting—or you can try bulimia. If you think they're equivalent, you probably better go back to your gastroenterologist.

CELEBRATE: Learn about Natural Family Planning from one of the many Web sites available, especially the Couple-to-Couple League (*www.ccli.org)* and the Billings Centre (*www.billings-centre.ab.ca*). Practicing NFP usually entails a woman checking for signs of fertility (doesn't sound too romantic, but neither are condoms or vasectomies, come to think of it).

Most women are likely to conceive for between eight and ten days a month. Which leaves two-thirds of the month as a free-fire zone. Compare that to the average married American couple—who have sex once a week, for about ten minutes—and NFP Catholics are making out like bandits.

NFP also helps if you're trying to conceive. Devout Catholics even today sometimes decide to have large families, trusting to God to sort out the details. They re-

---

10. Sure, it says in the Bible, "Be fruitful and multiply." It also says, "Take ye no thought for the morrow." But the Knights of Columbus still sell insurance.

port that it's loads of fun, on top of the hard work, to fill one's rural home with Brigids, Patricks, Marios, and Philomenas—little blurred Xeroxes of either parent, who can be taught to sing, play harpsichord, mow the grass, or cook you dinner. Big families often form home-schooling groups with other, even bigger families—gathering periodically to stage *A Midsummer Night's Dream,* feast outdoors on picnic tables, or act like soccer hooligans in the yard. You'll see these folks at Latin Masses usually, pouring out of a battered minivan, the little girls all in veils and the boys with looks full of mischief, in which they are thoroughly versed, having had many sisters handy to torment. We should be grateful to these people: they're propping up the Social Security system.

March 1

Cunegundes (+1040): A Holy Hot-Foot

This daughter of Flemish nobility was torn between her vocation and her family's plans for her. As an heiress to the County of Luxemburg, she was expected to marry. But Cunegundes had already fallen in love with the religious life, after being educated by nuns. (Hey, it happens. Just not so often, anymore.) Like a good daughter, Cunegundes obeyed her family's wishes and humbly accepted the worst of both worlds—marriage without sex. Cunegundes convinced her husband, Henry the Duke of Bavaria, to honor her private vow of virginity. For his pains, he would someday be canonized as well. With lots of energy to sublimate, Henry managed to win the throne of the Holy Roman Empire in 1014. He spent the next ten years distributing most of his wealth to the poor. A year after he died, Cunegundes fulfilled her lifelong wish and became a nun.

At one point during her monastic marriage to King Henry, Cunegundes was accused of adultery. It caused a royal scandal and could even have threatened her husband's hold on the throne: medieval cuckolds who failed to hunt down and punish their wives' lovers were customarily driven out of town by a jeering crowd, in a ritual called a "charivari." So to set wagging tongues at ease, Cunegundes came upon a solution that would satisfy the thinly Christianized Teutonic warlords—and, more importantly, their wives. She gathered the court, had the ground spread with hot coals, and after a prayer walked over them calmly and uncomplainingly—without injuring her feet.

CELEBRATE: Wives, demonstrate your ongoing romantic interest in your husband by picking up a pair of particularly sexy, impractical high heels—the kind that make you totter, precariously, like a melting ice sculpture. Put those "sensible" sneakers or Birkenstocks out of sight. Like good King Henry, he'll appreciate the effort.

March 3

Katherine Drexel: What You Get for Pestering the Pope

This saint's story can be seen as a cautionary tale about making demands of Church officials. The lovely, carefree American Katherine Drexel, daughter of a railroad baron, was traveling Europe in 1887, enjoying her trust fund, which paid her $1,000 a day (serious money, back then). Like her parents, Katherine had spent treasure and time helping the poor; the family founded schools for rural orphans and freed slaves in Virginia. Now, as she completed her grand tour of the Continent, she stopped in to see Pope Leo XIII. As one of the richest Catholics in the world, when she asked for a personal audience, she got it. She approached the pontiff boldly to beg a favor for a friend, Bishop James O'Connor of the Wyoming Territory. He needed more missionaries to preach to the Indians. The pope thought for a moment, looked into Katherine's eyes, and then asked the question that ended her carefree life: "Why don't you become a missionary?"

Katherine wound down her tour and returned to America, traveling to visit Sioux Indians and set up missions. Deciding that black and native Americans were underserved by the Church, she founded her very own order, the Sisters of the Blessed Sacrament for Indians and Colored, in 1891. Renouncing all her wealth, she devoted herself to running the organization, which founded black Catholic schools in thirteen states, fifty missions on reservations, and America's first university for African Americans, the still-thriving Xavier in New Orleans. Inspired by her example, wealthy Catholics visiting the Vatican have been careful not to make requests.

> **CELEBRATE:** Use your railroad inheritance to found a university devoted to your favorite ethnic group.

March 9
Frances of Rome (1384–1440): Exorcise that Gremlin!

Anyone who has ever driven a Yugo or struggled with road rage should have recourse to this saint, patroness of everything from gear boxes to turn signals. Every year, local drivers clog traffic in their taxicabs, Vespas, and Fiats on her feast day for the annual Blessing of the Cars. (The same tradition is honored in Los Angeles and several other American cities.)

St. Frances was born into Roman aristocracy during the Renaissance. She married and raised six children. After her husband's death she founded a women's religious order that served the sick and the poor. She opened Rome's first foundling hospital, and her basilica sits in the Roman Forum.

What does this holy widow have to do with your dinged-up Volvo? Well, the plucky Frances didn't restrict herself to daylight hours. By night, she'd wander the pitch-black streets of Rome, tending to needy travelers and crime victims, and collecting abandoned children. In her travels, she was guided by her guardian angel, who lit her way all through the night. So Pope Pius XI thought her a fitting patron for the newfangled "horseless carriages." If you've ever seen how Romans drive, you know that they're keeping Frances busy.

> **CELEBRATE:** If you have a functioning car, drive it over to the rectory today and ask a priest to perform a simple blessing over the hood. Here's one we found, by the Hawaiian priest Fr. Bruce Graft:
>
> *Gracious Lord: We give you thanks for the gift of this automobile for our convenience, recreation, and livelihood. Help us, Lord, to use this gift thoughtfully, carefully, and never while under the influence of alcohol or any chemical substance that might impair our ability to safely drive this vehicle. Lord, give us patience and a loving spirit, and take away from us all anger and impatience that might either put others or ourselves in danger. Amen.*

March 10

John Ogilvie (1579–1615): Death before Haggis

This Scottish nobleman was possessed of the spiritual gift that mystical theologians have called *cajones.*[1] At a time when Catholics were being massacred wholesale in parts of his country, John Ogilvie shook off the state religion, Calvinism, at age seventeen. He went to Paris to join the Jesuits. Their mission in the British Isles was to keep the faith alive, however many of them died in the attempt. (Saying Mass was considered an act of treason, and priests were commonly disemboweled slowly before being hacked to pieces, like William Wallace in the movie

Braveheart.) John pestered his superiors, who kept warning him away, until they sent him back to Scotland, where he traveled in disguise, dispensing sacraments in hidden chapels for only eleven months before he was arrested. After many hours of torture, he still wouldn't name names of fellow priests, scoffing at the men with the sharp implements: "Your threats cheer me; I mind them no more than the cackling of geese." He said he no more feared to die "than you do to dine." Of course, he knew that they'd be eating haggis. . . .

> **CELEBRATE:** Roast a goose in honor of brave St. John and wash it down with a single-malt Scotch. For entertainment and insight, rent the movie *Braveheart.* During the torture scene, mock his tormentors by practicing goose calls at the top of your lungs. (More than one glass of Laphroig is clearly indicated.)

March 12

Serafina (+1253): Bring Yapping Dogs to the Housebound

Another saint with a cinematic connection is the humble Serafina. Her image, painted by Michelangelo's mentor, Ghirlandaio, is the painting Judy Dench's character is striving desperately to save from the effects of Allied shelling in Franco Zeffirelli's *Tea with Mussolini.* If we peel away the sandbags that protected the lovely Renaissance picture, we see the story of a young woman who wove immense suffering into holiness. Born to a family that had recently lost its wealth, Serafina was soon left an orphan and stricken with a mysterious paralysis that left

---

1. To be fair, plenty of women have displayed this quality as well, from St. Agatha to St. Joan of Arc.

her flat on her back for the rest of her life, afflicted with sores. She was kept alive only by the visits of a devoted friend, and she spent that life in prayer, uniting her own pains to Christ's. She was excited to learn that one saint, Gregory the Great, had suffered similarly. She developed an ongoing relationship with the long-dead pope, who would come to visit the impoverished Italian girl, finally predicting to her the day when she would die and enter heaven. She's now a patron of shut-ins.

CELEBRATE: In honor of St. Serafina, you might take time to pay a visit to a shut-in you know—perhaps someone who's handicapped or an agoraphobic— bringing along some spicy food treats, all your kids, your pets and CDs of lively, danceable music. Show up early and don't leave till late; make sure to fill the person's usually empty house with chatter, strange smells, mariachis, and the yapping of tiny dogs. Leave them, after seven hours or so, so they can sit back and realize how lucky they are that they don't go out into the world every day and have to deal with people like you.

March 17

Patrick: Bobbing for Potatoes

If there's one thing the long-suffering people of Ireland came to be known for, it was their ability to transform misery into joy. Listen to Irish music: the songs that aren't about hopelessly unrequited love are tales of rebellions gone astray, betrayals by trusted allies, and drinking entire barrels of beer on board a sinking ship. Irish wakes—held in the home, around the body, which is frequently plied with the deceased's favorite brand of whiskey—end with friends of the deceased hiding the body from the family, who then have to ransack the house to locate the corpse so it can be buried.

In this spirit, we'd like to suggest a way to celebrate the great Apostle of Ireland, St. Patrick, that doesn't involve green beer, paper shamrocks, or tipsy parades full of scheming politicians. This year, invite your Hibernian friends to a Potato Famine Party.

Of course we don't intend to make fun of the people who suffered in the great famine, which struck Ireland between 1845 and 1850, leaving millions dead or malnourished while a complacent British government debated the merits of free

market economics. Hundreds of thousands died, while millions were forced to emigrate, half-alive, in "coffin ships" to Boston, New Brunswick, New York, and other ports. Instead, we propose this party to honor their endurance and faith—and offer those who died the Irish wake they never had.

Your party should embody the great Christian theme of earthly suffering—interrupted by a sudden explosion of joy. To make this work, it should begin as miserably as possible: try to create the atmosphere of a ramshackle, nineteenth-century Irish hut. Strew your floor with straw, hang your walls with old-fashioned religious pictures, and drape the entertainment center with burlap potato sacks. Dress the hostess, host, and kids in peasant clothes and cover your coffee table with fresh-cut moss. As guests arrive, greet each with a deep, long sigh, and a roll of the eyes. When they ask, "How are you?" answer: "As best as can be expected," or "I'll be offering it up." Smudge the children's faces with a little charcoal, and give each one a can to beg the guests for change "for charity's sake." Make sure each can bears a big green cross and is clearly labeled "IRA."

To set the mood, your hidden CD player should be set on a continuous loop of Irish dirges, and the hostess should lead the guests in a "keening" contest, encouraging each arrival to practice the deep, guttural howl which legend attributes to banshees, the female ghosts rumored to haunt the Irish countryside. If your friends seem disinclined to keen, just wait until they get a load of the food.

Of course, you'll serve only potatoes. But you won't serve enough of them.

To reinforce the scarcity theme, make sure there's only one potato for every two guests, who'll have to compete if they wish to eat. You might propose arm wrestling, a hurling match, or the traditional Irish party game of *bobbing for potatoes, in the water where they were cooked.* Blindfold the guests with gray, moist rags and encourage them to seek out their potato with their teeth. (Make sure the skins are still on, and that the water has cooled.) Let the winners wash down their dinner with bad American beer (such as Killian's "Irish" Red), served lukewarm. Then go back into the living room to keen about your hospitality.

When guests begin to head out the door, shaking their heads and vowing never to return, it's time to spring on them the sudden explosion of joy: change the music to jigs and reels and lively songs by modern Irish groups (the Cranberries, Rogue's Progress, and the Pogues come to mind), and pull out your carefully hidden stash of excellent Irish alcohol, such as Guinness, Magner's Cider, and Black Bush Irish Whiskey. Quickly save the party by serving an array of gourmet Irish food—such as cold baked salmon with dill, au gratin potatoes, warm cabbage salad with bacon, and buttered Irish soda bread. Give each of your guests one of the "contest" potatoes to take home as a keepsake—and hope they don't hurl it at your windows as they drive away.

Apart from the boiled potatoes, today's menu is composed mostly of cold dishes so that you can fool your hungry guests. The seafood and apple crisp can be put in the oven at the last minute. Serve the meal buffet style. We've chosen traditional Hibernian dishes which were popular in medieval Ireland—before it was conquered and the English took all the . . . (*insert tipsy, semicoherent, thirty-minute rant about ancient historical wrongs here*). Made from ingredients abundant in the Emerald Isle and promoted by the Bord Bia (Irish Food Board), these recipes are part of the culinary renaissance now sweeping Ireland.

CELEBRATE

Steamed Lobster and Crabs with Herb Butter

Oysters on the Half Shell

Vegetable Platter of Pearl Onions, Radishes, and lightly dressed Baby Greens

Salt Roasted Shrimp in the Shells (see recipe)

Apple Oatmeal Crumble (see recipe)

Salt Roasted Shrimp in the Shells

2 pounds shell on medium shrimp
Coarse sea salt
2 bunches rosemary

2 tablespoons whole coriander
2 tablespoons pink peppercorns,
   lightly crushed

Preheat oven to 550 or as hot as it will go.
   Rinse and pat dry shrimp.
   Cover large baking pan with salt.
   Distribute rosemary on salt.
   Toss shrimp with coriander and pink peppercorns.
   Lay in an even single layer on salt.
   Roast for 8–10 minutes. Shrimp will turn pink. Toss gently to cook other side.
Cook another 2–5 minutes. Serve on a platter garnished with rosemary branches.

Makes 2–4 servings

Apple Oatmeal Crumble

1 cup golden raisins
1/4 cup Irish whiskey
3 Gala apples
1 cup rolled oats

1/2 cup brown sugar
Pinch of Himalayan salt
1/2 cup butter (1 stick)

Preheat oven to 375 degrees.
   Lightly butter 1-1/2 quart casserole dish.
   Simmer raisins and whiskey on low until whiskey is absorbed and the raisins are plump.
   Meanwhile quarter, core, and slice unpeeled apples. Toss with raisins in baking dish.
   Mix together oats, sugar, and salt. Beat in butter and work until evenly combined. Spread over apples evenly. Bake for 45–50 minutes. Allow to cool briefly before serving allowing crust to crisp.

Makes 6 servings

Joseph: He Couldn't Get No Respect

According to art historians, Joseph, the spouse of the Virgin Mary and earthly father of Jesus, was once the Rodney Dangerfield of saints. In the early Middle Ages, the rough, recently Christianized barbarians couldn't muster much admiration for a husband who'd never laid a hand on his wife. Legends of the saint cast him as someone virtually cuckolded by God the Father, who lived in the shadow of his sinless, virginal wife and divine adopted Son. Painters and writers explained his celibacy away by depicting him as a feeble old man at the time of his betrothal, who presumably didn't mind contracting a monastic marriage. (Outside the ascetic sect of Essenes, which might have included John the Baptist, there were few Jews

who considered celibacy virtuous. Quite the contrary.) This is surprising information to modern Catholics, who grew up thinking of St. Joseph as one of the most powerful intercessors in heaven, the Patron of the Universal Church, a skilled craftsman and noble exemplar to his foster son, who "grew in age and wisdom" under Joseph's tutelage. There's barely an Italian-American front yard in New York City or New Orleans that doesn't have a statue of St. Joseph watching over the tomato plants and peppers.

What happened to transform the image of this saint? The economy, stupid. As manufacturing exploded in the High Middle Ages, craftsmen and other working people began to demand their place in society, alongside clerics, knights, and kings. The Church in the West had already developed a theology of work, replacing the classical disdain for "servile" labor with St. Benedict's injunction to "work and pray," even seeing work *as* prayer. Workingmen's guilds arose (think of labor unions, with patron saints and festive banners) and grew rich, particularly in northern Europe. These guilds began to sponsor artworks that showed workingmen in a more respectful light—such as Robert Campin's "Triptych of the Annunciation," which depicts a healthy, vigorous Joseph, with an only partly graying beard, doing detailed woodwork with all the dignity and grace of a monk saying Mass. St. Joseph's celibacy began to be seen as a heroic act that he'd undertaken long before the Annunciation to Mary, and that the angel's message only confirmed. Tales about the Holy Family started emphasizing Joseph's role as earthly patriarch, an heir of royal blood to his Old Testament forebears.

On a more pragmatic level, St. Joseph himself began to undertake some image management, interceding from heaven in several spectacular instances, for instance, to avert a famine in Sicily by answering prayers with a bumper harvest of fava beans. To this day, these beans are cooked up and served festively on his feast by inhabitants of the island, who sponsor elaborate "St. Joseph Altars" in homes and parish halls. These lavish feasts, which usually fall in the midst of Lent, are thrown open to the public in an act of generosity that's meant as gratitude to Jesus's foster father.

CELEBRATE: Cook up a plate of St. Joseph's miraculous fava beans. If you plan to celebrate this day as a family, promote interpersonal harmony by handing out Beano to each guest.

St. Joseph's Day Fava Beans

1-1/2 cups dried, split fava beans	3 cloves garlic, minced
5 cups water	2 tablespoons extra virgin olive oil
1 medium potato peeled, cubed	Salt and freshly ground pepper

Rinse fava beans under cool running water. Put beans in heavy bottomed pot, add water, bring to a boil. Reduce heat and simmer on low 10 to 15 minutes. Add potatoes and garlic and continue to simmer until potatoes are soft and most of the liquid is absorbed. The beans should be somewhat thick. Purée through a food mill or potato ricer. Beat in olive oil and season to taste.

Accompany with capers, assorted olives, soft cheeses, pickled eggplant, roasted red peppers, and foccacia or Italian bread—and plenty of olive oil!

Makes 4–6 servings

March 23

Sibyllina Biscossi (1287–1367): Patroness of Church Ladies

This reclusive, orphaned, housebound saint was blind and lived bricked up in the walls of a local church in Pavia. After losing her sight at age twelve, she was taken in by Third Order Dominican women and invited to join their community. She accepted and gained a reputation as the most prayerful nun in the cloister. But this wasn't enough for Sybillina, who'd developed a close friendship with St. Dominic himself, founder of the order. She prayed to him regularly to get back her sight, and one day he appeared to her in a lengthy vision in which he explained that God had answered her prayer. And the answer was no.

Undaunted, Sybillina increased her devotion, gaining permission to live as an anchorite— a hermit, locked up in a tiny cell adjoining the parish church. She suffered in the winters and lived on practically no food, communicating with the world only through her window—through which she would occasionally speak, accepting prayer requests and working miracles. Needless to say, she became a popular attraction in the town. Although she had no physical sight, Sybillina had been granted spiritual visions and a keen sense of the presence of God. Once she heard a priest passing by to bring the Eucharist to the sick, and she called out the window to tell the priest that he was carrying unconsecrated hosts. He sighed, shook his head, and agreed to check—only to find that in his haste he'd grabbed the wrong container.

Sybillina is the rightful patron of little old ladies who hang around the rectory, critiquing the priests' sermon, his choice of vestments, his choir director, and infidelity to liturgical directives from the Vatican.

CELEBRATE: Download the latest liturgical decrees from the Roman Congregation for Divine Worship (*www.vatican.va*). Attend Mass at your local parish with a pen and notebook, marking down any deviations from the rules. Then drop by the rectory on St. Sybillina's feast day to discuss the results of your research with the pastor. He'll thank you. Pastors always do.

March 25

The Annunciation: Salvation is from a J.A.P.

In medieval England this feast was reckoned as New Year's Day, since it marks the beginning of the Incarnation of Christ, in Mary's womb. It's interesting to think that when the angel came to Mary, offering to make her the mother of the suffering Messiah, she was free to say no. It wouldn't even have been a sin. In his theology, Pope John Paul has made much of Mary's choice, her decision to say "yes" to God, "Let it be done unto me according to thy word."

Since Mary was descended from King David and spoke the local dialect, it's accurate to call her a Jewish-Aramaic Princess. How different the world might be if that teenaged J.A.P. had looked at the fiery angel in her window who offered her a life of perpetual virginity and co-redemptive suffering, cracked her gum, and said, "As if. I don't *think* so. . . . " Would God just have crafted another immaculately conceived Jewish virgin? (Hebrew legend said that when Adam's first wife, Lilith, displayed a little too much *chutzpah,* Adam returned her within the warranty period and exchanged her for a new model, Eve.)

What would God have done? Given up on the whole Redemption thing? Or sent the Messiah to the Vikings? Might the Sermon on the Mount—delivered in Danish—have urged each of us, like Conan the Barbarian, to crush your enemies, to see them driven before us, and to hear the lamentation of the women? It's pointless to speculate.

Instead, why not reflect on this holy day in the light cast by one of the greatest poets of the nineteenth century, Oscar Wilde, who wrote a meditation on this feast "Ave Maria Gratia Plena". Wilde, who tragically lived closeted for most of his life, was able only on his death bed to "come out" and be received into the Church—thus admitting that all along he hadn't been a Decadent, or a "sodomite," but just another Bad Catholic—like us.

A BOWL OF MARY, WITH VIRGIN OIL

In the Middle Ages, almost every plant was named for a saint, a mystery of the faith, or the Blessed Virgin Mary. Most of the gardeners and herbalists who recorded the attributes of plants were monks, who often designed cloister gardens. The religious names of flowers mostly disappeared during the Reformation, but the names have come down to us in books, and around the world people are reviving these names in "Mary Gardens." To learn more, see *www.mgardens.org.*

For your salad on the Feast of the Annunciation, serve some of the flowers, and make sure to tell your guests the plants' original religious names. The flowers are readily available at your local farmers' market and in your own yard. Don't be tempted by the flowers at the florist's; they are full of pesticides and other inedibles.

Virgin Petal Salad

4 cups mesclun greens
1 cup St. Joseph's Flower (nasturtium) leaves
1 cup nasturtium blossoms, shredded
1/2 cup Our Lady's Delight (pansies) leaves
1/4 cup blossoms from Our Lady's Garlic (chives), petals torn from stem

1/4 cup Mary's Gold (marigold) blossoms, petals removed, reserved
Salt and freshly ground black pepper
Ever-virgin olive oil
Sherry vinegar
3 tablespoons sour cream

Toss lettuces and blossoms together. Toss consecutively with salt, pepper, drizzled olive oil (extra virgin!) and vinegar. Finally, gently toss with sour cream and sprinkle with Mary's Gold petals.

Makes 6–8 servings

Season of Lent
Shrove Tuesday: Pancakes and Proxy Penance

Shrove Tuesday (also known as "Fat Tuesday" or "Mardi Gras") is the last day of Carnival season. It may surprise you to learn that Carnival is celebrated as far north as England. It's true that the Reformation dulled the edge of British Lent, just as it pulled out the statues from the niches at Oxford University—although the elder dons keep up the poignant, ancient custom of bowing their heads to saints who aren't there.[2] Could there be a better illustration of the English devotion to tradition for its own sake? That's what keeps the guards outside Buckingham Palace stiff-

---

2. When Yale University in the late 1920s and early 1930s constructed an exquisite series of "residential colleges" using Oxford as a model and cheap Depression labor as a means, several of the complexes were built in classic British Gothic style. Ingenious architects used acid to age the stones, and carefully cracked the stained-glass windows, so they could be "repaired" in medieval style, with lines of lead. The result was a group of buildings that, when new, looked almost eight hundred years old—a kind of intellectual Epcot Center. The Oxford-style buildings contained all the old saints' niches—most of which were left empty.

lipped in tall bearskin hats, the queen on her throne, and Americans with digital cameras landing by the planeload to gawk. You can recreate a bit of misty, dreamy England in your very own home by throwing a traditional British Shrove Tuesday party.

This celebration was certainly invented by women, since it involves clearing things out of the house. (Men are interested only in bringing things in—especially if they're "really old, probably an antique," "incredibly unique and cool," and "worth something, it's gotta be.") Shrove Tuesday entailed using up all those food items that weren't allowed according to the old, strict rules of medieval Lent: eggs, butter, sugar, lard, and meat. Yep, life pretty much wasn't worth living for forty days every year back then—especially since the Church also strongly recommended married couples remain celibate until Easter. Not that anybody would have had much strength for the tussle, on a diet of bread, gruel, and herring—pretty much all that's left in an English diet when you take out the fats and meats.

Before the medieval English lurched forward into six long sexless, sunless, meatless weeks, the ladies cooked up treats that would use up all the forbidden items in the cupboard and put a little fat on the family's bones to last through the

fast. Traditionally, that meant whipping up the richest, ripest pancakes ever invented, accompanied by every kind of meat— bacon, ham, sausage, pork chops, you name it.

It's said that one woman was making her pancakes so assiduously that she ran out of the house to church with her pan in hand and flipped the cakes all the way to Confession. This story inspired a curious custom: pancake flipping races. Even today, on Shrove Tuesday, wives and mothers gather in village squares and on parish greens to race each other down appointed paths, while flipping pancakes in hot, greased pans, without the use of spatulas.

CELEBRATE: The very name of this holiday reminds us of a spooky, theological reality: shrove comes from "shrive," which means to confess your sins. So the medieval English gathered the family after the pancakes were done and took them all to church to confess their sins. After the Reformation, this custom continued in a muted form; since priests don't hear confessions in Anglican churches, and most English don't quite believe in God (though they're too polite to tell Him), instead they end up at the pub, where holy water has been replaced by tepid ale, and the priest behind the grille by a barman behind his rail, who listens, dispenses advice, and offers libations (if not absolution).

You can start to revive the deeper meaning of Shrove Tuesday by gently adapting the medieval customs to suburban, modern usage. Remind your friends that Christ suffered hideously and died not for the sins of all humankind *in general,* but for *each one* of them in particular, and their individual sins. To mark this profound theological truth, we suggest a fun family game: invite each guest to "confess" the particular sins of his spouse, date, or child, for which Christ had to die. We call this game "Proxy Penance."

Few of us like relating our own sins anymore—except for the really glamorous ones, which mostly took place years ago in an alcoholic fog. But you'll find no such resistance when it comes to confessing the sins of others. The guests can take turns, offering thanks to Christ in the form of a toast for "forgiving my wife's habit of rampant, almost random infidelity," or "helping Peter here with the whole methadone thing," or "giving Mary some insight about her eating disorder."

You'll find that once they get started, people are happy to play Proxy Penance for hours at a time. In fact it's hard to get them to wait their turn. As the cocktails flow, the sins will pile up on the floor of the living room, where your clean-up crew can collect and discard them at evening's end. It feels wonderful to go into springtime with a clean conscience. Don't be selfish, and hoard that feeling for yourself; help someone else attain that fresh-scrubbed sensation by spilling his sins for him. He'll thank you later.

Crepes

The heart of the party. Serve with strawberry orange sauce, blueberry pomegranate sauce, maple syrup, whipped cream and nuts.

2 cups all-purpose flour	3 cups milk
2 tablespoons sugar	Zest of 1 orange
Pinch of salt	Zest of 1 lemon
6 large eggs	4 tablespoons clarified butter

Add flour, sugar, salt, eggs, and milk to blender and process until smooth. Pour through a strainer and add fruit zest. Let rest for at least 1 hour, or overnight.

Heat a nonstick 6 to 8 inch skillet and brush with a dash of clarified butter. Add just enough batter to cover pan in a thin layer. Working quickly, flick the pan with your wrist so the batter will cook evenly.

Flip pancake and cook other side. It is helpful to use a spoon to loosen edges of crepe to turn. Repeat until batter is consumed, stacking crepes on a plate.

Makes 10 servings

Strawberries in Orange Sauce

2 pints strawberries
1/2 cup sugar

1/3 cup orange juice
1 teaspoon orange blossom water

Rinse strawberries in colander, remove stems, and cut into quarters. Sprinkle with sugar and toss. Allow to sit half an hour. Add juice and blossom water. Macerate for an hour. Serve in bowl alongside crepes.

Blueberry Pomegranate Sauce

12 ounces blueberry pomegranate
    juice
1 10 ounce bag frozen blueberries

1/4 cup sugar
Zest of one lemon

Combine frozen berries and juice in medium stainless steel saucepan. Heat gently and add sugar. Stir to dissolve. Add zest. Lightly simmer 5–6 minutes. Remove from heat. Serve warm or chilled. Extra sauce is great for breakfast with yogurt.

I'd Zing the Better Vor a Nut

A traditional Shrove Tuesday song, from W. H. Long's *A Dictionary of Isle of Wight Dialect*.

> *Shroven, Shroven,*
> *I be come a Shroven,*
> *A piece of bread, a piece of cheese,*
> *A piece of your fat bacon,*
> *Doughnuts and pancakes,*
> *All o' your own maaken.*
> *Vine vowls in a pie,*
> *My mouth es very dry,*
> *I wish I was zo well-a-wet,*
> *I'd zing the better vor a nut.*
> *Shroven, Shroven,*
> *We be come a Shroven.*[3]

---

3. We have no idea what any of this means.

Ash Wednesday:
Catholic Mating Identification Day

This is one of the most solemn days on the liturgical calendar, marking Jesus's departure to pray and meditate—and endure diabolical temptation—in the desert, in preparation for the culmination of His earthly mission, entry into Jerusalem, and death on the cross. Our Lord spent forty days in the desert—a profoundly symbolic number in the scriptures, which also marked the number of days the skies poured rain during Noah's flood and the years the Israelites wandered in the desert after leaving Egypt, before they found the Promised Land. (Look at a biblical atlas some time to see how they must have wandered; it's not that far from Egypt to Israel. Those Jews were good and *lost*. They were probably using Mapquest, which has sent the authors two  hours astray in the snow on to service roads of Newark Airport, simply to avoid a seventy-five-cent toll on the New Jersey Turnpike. But we digress.)

To mark the onset of penance, the Church distributes ashes to Catholics, which are rubbed on the forehead with the timeless warning "Remember, man, that thou art dust, and unto dust thou shalt return." This ceremony is so vivid that it has the power to draw people to church who almost never otherwise attend. (So Catholics like free samples—what's wrong with that? See you on Palm Sunday!) Our favorite Ash Wednesday anecdote concerns an old parish of ours near Grand Central Terminal that had a fire, and hence an abundance of ashes, but no place to hand them out. So the priests put on their stoles and stood in the main concourse of Grand Central Terminal—as fearless as Hari Krishnas in an airport—and smudged the foreheads of anyone who stopped by. This sort of "drive-through" Ash Wednesday service proved much more popular than any actual liturgies that day, and was soon discontinued. But it shows the enduring power of this public sign of penance, which serves to mark one's intention to lead a truly penitent Lent.

It's also a handy way for single Catholics to spot each other and meet. For one day a year, that cute intern you've been eyeing in the elevator, the distinguished executive who doesn't have a wedding ring, the pink-faced Polish waitress or Irish construction worker, walks around all day with a sticker on his or her head that says "Marriage Material." We know that there isn't the same opprobrium attached to mixed marriages as there used to be; mixed couples no longer have to hold the wedding ceremony in the rectory. But there is still something powerfully appealing about finding someone who shares your deepest beliefs about the world, who speaks in the same vocabulary of faith—and feels guilty about all the same things. It clears away any number of potential areas of conflict, such as which religious services you're going to attend, and to which sort of miserable school you're going to send your kids.

So if you're a single Catholic, take full advantage of the solemn fast we like to call "Mating Identification Day" by making a point of meeting those unhitched papists you've been ogling all year. Here is a list of classic "Catholic pick-up lines" that have been circulating in church vestibules and email inboxes for years, which Catholic writer Patrick Madrid sorted out, edited, and (most importantly) copyrighted in his delightful magazine *Envoy*. Clearly, they're designed for Catholics of a particular sort—the serious, self-described "orthodox" believers who have probably already slammed this book shut with a guilty smile.

TOP TEN CATHOLIC PICK-UP LINES

10. May I offer you a light for that votive candle?
9. Hi there. My buddy and I were wondering if you would settle a dispute we're having. Do you think the word should be pronounced HOMEschooling, or homeSCHOOLing?
8. Sorry, but I couldn't help but noticing how cute you look in that ankle-length, shapeless, plaid jumper.
7. What's a nice girl like you doing at a First Saturday Rosary Cenacle like this?
6. You don't like the Culture of Death either? Wow! We have so much in common!
5. Let's get out of here. I know a much cozier little Catholic bookstore downtown.
4. I bet I can guess your Confirmation name.
3. You've got stunning, scapular-brown eyes.
2. Did you feel what I felt when we reached into the holy water font at the same time?
1. Confess here often?

If none of these appeal to you, we can offer a more mainstream approach, which combines good humor, ancient tradition, and contemporary forthrightness: Here's My Number, I Think You're Kind of Hot Cross Buns (see recipe).

It has been customary since the Middle Ages to bake sweet, sticky buns marked with a cross to serve as one of the light meals permitted during fast days, like Ash Wednesday. Why not take part in this tradition and turn it to ruthlessly pragmatic use by baking your name and phone number into these buns and then distributing them throughout the day to eligible, clearly labeled Catholics who interest you? They're a light way to break the ice with a total stranger to whom you're attracted, and about whom you know nothing more than that he will someday return to dust.

"Here's My Number, I Think You're Kind of Hot" Cross Buns

BUNS:

1 package yeast
1 cup milk, warm
2 large eggs
1 teaspoon salt
1/3 cup turbinado
3-1/4 cups flour
4 tablespoons unsalted butter, softened
2/3 cup currants or raisins

4 teaspoons spice mix (grind and combine the following spices: 1 teaspoon whole allspice, 1/4 of a nutmeg, 1/4 cinnamon stick, 1 teaspoon whole cloves, 1 teaspoon ground ginger, 1/2 teaspoon white peppercorns, 1/4 teaspoon whole cumin)

GLAZE:

1/2 cup milk

1/2 cup sugar

Cream yeast with 1/4 cup warm milk for about 10 minutes.

Combine yeast mixture with salt and sugar in bowl with 1 cup flour. Add spice mixture to remaining flour.

Add remaining milk and eggs to yeast mixture, stirring with wooden spoon. Gradually add remaining flour. Add butter in pieces.

Remove from bowl to counter and knead until smooth and elastic, sprinkling lightly with flour as needed. Put dough into a bowl and cover with a damp cloth. Allow it to rise in a warm, draft-free spot for approximately 2-1/2 hours, until doubled in size.

Punch down and gently knead in currants. Allow to rest 10 minutes.

Divide dough in half and form two long ropes. Cut each rope into 10 pieces. Roll pieces into smooth balls and place on lightly greased sheet pan. Cover with cloth and allow to rise again, until doubled in size (about 1 hour). Preheat oven to 350 degrees.

Slash cross-shape into tops of buns with very sharp knife and fill with currants. Slip your business card—or (better) a blank Chinese fortune cookie slip with your number written on it on one side and one of the Top Ten Catholic Pick Up Lines on the other, into each bun.

Bake for 15–20 minutes until golden. Meanwhile, make glaze, boil sugar and milk in saucepan until thick and syrupy. Remove buns from oven, and brush with glaze.

Allow to cool on wire racks.

Makes 20 buns

Not Particularly Penitential Recipes for Lent

The season of Lent used to be a real penance. The "fast" imposed now on Catholics just two days a year—one full meal, and two snacks—used to apply for forty. In the East the fast gets stricter as it approaches Holy Week. Russian and Ukrainian Christians give up, successively: meat, cheese, sex, wine, oil, and eventually, oxygen (eaten up by all those candles they're lighting in front of the icons). Nowadays, the Church encourages penitential practices for Lent, but imposes very few. The reason for this is suggested in the Vatican II document *Gaudium et Spes.* It seems that Western man has grown so much more faithful, hopeful, and loving in the past few centuries that by now we're just about perfect. So we don't really need to fast. Hurrah!

Just about all you have to give up during Lent nowadays is meat on Fridays. Here are a few nice dishes you can make for your family instead:

Mussels in White Wine

1 pound mussels	1 sprig thyme
1 tablespoon olive oil	2 cups Burgundian Petite Chablis
1 teaspoon garlic	White pepper
1/2 leek, sliced	Freshly ground black pepper

Clean and purge mussels. Cover in cool water and sprinkle with white pepper. The mussels will "sneeze," spitting out impurities. One by one clean each mussel of seaweed and dirt on shell and pull away beards—using pliers where needed. Put mussels through several more changes of water, drain, cover with a damp towel and set aside.

In large skillet heat oil and garlic. Add leeks and cook until translucent. Add thyme and wine. Bring to simmer for a few minutes. Add mussels. They will open up and steam. Discard any that are broken or do not open. Serve in bowl with juice and French fries or crusty bread.

Makes 2 servings

Spinach with Raisins and Pine Nuts

2 pounds fresh spinach	1 small onion, finely chopped
3 tablespoons olive oil	3 cloves garlic, minced
1/4 cup pine nuts, toasted	1/3 cup raisins, plumped in hot water and drained

Wash spinach in several changes of cool water. In sauté pan, warm 1 tablespoon oil over medium heat. Add pine nuts, gently shaking the pan until they turn golden. Remove pine nuts from pan and set aside. Warm remaining oil, add onions, and sautée until translucent. Add garlic, stirring until lightly golden. Add spinach in handfuls, stirring until wilted. Add raisins and pine nuts. Season to taste and serve warm.

Makes 2 servings

Potatoes Aoli

This recipe consists of two simple preparations: potatoes, and aoli—a garlic and lemon mayonnaise eaten all over the Mediterranean. (You'll have plenty left over to use on salads and sandwiches!)

2 pounds red potatoes
3 egg yolks
1 tablespoon Dijon mustard
1/2 teaspoon salt
1 tablespoon chopped garlic

2 cups premium extra virgin olive oil
1/4 cup fresh lemon juice
1 tablespoon red wine vinegar
6 tablespoons chopped parsley
1 tablespoon capers

Bring potatoes to a boil in salted water. Simmer covered 15–20 minutes until tender to the knife. Drain and cool. Peel and cut into medium-size chunks. Set aside.

To make aoli, add egg yolks, mustard, and salt to large bowl and whisk together. Begin adding olive oil drop by drop and whisk to incorporate. When the mixture has formed a thick emulsion, add half of the lemon juice. Add remaining oil, drizzling it into the middle and whisking to incorporate. Add remaining ingredients and adjust seasoning. Remove all but 1/2 cup of the aoli and set aside for future use. Add potatoes to bowl and combine with aoli until all chunks are moist. Serve cold.

Makes 4–6 servings

Shrimp in Garlic Sauce

1 pound small shrimp, cleaned
1/2 cup sherry
Coarse salt
3 tablespoons olive oil

2 teaspoons garlic, finely minced in processor
1/2 teaspoon red pepper flakes
Several sprigs fresh thyme
1 tablespoon minced parsley

Rinse shrimp and marinate for 3 hours in sherry and 1 tablespoon olive oil, with one teaspoon garlic and thyme. Heat remaining olive oil in sauté pan. Add remaining garlic and thyme, cook until lightly golden. Drain shrimp, reserving liquid.

Add shrimp to pan, cooking until it starts to turn lightly pink. Add marinade and parsley to pan, reduce, and thicken. Adjust seasonings to taste.

Makes 2 servings

Manchego Cheese and Quince Paste

This Catalonian specialty serves as an exotic five-minute dessert. Which you really shouldn't be eating during Lent. You worldly wretch.

1/2 pound Spanish Manchego cheese

1 package quince paste or 12 ounces quince preserves

Bring cheese to room temperature for 3 hours before serving. Serve with quince.

Makes 2–4 servings

Cuban Style Black Bean and Rice Soup

1 pound dried black beans, rinsed
6 cups water
4 cups vegetable stock or water
1/4 cup olive oil
1 bay leaf
1 large onion, chopped
4–6 cloves garlic
1-1/2 teaspoons cumin

1-1/2 teaspoons oregano
1-1/2 cups cooked rice
2 teaspoons salt
2–3 tablespoons, sherry vinegar
Garnishes: Sour cream, chopped
  scallions, sliced radishes, lemon
  wedges, freshly ground pepper,
  chopped fresh oregano

Boil beans in water for 45 minutes to 1 hour. Heat oil in skillet. Sauté onions and garlic in skillet until golden. Add cumin and oregano to mixture. Add vegetable stock, sautéed seasonings, bay leaf to cooking beans.

Simmer on low for 1–2 hours until beans are tender. Add cooked rice, salt, and vinegar to beans. Purée 2–3 cups of beans in blender. Return to soup. Stir until combined. Adjust seasonings to taste. Serve in soup bowls, with garnishes.

Makes 6–8 servings

Soft Olive Oil Bread

1/2 cup warm water
1 teaspoon yeast
1 teaspoon sugar

2 cups flour
1 teaspoon salt
1/4 cup olive oil

Combine water, yeast, and sugar. Let proof in a warm spot 10 minutes.

Whisk together flour and salt and form a well in middle.

Add yeast mixture and olive oil.

Form into a soft ball and knead until soft and elastic.

Place in an oiled bowl, cover with a damp kitchen towel and let rise until doubled 1-1/2 to 2 hours.

Punch down and form into a round boule. Let rise until doubled once more.

Meanwhile heat oven to 450. Use a baking stone if available.

Slide onto stone, or on oiled pan, and bake 45 minutes or until dark brown and hollow sounding.

Allow to cool on a rack 15 minutes before slicing.

Makes 1 small boule

Provençal Bouillabaisse

This is a particularly lavish dish, which we're almost embarrassed to be suggesting during Lent. Cook it on a Sunday. Sundays don't count (we looked it up!).

1 cup olive oil
1 onion, finely chopped
3 leeks, white part, sliced
1 28-ounce can plum tomatoes
2 fennel medium, diced
1/3 cup parsley, chopped
Few sprigs thyme
1 bay leaf
Peel of 1 small orange
2 pounds shellfish

2 pounds firm fish (sea bass, snapper, halibut, or striped bass), cleaned, cut into uniform size pieces
Salt and freshly ground pepper
Generous pinch of saffron
16 ounces clam juice
2 cups dry white wine
2 pounds delicate fish (flounder, whiting, tilapia), cleaned, cut into uniform size pieces

Heat a large soup pot. Add one tablespoon olive oil; sauté onion, leek, tomatoes, garlic, fennel, parsley, thyme, bay leaf, orange peel until soft.

Clean and bone fish and then cut into uniform pieces. Add shellfish and firm fish to pot. Drizzle with remaining olive oil. Season with salt, pepper, and saffron. Add clam juice, white wine, and water to cover.

Bring to a rapid boil and allow to boil 7 or 8 minutes. Then add delicate fish. Allow to cook another 5–6 minutes. (Total cooking time should not exceed 14–15 minutes.) Adjust seasonings and serve with French bread.

Makes enough to serve a party

April 4

Isidore of Seville (560–636): Urban Legendary

This early medieval historian and encyclopedic writer compiled and preserved much of the classical learning that had survived the fall of Rome, introduced the works of Aristotle to Spain, and was instrumental in several important Church councils. The scope of Isidore's major work, the *Etymologies,* was a tad ambitious: he intended it as a collection of all previously available knowledge and a universal history of the human race. What it turned out to be was a grab bag of genuine lore and misinformation, philosophical insights and urban legends, reliable history and "well-attested rumors." It wasn't Isidore's fault: he was working against time, as barbarians roamed at will, burning libraries and massacring the teaching monks who manned them, trying to save as much knowledge as he could. He didn't have the leisure of skeptical sifting.

Because of his historical method—collecting information, accepting at it face value, then piling it higher and deeper[1]—St. Isidore has been proposed by Vatican officials as patron saint of the Internet.

⋯⋯⋯

---

1. Making him, logically, the first Ph.D.

April 14

Lidwina of Schiedam (1380–1433): Let's Go Skating, Kids!

Feeling sorry for yourself as you fill out your taxes? Here's a saint's story to meditate upon and make you thoroughly ashamed of yourself. Indeed, it should stop you from complaining about anything that happens to you, ever again.

Bl. Lidwina was a normal, pious Dutch child up until the age of sixteen, when she discovered her frightful vocation—as a "victim soul," one of those unlucky few who are specially called on this earth to help "make up what is lacking in the sufferings of Christ" by enduring a lifetime on the Cross. Paralyzed in an ice-skating accident, Lidwina spent the rest of her life as an invalid, suffering ulcers, insomnia, bedsores, blindness, and finally the Black Plague—not to mention constant spiritual temptations to despair. For thirty-seven years she endured, offering up her sufferings to win mercy for unrepentant sinners and uniting herself to Christ. Toward the end of her life, Lidwina was rewarded with spiritual ecstasies and visions of Jesus, finally coming to live (for nineteen years) on nothing except the Eucharist. In classic Catholic fashion, Lidwina has been named the patroness of ice-skaters.

CELEBRATE: If you haven't already succumbed, Lidwina's feast day is an excellent occasion to take your children shopping for those roller blades they've been hounding you to buy. As they try on the skates, tell them Lidwina's story, dwelling on each detail of her sufferings, ignoring their shrieks of protests and the salesman's mournful looks. Promise the kids that Lidwina will be watching over them as they whiz in and out of traffic. . . .

Bl. Lidwina just saved you eighty bucks. Per kid.

April 16

Bernadette of Lourdes (1844–1879): Kitsch and Miracles

This simple shepherdess was granted, in less than half a year, some seventeen visions of the Blessed Virgin Mary. Anticlerical Frenchmen of her day and skeptics ever since have dismissed Bernadette's apparitions as evidence of madness or religious hysteria. They've had a harder time explaining the seemingly impossible medical cures that have piled up around the shrine built in her honor, on the site of

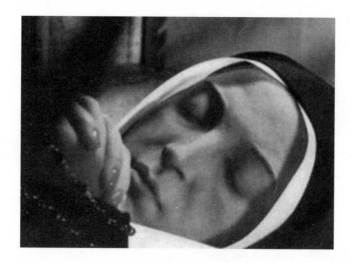

the apparitions at Lourdes. The Church, afraid of superstition, hires the most skeptical, non-Catholic scientists it can find to test all claims of miraculous healings at the shrine, of which there are hundreds every year. These irreligious researchers, at the bishop's request, throw out any cure for which there is a remotely plausible natural explanation—leaving some sixty-six inexplicable recoveries, dating from 1858 to 1987.

And then there's the matter of Bernadette's body. After she died of tuberculosis in the convent, Bernadette's corpse didn't change very much. In fact, it hasn't changed at all. Never embalmed or preserved in any way, her body lies still in the chapel at Lourdes, pink and fresh, as if she were taking an afternoon siesta and might awaken at any moment. We wouldn't be too surprised if she did.

The little spring that Bernadette dug up with her bare hands at Mary's request produces water that is revered for its healing qualities worldwide and is typically encased in plastic replicas of the Virgin Mary, which hide among the Hummels in millions of Catholic homes. The site of perhaps the world's largest concentration of religious article shops, Lourdes has rightly been dubbed the Marian Disneyworld; to cradle Catholics, its very tackiness is proof of the shrine's authenticity. If the stuff the place sold was in solid good taste—like those nifty gargoyles you get at the Cloisters in Manhattan—we'd suspect that something Anglican was going on.

April 19

Expeditus (dates unknown): Saint Overnight of Delivery

Here is a saint whose name and legend may well be the result of a pun. His image is venerated in New Orleans (where else?), where just about any native will tell you with delight that he got his name when a band of Spanish nuns received among a shipment of other saints an unmarked statue of a Roman soldier, whose crate said only "Expedite." Instead of wondering exactly why an anonymous statue had to be a rush delivery, the story goes, they decided this must be the saint's name, and put it up in their chapel, Our Lady of Guadalupe. Fittingly, Expedite has been dubbed the unofficial patron saint of impatient creditors, procrastinators, and deliverymen.

....

April 20

Agnes of Montepulciano (1268–1317): The Flying Nun

According to the authoritative Butler's *Lives of the Saints,* Agnes was quite a precocious little mystic, displaying behavior that today would probably get her labeled as autistic. As a toddler, Agnes "spent whole hours in reciting the Our Father and Hail Mary on her knees in some private corner of a chamber." Instead of putting her in a protective helmet, her wealthy parents placed Agnes in a convent at the tender age of nine. She thrived there among the nuns, eventually joining a Dominican house near Orvieto, where she was quickly appointed abbess by the pope. Agnes inspired her subordinates with her penances—for instance, by sleeping on the ground with a rock for a pillow and living for fifteen years on San Pellegrino and dinner rolls. She attracted notoriety by healing people miraculously, predicting the future, levitating several feet in the air while in ecstatic prayer, and multiplying Italian bread simply by blessing it. Jealous that they had lost a spiritual luminary, the people of Montepulciano decided to lure Agnes back to her home town. They knocked down a favorite bordello and built a convent there instead. This was an offer Agnes couldn't refuse, and she came home, living until the ripe old medieval age of forty three.

CELEBRATE: See if by praying with sufficient sincerity you can levitate. If you can't, your prayers are probably shallow and useless, and maybe you shouldn't even bother. That's what a scrupulous Catholic might decide. But we're unscrupulous Catholics, so we're willing to compromise. So we suggest getting a small trampoline and using it as you pray the Rosary, gradually moving toward purely contemplative union with Christ—and eventually, toward getting the hang of defying gravity. At the very least, you'll get your kids' attention.

Bonus Saint: John Payne (1574–1582): *So Long and Thanks for the Martyrs*

This fearless Englishman converted to Catholicism at the height of Elizabeth's persecution, going to Douay to be ordained a priest and then returning to serve the underground Church. He was caught and sent into exile but returned within two years to continue saying Mass in secret, living in "priest holes" and traveling incognito. (For a gripping picture of how such priests lived, see Msgr. Robert Hugh Benson's theological spy-thriller, *Come Rack, Come Rope*). John was eventually caught by one of Elizabeth's army of professional "priest-hunters" and falsely accused of plotting to kill the queen. After lengthy torture, he was partially strangled, cut open while still alive, and disemboweled before a crowd of cheering football hooligans. His feast makes a nice day for an ecumenical gesture. If you happen to know any of America's 2.5 million residual Episcopalians, be sure to thank them for the contributions made by their mother church to our list of martyrs.

Catherine of Siena (1347–1380): Grabbing the Pope by the Collar

This late medieval mystic harnessed her particular talents—anorexia, for instance—to the service of Christ. Living only on the Eucharist and a few handfuls of herbs, Catherine became famous throughout Christendom and transformed the Church in her time. A Third Order Dominican who never learned to read or write, Catherine dictated to others the theological insights she accumulated through a series of spiritual experiences—which included a mystical marriage to Jesus Himself, who appeared to her and gave her a wedding ring. (See what happens to Italian girls when they don't get enough to eat?)

Catherine's hunger for holiness was contagious. She soon attracted followers and fame and was called upon to represent Florence in an embassy to the pope. Some fifty years before, the popes had left the chaotic, plague-ridden city of Rome and moved to greener pastures in lovely Avignon, France. There the French king kept them as happy prisoners, appointing bishops as he chose and stacking the College of Cardinals to keep the Church under his thumb.

Catherine was determined to drag the pope back to Rome. The unlettered, half-starved mystic made her way to Avignon, where she rebuked Pope Gregory XI for leaving Rome an orphan. In one of her screeds she told him: "Since [Christ] has given you authority and you have accepted it, you ought to be using the power and strength that is yours. If you don't intend to use it, it would be better and more to God's honor and the good of your soul to resign." Catherine made such an impression on Gregory that he agreed—and left behind his gilded cage, rolling estates, and casks of Chateauneuf-du-Pape, restoring the papacy to Rome. She was the first woman to be declared a Doctor of the Church.

CELEBRATE: For her boldness in admonishing the pope and other bishops, the brilliant but illiterate Catherine is invoked by critics of the Vatican on the far left and far right alike. In her honor, compose a semiliterate critique of the current pontificate, single-spaced, using both sides of the paper, and send it to the Vatican. Send your letter registered mail, forcing the Vicar of Christ himself to sign for it. Address it simply: The Pope, Vatican City—as with letters to Santa, the Post Office will know just what to do.

Holy Week and Easter

Holy Thursday: Sangria in the Streets

This is a big day in the Church calendar, packed with theological significance: on one night, Jesus held His last dinner with His apostles, washed their feet, said the first Mass, established the priesthood and episcopate, offered up His perfect obedience to His father in the garden of Gethsemane, rebuked His disciples for napping, and was betrayed by Judas and arrested. Whew! Where to begin to mark such a feast? Too many Catholics feel overwhelmed by its sheer solemnity and discreetly spend the evening at home watching *Law and Order* reruns. We don't believe in criticizing popular devotions, but we'd like to suggest a few alternatives.

The Church celebrates two liturgies on this feast—one "chrism" Mass in the morning, when the bishop consecrates all the holy oils that will be used to sanctify church buildings, automobiles, motors, and hinges throughout the year. At night, parishes offer the Mass of the Lord's Supper, a particularly festive event that often includes the "Gloria of the Bells," after which the pastor joyously gets to switch off the church's electronic carillon system until Easter Sunday. The plaster statues are draped in purple Dacron, and electric candles unplugged. The celebrant of the Mass ceremoniously washes the (carefully prewashed) feet of twelve laymen in the sanctuary—an act of service and humility that commemorates both the twelve Apostles and the twelve people who actually go to Confession in the parish every week. The rest of the congregants wrinkle their noses and wriggle their toes, as the priest towels dry.

After the liturgy, the Eucharist is removed from the tabernacle and transferred to a side "altar of repose," which in many parishes is made to look like a tomb and surrounded with lilies and candles. It's customary for the devout to spend an hour or so before the Blessed Sacrament, "watching with" Christ as he prepares for His passion. Another old tradition, credited to St. Philip Neri, is to visit seven churches on this night, stopping in to say some prayers at each. This commemorates the historic pilgrimage the pope used to make on this night to seven churches in Rome.

CELEBRATE: Mark this multifaceted feast by making a pilgrimage to seven churches in your city—preferably visiting congregations you wouldn't normally see, in neighborhoods you might avoid, to remind yourself of the universality of the Church and why you moved to the sterile suburbs in the first place. Since the authors dwell in New York City, it's easy for us to make this trip on foot. Each year, we go from a Russian Catholic liturgy to a cathedral built by the Irish, a parish in Little Italy, a Slovenian and then a Polish church, then to a succession of parishes populated by Catholics from Ecuador, China, Peru, and Puerto Rico, ending up at a Gothic church full of devout Filipinos. Chances are that your own city has almost as many ethnic opportunities, though you might have to do some driving. Pile the kids in the minivan[2] and stock up in advance with a good supply of sangria, the drink that Spaniards traditionally chug on this feast (*sangre*=blood). A few sips should quiet down the most rambunctious five-year-old. Eat heartily. There's a strict fast starting at midnight, and the fun should certainly end as Good Friday begins.

Holy Thursday Sangria

1 bottle Spanish red Penedes	1 lemon
1/4 cup brandy	1 Golden Delicious apple,
1/4 cup sugar	quartered and thinly sliced
1 Valencia orange	1–2 cups sparkling Apollinaris,
2 clementines	chilled

Scrub citrus with vegetable brush and slice into thin rounds. Combine all ingredients except mineral water and stir. Chill 24 hours. To serve, add water and pour over ice.

This recipe can be multiplied to serve as many rounds as you need to prepare for Good Friday.

Makes 8 servings

2. So-called "subculture Catholics," typically quite conservative, can be picked out from other churchgoers by their large, often home-schooled families, Fatima/Medjugorje/Rosary/Prolife/NRA bumper stickers, and older-model minivans. Social-justicey Catholics are more likely to drive modest Volvos with slogans such as "If You Want Peace, Work for Justice," "Think Globally, Act Locally," and "Visualize Whirled Peas."

Good Friday: No Laughing, No Talking, No Showing Your Teeth

This day, the most solemn in the Church's calendar, is an occasion to avoid any kind of frivolity or mirth. The feast is important, especially to wretched, lukewarm sinners like us who spend the whole year trying to wriggle out from under the Cross. Today, it's standing right in front of us, and we really can't turn away. So let's take a good long look—if only for this one day—at the shape divine love takes when it encounters human sin.

The Church's service today is stark and sober—not even a Mass, but only a Communion service, culminating in the veneration of a crucifix. At some parishes, a preacher will give meditations on the Seven Last "Words" (really sentences) of Christ. We like to attend a Byzantine Catholic service called the "Burial of Christ," which ends with parishioners coming up in silent procession to kiss a burial shroud emblazoned with Jesus's corpse. In fact, since we can't think of anything else appropriate to do today, we try to spend most of it in church. If you find that your company is open today, why not call in sick—as in, you're sick of having to work on major religious holidays.

For adults, this is an occasion of abstinence and fast—a pretty wimpy penance nowadays, allowing you one real meal, two light snacks, and no meat. You might choose to revive the old-fashioned Irish "black fast"—which means consuming nothing but unsweetened black tea. We recall that as we grew up, our parents would turn off the television and radio precisely at noon, and leave it off until three. To modern kids like us, there was no better way of making us feel like we were on the Cross.

This might be a day to unplug the TV, Internet, and Game Box altogether, and leave the stereo off. If you really want to serve up the solemnity, you could shroud the entertainment center in black silk, cover the mirrors, switch off the circuit breakers, and insist that everyone huddle by candlelight. That should make the day memorable.

If you insist on electricity, program your home with appropriate music for the day, such as Haydn's "Seven Last Words of Christ," one of Bach's three powerful Passions, Mozart's Requiem, or some Gregorian chants. If some family members simply cannot get by without moving images on an electronic screen, today's a good day to rent a movie life of Christ,[3] or a parabiblical epic such as *The Robe*. A truly great and fitting film available on DVD is *The Passion of Joan of Arc*.[4]

Jesus's Reproaches from the Cross

This classic prayer of the Church, which pictures Jesus addressing the crowd that called for His death, speaks to every sinner. It's fitting that you feel good and rotten today—and we're here to help:

O my people, what have I done to you? How have I offended you? Answer me! I led you out of Egypt, from slavery to freedom, but you have led your Savior to the cross.

For forty years, I led you safely through the desert. I fed you with manna from heaven and brought you to a land of plenty, but you have led your Savior to the cross.

What more could I have done for you? I planted you as my fairest vine, but you yielded only bitterness; when I was thirsty, you gave me vinegar to drink, and you pierced your Savior's side with a spear.

O my people, what have I done to you? How have I offended you? Answer me.

I led you out of Egypt, leaving Pharaoh drowned in the Red Sea: but you have delivered me to the chief priests.

I opened the sea before you; and you opened my side with a spear.

I went before you in a pillar of fire: and you have dragged me into the judgment hall of Pilate.

I fed you with manna in the desert; and you have beaten me with fist and whip.

I gave you water of salvation to drink: and you have given me gall and vinegar.

For your sake I struck the kings of the Canaanites: and you have struck my head with a reed.

I gave you a royal scepter: and you have given me a crown of thorns.

I raised you up with great strength: and you have hanged me on the gibbet of the Cross.

O my people, what have I done to you? How have I offended you? Answer me.

---

3. We heard that quite a good one was released in 2004, but can't recall the name, since it went unmentioned by the media. . . .
4. And you thought we were going to recommend *The Life of Brian*. What is *wrong* with you people?

Celebrate the Resurrection: Roasting the Easter Bunny

On this most festive day, we celebrate for a glorious mixture of Christian and pagan reasons: because the winter's ending, because Christ is risen, and because that means each one of us gets a shot at joining Him. (Actually, in the end, we'll have no choice. According to St. Thomas Aquinas even the souls of the damned will regain their flesh at the end of time, to perfect their punishment. So everybody has something to look forward to!) After a dismal winter, maybe even a penitential Lent—more likely a season of dimly remembered good intentions that puddle in the corner and breed mosquitoes—there's nothing finer than a spirited Easter dinner to crown the day and change your mood. Kids love the day, of course—because when Jesus returned from the grave, He brought with Him great big baskets of jelly beans and marshmallow bunnies! As He hippity-hopped around Jerusalem, He distributed these treats on suburban lawns and under sofabeds, and filled every child's candy dish with colorfully painted eggs He laid Himself, as reminders of—well, something or other. We can't quite keep all of this straight. . . . Let's check the Catechism again. . . .

The Easter holiday in fact marks the Resurrection of Christ, which has less to do with hollow milk-chocolate animals than you might think. But it has for centuries been celebrated throughout Christendom by an inextricable tangle of pagan fertility rites, folk customs, and liturgical events designed to baptize all of the above and harness the natural good cheer at the return of decent weather, flowers, and fresh fruit to the hope for eternal life. The Easter Vigil incorporates some of the most powerful natural symbols in its liturgy—the blessing of fire, a darkened church, the slow procession of candle flames through a hushed congregation, and the consecration of water.

For centuries in Europe—and still in the eastern regions—laypeople would bring water with them to Mass in bottles, so it could be blessed by the priest. Then they'd take it home for use around the home—warding off household demons, or serving as a beauty wash for the women and a cure for illnesses; it was the medieval equivalent of baking soda. In fact, the belief arose that all water on Easter Day "had a blessing in it," so peasant folk would take that day for one of their semiannual baths, cavorting in rivers and streams, consuming long-forbidden treats, and sneaking around back to repopulate the village. The Lithuanians used to rush home from church with their holy water, convinced that this would make their farm chores go faster that year. They'd sprinkle their homes, fields, barns, and

orchards with holy water, wash old people's eyes with it, anoint their seeds and plants, and even the udders of the family cow—just to be on the safe side. Why not make like the Lithuanians? After all, it is a feast of new life. . . .

CELEBRATE: If you decide to start the day with an Easter egg hunt, here's a clever way to make your celebration a little different from the neighbors', and memorable for all. On Holy Saturday night, as you decorate eggs, don't bother to boil them first. That's right, color them raw and plant them all over the yard and bushes outside your house. When you put the kids to bed, suggest they wear their rattiest, oldest, most easily washable clothes. When they ask why, promise them a big surprise in the morning. Do the same yourself. Then come morning, awaken the little ones at sunrise for the Easter egg hunt. But as you collect them, instead of peeling and eating hard-boiled eggs—let's face it, who really wants to eat them?—have a raucous egg-fight, boys against girls, on the lawn in front of your home. You might even want to lead them in an Easter hymn as they hunt and hurl, hunt and hurl, such as "Jesus Christ Is Risen Today," "Victimae Paschali Laudes," or the beloved Polish "Chodzimy po dyngusie i . . . piewamy o Jezusie."

This is sure to attract the attention of curious neighbors, who'll want some explanation of what's going on at 6:00 a.m. As Catholics, it's our duty to offer such accounts of our creed and customs to anyone who asks, so wait until they've crossed your property line. Then shout "Christ is Risen!" and include them in the fun. Remind the boys not to aim for the head.

Our favorite Easter custom persists among the Poles and bears the evocative name *Dyngus.* It differs from town to town—for instance, from Buffalo to Chicago—but in general the custom invites young men to walk from house to house singing songs, along the way swatting young women with rods of willow and pouring water all over them. While it's obviously rooted in some ancient fertility rite—and soaking wet Polish blondes can prove surprisingly fertile—the practice also lays claim to some Christian roots. The water is said to be symbolic of Christ's blood, which washes the sinner; another tale says that the crowds who rejected the Gospel threw water to scatter the noisy Christians who proclaimed the Resurrection.

When you serve up dinner, provide each guest an inexpensive but festive-looking Jack-in-the-Box to drive home the theme of Resurrection. As the centerpiece of a lavish, Slavic Easter dinner, make the main course a fricasseed rabbit. The meat is healthy, versatile, and delicious, but you'll serve it mostly for the sake of the children. Encourage them to poke the Easter Bunny as hard as they like. He won't rise from the dead.

Champagne (of course)

Tangy Plum Soup

Beet Salad

Eggplant Salad

Spring Potato Salad

Easter Bunny Fricassee

Resurrection Cheese Cake

Cheese Pascha

Tangy Plum Soup

3 pounds plums
5 cups orange juice
2 cups mango juice

1/4 cup clover honey
Plain Greek yogurt

Pit and cut plums into small pieces. Place in stainless steel pot with juices. Bring to a simmer for about 20 minutes, until fruit is soft. Purée in a blender and add honey to taste. Chill thoroughly and garnish with yogurt.

Makes 12–15 servings

Beet Salad

4 medium size beets	Salt
1-1/2 cups sliced, pitted prunes	Sugar
1 cup walnuts, coarsely chopped	Juice of one lemon
or quartered	Sour cream or mayonnaise

Boil beets in their skins. When cool, peel them and grate or julienne them. Add prunes and walnuts. Season with salt, sugar, and lemon juice to taste. Add sour cream and mayonnaise to make a smooth salad.

Makes 2–4 servings

Eggplant Salad

1 medium eggplant	2 medium Bermuda onions, diced
1 tablespoon vegetable oil	3–4 cloves of garlic, mashed
2 green peppers, diced	Ketchup
2 red peppers, diced	

Peel and dice eggplant. Place into a bowl and salt. Let stand for 30 minutes. Warm oil in pan; sauté the onion. When it is translucent, add the peppers. When they are nice and soft, add the eggplant but squeeze out the water before adding to the frying mixture. Add mashed garlic. Sauté everything for about 10 minutes, stirring occasionally. At the end, add ketchup to taste. Let fry for another 5 minutes. Turn off the heat and cool. Can be served hot or cold.

Makes 2–4 servings

Spring Potato Salad

3 medium red potatoes	1/2 cup dill, chopped
10 ounces frozen baby peas	1 cup mayonnaise
2 cucumbers peeled and diced	1/2 cup sour cream
1 bunch scallions, sliced	

Boil potatoes in skins 15–20 minutes, until tender to knife; peel and cube. Allow to cool. Simmer frozen peas 1 minute and allow to cool.

   Mix ingredients together and adjust seasoning. Add more sour cream or mayonnaise if necessary to make salad nice and smooth.

Makes 2–4 servings

Resurrection Cheese Cake

CRUST:

1/2 cup butter	2 tablespoons sour cream
1/2 cup sugar	1 1/2 cups sifted flour
3 egg whites	1 teaspoon baking powder
1 whole egg	2 cups heavy cream
Zest of 1 lemon	1 pint blueberries

Cream butter. Add sugar, egg whites, grated lemon rind, and sour cream. Blend flour with baking powder. Pour into 9 inch springform pan. Bake at 350 degrees for 20 minutes, until lightly browned.

FILLING:

1 pound fresh ricotta	Zest of one orange
1 tablespoon butter	1 tablespoon rum
1/4 cup sugar	1/2 teaspoon vanilla extract
1 cup powdered sugar	5 egg whites
5 egg yolks	Pinch of salt
1/2 cup sour cream	1 teaspoon cream of tartar
1/4 cup raisins	

Pass cheese through sieve. Cream butter thoroughly. Add cheese and sugars and blend thoroughly. Add egg yolks one at a time, beating well after each. Gently stir in sour cream and then add raisins, orange rind, flavorings.

Beat egg whites with cream of tartar into stiff peaks. Fold into cheese mixture. Pour over baked base and bake at 325 degrees for 40 minutes. Allow to cool, and top with freshly whipped cream and berries.

Makes 12–16 servings

Cheese Pascha

2 pounds fresh ricotta	5 egg yolks, hard-boiled
3/4 cup soft butter	1 teaspoon salt
1/4 teaspoon cloves, ground	3/4 cup heavy cream
1/4 teaspoon cinnamon	1 tablespoon vanilla extract
1-1/2 cups powdered sugar	

GARNISH:

Approximately 8 tablespoons whole cloves	5 dried apricots
	1/3 cup honey

Purée cheese or press through sieve. Cream butter. Add sugar and spices to butter. Pass yolks through sieve and add to butter. Add cheese to butter mixture. Add cream and mix thoroughly. Add 1 teaspoon vanilla.

Boil cheesecloth in water with two teaspoons vanilla. Cut cloth in pieces to line small clay flowerpots. Spoon mixture into pots. Fold cheesecloth to cover filling. Refrigerate at least 24 hours. Unmold.

To decorate, slice dried apricots in half, lengthwise and then into thirds. Put three slices on side of each Pascha. Garnish top with cloves in shape of cross. Drizzle honey over finished cakes.

Makes 4–8 servings

Easter Bunny Fricassee

2 rabbits, cut into serving-sized
    pieces
Fleur de Sel and freshly ground
    pepper
Flour
1 tablespoon grapeseed oil
1/2 tablespoon butter
3 pounds kielbasa, sliced

1/2 cup shallots, finely chopped
1/2 pound cremini mushrooms,
    sliced
1/2 pound shiitake mushrooms,
    sliced
1/2 cup Armagnac
1/2–3/4 cup Pic-St-Loup red wine

Preheat oven to 400 degrees.

Rinse and pat dry rabbit. Sear and then dredge in flour. Brown rabbit on all sides in large roasting pan with oil and butter. Set on stove over medium heat until oil and butter begin to foam.

Remove bunny and set aside.

Add kielbasa to pan. Stir with a wooden spoon. After about 2 minutes, add shallots. Stir and sizzle briefly before adding mushrooms. Season lightly and stir. The mushrooms' aroma will begin to mingle with the kielbasa's. Pour brandy over all and allow to warm up before flaming with brandy. Stand back and enjoy. Flame will diminish and then go out completely. Add wine.

Stir gently to loosen all the good bits from the pan. Bring to a gentle simmer, add rabbit back, and cover. Transfer to oven. Cook 1-1/2 to 2 hours, stirring occasionally.

Adjust seasoning and serve with buttered egg noodles seasoned with Fleur de Sel.

Makes 6 servings

Sacramental Executive Summary #2: The Eucharist

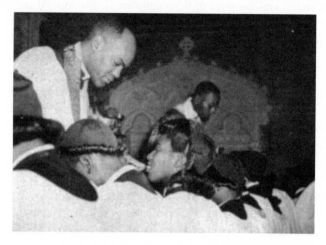

Which of us can forget our preparation for First Holy Communion? The nervousness about making a mess of this puzzling big day—for instance by gagging on the Host—the bustle of family preparations for the party afterward, and most of all the unspoken, creepy anxiety we felt in our seven-year-old minds about—well, you know, eating and drinking Jesus. Older folks might remember such sonorous, impenetrably adult hymns as "Soul of My Savior." We Gen X Catholics recall sitting in second grade class learning the sing-song, "Eat His body / drink His blood. / Now we sing / Our song of love." No wonder so many horror novelists, violence-heavy filmmakers, and members of heavy metal and Goth bands turn out to be cradle Catholics. (We go to Mass sometimes at the parish where Martin Scorcese was an altar boy, from which he joined the seminary, briefly.)

The Eucharist is not a mystery most parents or grammar school teachers are well equipped to distinguish from literal cannibalism—at least without reducing the presence of Christ in the Eucharist to some vague, not terribly suggestive symbol. But as Flannery O'Connor once said, "Well, if it's a symbol, to hell with it." And it's pretty hard (though Judas tried) to get around such words of Christ as these:

> I myself am the living bread come down from heaven. If anyone eats this bread he shall live forever; the bread I will give is my flesh, for the life of the world. Let me solemnly assure you, if you do not eat the flesh of the Son of Man, and drink His blood, you have no life in you. He who feeds on my flesh and drinks my blood has life eternal, and I will raise him up on the last day. For my flesh is real food, and my blood real drink. The man who feeds on my flesh and drinks my blood remains in me, and I in him. (John 6:51, 53–56)

As uncomfortable as this doctrine sometimes makes us—it helped send thousands of early Christians into the jaws of lions and bears—it's so well attested by Scripture and tradition that it took until 1047 A.D. for anyone in the Church to publicly deny it.[5] Of course, during the Reformation, as the interpretative authority of the Church was shattered, "This is my body" was one of the first "hard sayings" of Christ to be explained away. (Next came the ever-popular "What God has joined together, let no man separate".) By 1577, the Protestant theologian Christopher Rasperger was able to compose a book entitled, *Two Hundred Interpretations of the Words "This Is My Body."* From doctrinal unity about an impenetrable mystery came a "gorgeous mosaic" of quarrelsome opinions.

Despite the ringing endorsement given the Church's doctrines on this and other matters at Vatican II and despite an easier-to-use liturgy (dubbed into English—no more subtitles!) American Catholics have become as confused as those German Reformers. In 1993, a Gallup Poll discovered that only 30 percent of self-identified Catholics asked about the Eucharist agreed with Flannery O'Connor and Christ. Among Catholics under thirty, that percentage dropped to 17 percent. The rest held that Jesus is present in a shadowy, symbolic fashion—a smiling ghost like Abraham Lincoln at a refrigerator closeout on Presidents' Day.

How could this happen? The younger generation of Catholics is more educated (quantitatively speaking) than their parents. One of us learned the faith from an Irish-American housewife who wouldn't park the family car in Chinatown because she was still angry about Pearl Harbor. But she could explain the Eucharist accurately while munching on cream cheese and jelly with a cigarette in her mouth. How'd she learn the faith? The same way millions of unlettered peasants did throughout the Middle Ages—from decades of subconscious catechesis that they drank in at Sunday Mass.

This book isn't the place for a critique of recent liturgical changes in the Church—particularly the method of dispensing Holy Communion. But we'd like to suggest an experiment:

From now on, to get a movie ticket, Americans should have to kneel before a consecrated celibate wearing ceremonial robes and take the ticket between their teeth—never daring to touch it with their hands. Within a generation or so, they'd all develop certain *ideas* about movie tickets and their significance.

Now take the Eucharist and reverse the process, treating it like a movie ticket. . . . Enough said.

---

5. The French theologian Berengarius argued that the Eucharist was simply a memorial of Christ's body and blood, a kind of Post-It note for the soul.

CELEBRATE: When the time rolls around for one of your offspring to attain the age of reason, and become a First Holy Communicant, help him or her begin to attain a lifelong appreciation for the Blessed Sacrament—by baking Baby Jesus cookies. Mold in gingerbread baby molds—they're conveniently cross-shaped—available from *www.kitchengifts.com* (search for "ginger baby"). To drive the point of the sacrament home to kids, mark each of Jesus's five wounds with a Red Hot candy, and serve the cookies at your kid's post-Communion party.

As you hand out the cookies, remind the kids that every Sunday they really are eating the Baby Jesus—body and blood, soul and divinity. Sure, some of them will cry. But as they dry their tears and then scarf down the snacks, they'll make important connections in their developing minds that could stay with them for life. You may well have implanted forever the profoundly consoling belief that Jesus is available to them, in intimate, nourishing union, at every parish in the world. Or you might have just created the next Alfred Hitchcock.[6]

Baby Jesus Cookies

1/2 cup butter, soft
1 cup confectioner's sugar, sifted
1 egg + 1 yolk
1 teaspoon white wine
2 tablespoons basil, finely chopped
1 tablespoon parsley, finely
  chopped

2 teaspoons dried
  Turkish mint
1/2 teaspoon vanilla
  paste
2-1/2 cups flour
1/4 teaspoon salt
Red Hots (5 per cookie)

Beat together butter and sugar. Add eggs and mix well. Add wine and herbs. Whisk together flour and salt. Stir in flour in two additions. Combine well without overmixing.

Form into a ball and flatten. Chill at least one hour.

Preheat oven to 350 degrees.

Roll out dough on lightly floured counter about 1/8 inch thick. Cut out and place on parchment-covered baking pans. Create "stigmata" by placing one Red Hot candy on each hand and foot and on the left side of each cookie.

Bake 10–12 minutes until lightly golden on edges. Leave on pan for 1 minute. Transfer to wire rack to cool.

Makes 2 dozen cookies

------

6. A cradle Catholic, of course.

May

May 1

Filling the May Hole

Here we have another delightfully convoluted holiday. It began as a pagan fertility feast, both among the Romans and the Celts, dedicated to the veneration of the forces that in an agricultural society were seen as giving food and life: sexuality, cows, and bees. It doesn't take a Viennese shrink to see in the Maypole a symbolic phallus, or to take a certain bawdy delight in the spectacle of virgins (ahem) dancing around it, carefully braiding it with ribbons and flowers, while eager lads fill their mugs with potently alcoholic mead. A favorite part of May Day preparations was the coed field trip into the woods to collect greens and flowers to brighten up the Pole.

Unlike the Puritans who came along later, the Church never tried to quash these festivities, only to steer them gently in a more Christian direction. So May Day was dubbed a festival of the Virgin Mary, whose profoundly mysterious fertility was the source of another sort of life altogether—as the order of Redemption perfects the fallen Creation. We still see in many parishes the lovely tradition of "May Crownings," in which young girls lead a procession to decorate the statue of Our Lady, which mostly has replaced the Maypole—an interesting and evocative symbolic substitution.

But the complications don't end there. Aware that May 1 was the most popular holiday among the increasingly starved and exploited working people, socialists and Communists in the nineteenth century transformed the day into a feast of labor. This custom began with folk celebrations that featured a gathering of the guilds—and ended with the glum parade of Soviet military hardware through Red Square before a steely-eyed rostrum of dictators.

The Vatican, eager to reclaim the allegiance of the secularizing masses, added another layer of symbolism to the day in 1955, when Pope Pius XII declared May 1 the Feast of St. Joseph the Worker—a solemn recognition of the dignity of labor.

Together, these many appropriations of the day made it so puzzlingly oversignificant that the name of the holiday "May-Day, May-Day!" is now used as a distress signal by desperate sailors at sea.

We're happy to report that the confusion continues to multiply. On the campus of the all-female college of Bryn Mawr in Pennsylvania, there's an old tradition of decorating a May Pole on the feast. Now campus feminists have added another layer to the celebration, by creating and ornamenting a "May Hole" right beside the Pole, an earthy celebration of what the painter Courbet depicted as the "Source of Life." Yet we hesitate a little: what if the "Mawrters" (as students there are called) were someday to *unite* the May Pole with the May Hole—thereby giving birth to a tiny universe, entirely contained within the campus, ruled by a race of all-powerful undergraduate goddesses. . . . Let's not give them any ideas.

CELEBRATE: To mark this cheerful feast, gather the kids on the front lawn with shovels to dig your family's very own May Hole. Surround this primal fertility symbol with decorative greens and flowers, and explain to your children and neighbors that you're helping to reverse millennia of profoundly sexist imagery. Leave this festive trench uncovered for seven days, or until you're contacted by the neighborhood zoning committee.

May 2

Athanasius (295–373):
But Don't Quote Him on That . . .

This Father of the Church is justly admired in the Eastern Orthodox and the Roman Catholic communions. In his time most of the bishops and clergy had fallen prey to a heretical notion of Christ called Arianism. Fashionable opinion said that Jesus wasn't really God, part of the mysterious, supernal, omnipotent Trinity—just an overachieving angel, who'd been promoted to number 2 as a part of divine meritocracy. For insisting that Jesus was really who He said He was, Athanasius was driven from his bishop's throne in Alexandria several times—once by a murderous crowd—and spent much of his career hiding in exile, conducting a guerilla campaign on behalf of Christ's divinity. Even the weak pope of the time gave Athanasius little support. But divinity won out, and Athanasius's teachings

were affirmed at the Council of Nicaea, which hammered out the Creed we say at Mass every Sunday. During his lonely crusade, Athanasius coined the phrase, "If the world is against truth, then I am against the world," which assured his place in *Bartlett's Famous Quotations*—and kept one of the authors out of Dartmouth. In 1982, that college's application asked students to name a famous phrase that expressed their worldview the best. A rash teen from Queens with a weird Slavic name chose to quote Athanasius, and follow it with a long screed about how he'd spent high school combating "modernist" religion teachers, eventually appealing to the Vatican. Dartmouth knew what to do.

....

May 4

The Feast of the Holy Shroud: Property of J. Arimathea Funeral Home, Inc.—Do Not Remove

Here's a feast established by the good Pope Julius II—who also gave us Michelangelo's Sistine ceiling—a day that is too often forgotten. What's more, the mystery that inspired it is typically dismissed. The Holy Shroud of Turin was for centuries regarded as the burial cloth of Christ, thanks to the mysterious image it bears of a crucified man. The faint outline that appears to the naked eye is much less impressive than the stunning, detailed image that appeared in 1898, the first time the Shroud was photographed—on the negative. Looking very much as if it had been blasted onto the linen by an unexplained burst of energy is a reverse-image of a Semitic male, with countless scourge-marks, holes in his wrists and thorn wounds on his forehead. The Shroud, long kept as a treasured relic (and tourist attraction) by the Archdiocese of Milan, quickly became a major object of scientific inquiry. In 1988, researchers obtained permission to test a tiny sample of the material, using the most current carbon dating—and discovered the Shroud was a medieval forgery. Their sample proved to be no older than 1290. For many, that settled that—though it remained a mystery why a medieval forger would ignore every painting he'd ever seen of the Crucifixion, which placed Jesus's wounds in His palms, not His wrists, or how that hoaxer predicted the development of photographic negatives.

But the story doesn't end there. Historians have long known that the Shroud was damaged in a medieval fire—and patched up by helpful nuns. In 2005, Raymond

N. Rogers, retired Fellow of the Los Alamos National Laboratory, published the re-sults of his own tests, which appeared in the academic journal *Thermochimica Acta.* He concluded that "the sample used to test the age of the Shroud of Turin in 1988 was taken from a rewoven area of the Shroud. Pyrolysis-mass spectrometry results from the sample area coupled with microscopic and microchemical obser-vations prove that the radiocarbon sample was not part of the original cloth of the Shroud of Turin. The radiocarbon date was thus not valid for determining the true age of the Shroud." Why didn't the Archdiocese of Turin make sure to give the sci-entists a sample from the "good part" of the Shroud? Keep in mind that we're talk-ing about Italians. They're really *good* at playing soccer, painting frescos, making wine, and writing operas. When it comes to administration—Who's prime minister this week?

To follow the latest research on this controversial relic, visit *www.shroud.com.* While one should not rest one's faith on a single relic, miracles have served throughout history as evidence of things unseen. Jesus performed His share of wonders; while He never made a big deal about them (okay, except for that whole Resurrection thing), they did convince people that He "spoke as one with author-ity." Of course, doctrinaire skeptics will not find the Shroud convincing—not even if further tests show up, stenciled on its back: "Property of J. Arimathea Funeral Homes, Inc.—Do Not Remove."

May 10
Damien of Molokai (1840–1889): Father Damien and Mr. Hyde

This "blessed" (soon-to-be-saint) has one of the most inspiring stories we've come across. Born Joseph de Veuster, this Belgian peasant traveled literally to the other end of the world to care for the most neglected people on earth—an island full of forgotten Hawaiian lep-ers. At the time, people thought that the wast-ing nerve sickness now known as Hansen's disease was instantly contagious, and it carried a moral stigma left over from the Old Testa-ment. Serving first as a missionary in the Con-gregation of the Sacred Hearts of Jesus and Mary in Honolulu, Father Damien volunteered to stay permanently on the quarantine island of Molokai. There he revolutionized the medical

and spiritual care of these desperate people. Unwilling to keep his patients and parishioners at arm's length, Fr. Damien eventually contracted the disease himself, which ultimately claimed his life. Damien soon lost his good name in a nineteenth-century sex abuse scandal—when rival, anti-Catholic missionaries claimed that he'd caught the disease by sleeping with the natives. (Ah, the irresistible allure of grass-skirted lady lepers!)

One of the most famous writers of the day, Robert Louis Stevenson (*Dr. Jekyll and Mr. Hyde*), went to Molokai to investigate—and found out the truth: that Fr. Damien had behaved as a second Christ on the island, keeping his vows and pouring out his life for the sake of his fellow-lepers—among whom he'd asked to be buried. Fr. Damien had been one of the very first to treat with dignity and love "the butt-ends of human beings lying there almost unrecognisable, but still breathing, still thinking, still remembering," Stevenson reported in a famous letter—directed, ironically, toward a "Mr. Hyde" who'd made the accusations. It served as one of the documents supporting Fr. Damien's beatification in 1995. You can see a statue of Fr. Damien in the U.S. Capitol, where he stands representing the state of Hawaii.

CELEBRATE: Tonight we suggest a rental and a recipe: *Molokai: The Story of Father Damien,* starring Kris Kristofferson, Peter O'Toole, and Derek Jacobi—and Pineapple and Torrontes Compote.

Pineapple and Torrontes Compote

1 fresh pineapple
1 tablespoon pink peppercorns

1 teaspoon Schezuan peppercorns
1 bottle Torrontes white wine

Peel and core pineapple. Cut into cubes. Sprinkle with peppercorns. Add wine to cover. Cover loosely and allow to macerate 2–4 hours. Serve with remainder of wine.

Makes 8–10 servings

Ascension Thursday: Did Christ Fly Standby?

This feast marks the end of Jesus's earthly ministry, when he was taken up at last, triumphant, to rejoin His Father: His Mission Impossible, now a Mission Accomplished. Since Jesus ascended from a mountain (probably Mt. Olivet), the day has traditionally been marked by Christians taking trips to hills or peaks, as if to watch for signs of Jesus's passing. Some shoot off rockets to celebrate and illustrate the miracle for the more literal-minded of the children. For centuries, popular superstition held that it was unlucky to work today, and that any project begun on this feast would surely fail. But lately, the Ascension feast itself seems to be ailing.

Most American Catholics have chosen to honor this holy day by skipping their obligation, to the point where a number of U.S. bishops have thrown in the towel and shifted the celebration of Ascension Thursday to the nearest Sunday. Many Catholics feel this is unfortunate—since it changes our image of the Ascension from Christ rising gloriously into the clouds before His awestruck apostles to Jesus camped out like Tom Hanks in an airport terminal for three days, waiting for His cancelled El-Al flight to be rescheduled. (He forgot about the mandatory Sabbath overnight stay.)

CELEBRATE: Tick off your local bishop: Go to Mass.

May 13

Fatima: Our Lady in the Sky with Diamonds

You probably know the story: On this date in 1917, a group of three apprentice shepherds in Portugal began to receive visits from the Blessed Virgin Mary. She brought these children, named Lucia, Francisco, and Jacinta, a profoundly consoling message: start praying to me or I can't be responsible for the consequences.

First, to get the kids' attention, she got them good and scared, revealing:

"a great sea of fire which seemed to be under the earth. Plunged in this fire were demons and souls in human form, like transparent burning embers, all blackened or burnished bronze, floating about in the conflagration, now raised into the air by the flames that issued from within themselves together with great clouds of smoke, now falling back on every side like sparks in a huge fire, without weight or equilibrium, and amid shrieks and groans of pain and despair."

Nobody ever said hell was rated "PG." But Mary wasn't finished. She went on to predict the rise of a violent, atheist regime in Russia, which would "spread its errors through the nations," and the eruption of a Second World War—this while the First was still going on. The only way to turn aside these disasters? For Russia to be consecrated to Mary's Immaculate Heart and a sufficient number of sinners to make reparation to her on the First Saturday of the month. Indeed, to those who attend Mass and say a few simple prayers for five such Saturdays, she promised the grace of final repentance (for some of us, this seems like our best shot).

Not a bad deal. So it struck Lucia, the only visionary to survive into adulthood. She passed the offer up the management chain, until it reached the pope's desk. He decided to greenlight the project, and Fatima was approved. (No private devotions are ever guaranteed with full Church authority, so you're free to accept or reject this apparition—as Our Lady said, at your own risk.)

Lucia also handed on Mary's prediction of a celestial fireworks show, which took place right on schedule: on October 13, 1917, the sun bounced in the sky like a basketball, scaring the wits out of some seventy thousand pilgrims and skeptics. As one journalist reported: "The sun began to dance and, at a certain moment, it appeared to detach itself from the firmament and to rush forward on us, like a fire wheel." Dozens of witnesses, some of whom had been miles away, tending their sheep and scrubbing their goats, confirmed the story—all this decades before Woodstock, or even the invention of LSD. The Fatima devotion soon became one of the most popular in the world.

Apparently not popular enough, though. The reparation quotient must not have reached the critical mass, since all the disasters of which Mary had warned came true—Communism, World War II, the miniskirt—leaving her like one of those scientists in a 1970s disaster movie, who started telling people in the first ten minutes that:

☺ Those sharks on the beach seem kind of hungry.
☺ The Poltergeist said, "Get out!" So GET OUT!
☺ That iceberg looks mighty solid.
☺ This ship will capsize, trapping us for days with Ernest Borgnine and Shelley Winters.

But no one ever listens.

Dymphna (dates unknown):
A Halfway House Party

On first blush, St. Dymphna's story is quite a sad one. According to her widely popular legend, this early medieval girl was the daughter of a petty pagan Irish king. Like her mother—whom she very much resembled—she was a Christian. When the queen died unexpectedly, the king was crazed with grief and announced that he would marry his daughter. Dymphna had the normal reaction: she went to Belgium. Her father tracked her down in the town of Gheel, where he watched as she was put to the sword. All in all, a dark family romance that sounds like a rejected first draft of a Faulkner novel.

But the story does not end here. St. Dymphna was buried in Gheel and a shrine was built in her honor. Several centuries later, a group of "madmen" who'd been driven from town to town happened upon the shrine—and were miraculously cured. Word of this cure spread quickly, in a world without Paxil or Lithium, and soon large numbers of mentally afflicted pilgrims began to descend on the town. Instead of locking them up or burning them as "witches," the Christian folk of the town admitted the pilgrims to their homes to await their cure. From this unlikely beginning came the West's first humane facilities for treating the mentally ill. To this day, pilgrims and patients come to Gheel and are welcomed by the locals.

CELEBRATE: To honor this saint and the heritage of her shrine, we suggest you turn your home into a little Gheel for a day, by throwing a party for your most insane friends and relatives. You know—the people you're afraid to invite other times, because you never know what they'll say, or onto whom they're liable to spill the punchbowl. The old man from the parish who takes you aside after Mass to explain that the Freemasons control the weather;[1] the Pentecostalist sister-in-law who burned the family TV on the lawn, your brother the failed seminarian, your aunt the Scientologist screenwriter. And of course, both your crackpot parents.

If you move in Catholic circles, you should have plenty of weirdness with which to work. There's something about a supernatural faith that can twist people's nature into a pretzel. Why not serve it up and enjoy it with melted cheese?

Remember: You're not inviting people who are genuinely suffering from some serious mental illness. There's nothing funny about schizophrenia or depression, while sociopaths are just plain *unsanitary*. Rather, you're summoning folks who fit the older definition of "eccentric," folks who are genuinely *happy* to spend the day researching the hidden connections between the Kabbalah and the stock market, or using Photoshop to place the heads of politicians on the bodies of farm animals. So resist the temptation to remake your house to resemble a state mental institution circa 1960.

Instead, think "wacky," think "Dada," think "fringe politics." Make up collages full of headlines and covers from tabloid newspapers, broadsheets of the far left or far right (if you can tell them apart) and tracts from hellfire sects that harass you at shopping centers. Just to keep people guessing, mix in cutouts from duplicates of beloved family photos—placing your eldest son "mysteriously" close to Lyndon Johnson during the Tet Offensive, or situating Mother Teresa squarely on the Grassy Knoll. Make your family dog a witness at Joseph McCarthy's HUAC hearings; lay in your infant in Bill Clinton's arms. Express your artistic inclinations—in a nice, harmless setting where no one will laugh at you. (They'll be too busy arguing.) Hang these collages squarely over the food and over the bar.

Since St. Dymphna was Irish—and she is venerated by countless bingo-playing, Entenmann's eating Hibernian agoraphobics throughout the Celtic Diaspora—you can also use your leftover St. Patrick's Day decorations in the theme. String angry boxing leprechauns from the ceiling lights and tape holy cards of St. Dymphna prominently throughout the house. (Find them, and a whole lot of other aquatint images at *www.holycards.com*.) You might also pin up Tarot cards, Black Muslim images of the Space Africans coming to save the planet, Hare Krishna devotionals, and selected villains from the U.S. Army's fifty-six-card Iraqi evildoers pack. Rebuff all requests for explanation with a whispered, "Surely you see the hidden connections—*you of all people*," and go back to the kitchen.

Don't serve green beer—you're not a sadist, for God's sake—but do make Guinness, Harp, and Magner's cider generously available. If you want to get really authentic, go online and order the brew made in Dymphna's final resting place, Gheel.

---

1. Why else does it always rain during papal visits? Eh, eh? Explain that away, *if you can*.

In a bit of that irony which has made God so justly famous, the local Gheel beer is called Kwak, and is marketed under the slogan "Kwak If You Want s Beer."

Aside from the inevitable quarrels that will erupt, you should really provide for some structured activities. We suggest beginning with Twister, and moving on, as the Kwak freely flows, into microwaving marshmallow Easter bunnies and chicks. Guests get to watch the sugary snacks distend ten to twenty times their size inside the oven and then consume the bloated treats—whose sugar has caramelized nicely, making them quite edible.[2] After a few more drinks, it's time to introduce "talking" games. Our favorite is called "Conspiracy or Dare," in which participants must either do something sickening—such as kissing another guest—or reveal the private conspiracy theory to which they secretly subscribe. Be sure to seat the JFK autopsy enthusiasts near those who insist that the Soviet Union still exists, and the people who believe that the European aristocracy is descended from a race of alien lizard men, who still rule the world (see *www. davidicke.com*) close to the anti-Semites. They should have plenty to talk about.

Irrelevant Anecdote

For an example of the kind of fun you may expect from your "special" guests, witness the interchange one of the authors overheard at a "Catholic Rendezvous" in the woods which began as a retreat but devolved into "a bunch of Irish-Americans singing and arguing around the keg." The two key speakers we will call "Andrew" and "Robert."[3]

Andrew argued that the Irish people had completely lost their culture when they gave up the Irish language. Robert insisted that they'd kept the Catholic faith—far more important.

Andrew disagreed: "You don't understand. The Word was made flesh. *The Word!*"

Robert paused. "Surely, '*the Word was made flesh and dwelt among us,*' refers to Our Lord Jesus Christ—not the Irish language."

Andrew replied: "You can't keep making these *arbitrary distinctions!*"

If you're blessed to have an Andrew in your acquaintance, make sure he's the guest of honor.

---

2. Find safety instructions at *www.weirdsnacks.com/peeps.htm.*
3. Their real names.

When it comes to food, it's important to stay thematic, without taking things too far. *Don't* order premade hospital meals and serve them on blunt-edged, light plastic trays that cannot be used as weapons against the orderlies. Feel free to make butter (*not* steak) knives available. Use real glasses—although not your finest crystal. Cheaper glass, when it's hurled across the room as a clincher to a rabid political argument, shatters into fewer, smaller pieces which are easier to sweep up.

And serve a nice, light eclectic meal that fits the party's theme by selecting tasty treats from around the world that happen to include some variant of the word "crazy" in their names. Here's a sample menu which will keep all your patients—er, "clients"—tranquil and cooperative.

Guinness Stout and or Harp Ale

Magner's Cider

Kwak Beer

Fruit Punch with St. John's Wort

Crazy Salad
This variety of salad, like a metaphysical poem, violently yokes
together opposite flavors—such as chickpeas and strawberries,
blueberries and cilantro—to wonderful effect.

Shrimp in Crazy Water (*Gamberoni al' Acqua Pazzo*)
An Italian favorite that recalls bouillabaisse. (See recipe)

Harvest Pazzo
A traditional Italian style of using recently gathered
fruits for a tempting dessert.

Individual Fruit Cakes
One for each fruit cake you invite.

Lunatic Cookies
Moon-shaped, with fruit and lots of nuts. (See recipe)

Coco-"Nut" Sorbet
(See recipe)

As an after-dinner treat, you might lay out Altoids, festively presented in empty bottles from your family's psychoactive medications—Ritalin, Neurontin, Effexor, or Viagra.

Shrimp in Crazy Water (Gamberoni al' Acqua Pazzo)

3 pounds shrimp, headless, unpeeled

1 tablespoon extra virgin olive oil

3 cloves garlic, thinly sliced

2 small red hot peppers, with seeds finely chopped

1 cup Acqua Panna, still mineral water

1 cup Verdicchio, light Italian white wine

1 tablespoon Sicilian sea salt

2 sprigs oregano, finely chopped

Freshly ground black pepper

Bring shrimp to room temperature while preparing the broth.

Heat oil in large pot. Add garlic and sauté 3 minutes. Add peppers and cook another 3 minutes. Add water and salt, bring to a boil, and simmer 10 minutes. Add shrimp and cook till all the shrimp turn pink. Do not overcook as they will continue to cook in broth.

At last minute add oregano and generous grinding of pepper.

Makes 4 servings

Lunatic Cookies

These delicious treats are based on the classic Mexican wedding cookies.

2 sticks butter, soft

Generous pinch fine sea salt

1/2 cup confectioner's sugar, plus additional for dusting

1/2 cup pecans, roasted, finely ground

1/2 cup walnuts, roasted, finely ground

1/2 cup almonds, roasted, finely ground

1 vanilla bean, seeds scraped, pod reserved for another use

1 teaspoon, Mexican vanilla extract

2 cups all-purpose unbleached flour

Preheat oven to 350 degrees. Line baking pans with parchment.

Beat together butter, sugar, salt, and vanilla seeds. Add nuts and combine thoroughly. Whisk flour and add, combining well. Roll into 1 inch logs and curve into a crescent.

Bake 12–15 minutes. Allow to rest on sheet 2 minutes. Transfer to cookie rack and cool completely. Roll in more sugar.

Makes 2 dozen servings

Coco-"Nut" Sorbet

2-1/4 cups coconut milk

1 cup unsweetened shredded coconut

1/2 cup sweetened shredded coconut

1/2 cup corn syrup

Combine all ingredients and chill at least 2 hours. Adjust sweetness to taste. Process in a blender until smooth and strain through a fine sieve. Blend solids once more until smooth and pass through sieve once more. Finally, discard remaining solids and chill. Turn in ice cream machine and magic! Enjoy.

Makes 1 quart

May 16

Simon Stock (1165–1265): Eternal Life Insurance

This feast commemorates a most unusual saint. He began his religious life living in a hollow tree as a hermit, later going on to run one of the Church's most austere and mystical religious orders, the Carmelites. But by formulating one of his devotions, St. Simon performed a great service for Catholic teenagers (especially boys) in all subsequent centuries: he introduced the Brown Scapular. In an apparition of the Blessed Virgin Mary, Simon was given the promise that anyone who wore the habit of the Carmelite Order at the moment of death would be granted the grace of

repentance and spared the pains of hell. (She made no representations about purgatory, but we'll take what we can get.)

If Mary had left it at that, this everlasting life insurance policy would probably be little used; most of us wouldn't have run around throughout our sex-crazed teenaged years in the full brown cloak of a Carmelite. But Our Lady looked ahead and foresaw the millions of pimply Irish, Italian, Bavarian, and Filipino boys to come, with sweaty palms and tortured consciences, and she offered a simpler way: the Brown Scapular, a sleek and minimalist version of the Carmelite habit—small enough to wear around your neck under your wife-beater T-shirt along with that golden horn against the Evil Eye—that itches just enough to remind you of the need for penance and prayer. Put it on before you go speeding in your Camaro. It will do the trick—or so the little Xeroxed pamphlet that comes with the scapular promises. If on the Day of Judgment we can't count on the little doodads we picked up in a parish gift shop, what hope is there for any of us?

··

May 17

Madron (+540): The Saint of Lost Socks

In case you were desperately seeking another medieval Cornish saint, we've dug one up for you. (Not literally, okay? We leave relic-hunting to the professionals.) This sixth-century hermit plays a part both in popular folklore and Arthurian legend. It's said that those making a vow can prove their sincerity by dipping their hands in St. Madron's Well, near the site of his private cell in Cornwall. Another tradition reports that if you require a miracle, you should leave a piece of cloth at the well. As the clothing rots, your illness will go away.

CELEBRATE: Ever wonder where all the lost socks of the world end up? Some theologians suggest that they are accumulating in Limbo, but here we differ. We think that St. Madron is taking them. King Arthur's knights are long dead, and most Corns today are post-Anglicans, leaving the old hermit feeling neglected up in heaven. So he's stealing our odd socks and hoarding them, waiting for us to wake up and start invoking his intercession. The next time you do the wash, offer up your missing footwear to St. Madron, in return for whatever favor you're seeking from God this week. If the socks do not return, feel confident your petition will be granted.

May 24

Simeon Stylites the Younger (521–597): A Treehouse for Dad

This saint was orphaned at a young age and adopted by a hermit—who promptly moved the two of them onto "prayer platforms" on top of pillars. (Foster care in late antiquity was better than it is today.) There they lived for decades, attracting hundreds of disciples. Eventually, Simeon convinced a bishop to climb up and ordain him a priest. Fr. Simeon gave out Communion to monks standing on ladders and lived on his pillar for sixty-nine years.

CELEBRATE: What a great occasion for a father/son project—building a platform treehouse in the yard! Gather the boys, the tools and materials, and build a big, spacious shelter behind your home, complete with a retractable rope ladder. Serve fruit punch and s'mores to the sweaty lads when all is done.

But when they try to clamber up the ladder, this is the time to teach them Christian renunciation. Dad should inform the boys that this isn't their treehouse;

it's his private "prayer platform," where he will retire for solitary contemplation. He'll climb up with rosary and breviary in hand, and pull up the ladder behind him. When they start crying, tell them to "offer it up."

May 25

Martyrs of Mexico (+1926): Trash for the Temple

Few of us *Norteños* know the story, but twentieth-century Mexico was the site of the most vicious persecution of the Church ever in this hemisphere. Starting in 1914, the "reformist" government of that one-party state began openly to attack believing Catholics, whom they saw as barriers to progress, which they identified with secularism.

If practicing Catholics organized themselves through parish activities, those who opposed the Church networked through Masonic temples.[4] (Because of the Masons' long history of anticlericalism, Catholics are still forbidden to join Masonic groups, on pain of excommunication.) The governing elite of Mexico had long been connected with the Masonic orders and jealous of the hold the Church had over the hearts of the common people. In 1924, an antireligious radical, Plutarco Elias Calles, took power in Mexico. He attempted to found a separatist "patriotic church," which used mezcal instead of wine at Mass—but people laughed at him.

Calles made it clear he was deadly serious in 1926, when he seized all Catholic schools, expelled religious orders, had his troops loot hundreds of churches, and arrested parish priests wholesale for refusing to break their vows and marry. Dozens of priests were shot simply for distributing the sacraments; most died with the cry "*Viva Cristo Rey!*" The persecutions (depicted movingly by Graham Greene in *The Power and the Glory*) mounted until they provoked a civil war, in which tens of thousands of humble peasants—who called themselves *Cristeros*—rose up to defend the Church. After a Vatican-sponsored truce, they laid down their arms—and were massacred. The profoundly corrupt and autocratic Party of Institutionalized Revolution (PRI) that sponsored these atrocities continued to rule Mexico until 2000, when free elections threw it out of power. For the first time in decades, it was legal for a Mexican priest to wear his religious garb in public.

---

4. North of the Rio Grande, Masonic temples were often built, provocatively, right across from a town's Catholic Church. In the 1920s, these temples were the seedbed of the revived Ku Klux Klan.

CELEBRATE: Read up on the stories of the Mexican heroes of the faith in Robert Royal's *Catholic Martyrs of the Twentieth Century,* and tell their inspiring tales to your children.[5] You might want to do so over a tasty Mexican feast. When dinner is over, carefully gather up the trash and drive with the kids to your town's nearest Masonic temple. Lead them in a zesty chant of *"Viva Cristo Rey!"* as you dump it on the front steps—and burn rubber on the way home.

---

5. New York: Crossroad, 2000.

June

June 3

Kevin (498–618): Milking the Wolf

This medieval Irish monk was one of the noble company of men and women who, in Thomas Cahill's famous phrase, "saved civilization" by recopying and disseminating books and cultivating intellectual disciplines that would otherwise have been utterly lost.

Kevin founded monasteries, built a cathedral, and started a lively intellectual tradition in his island refuge of Glendalough, for which he is still revered by Irishmen today—especially by those living in Woodside, Queens, who name every third boy "Kevin" (which can get confusing in large families). But Kevin is perhaps best known for the charming legends that grew up around him because of his famous tenderness toward animals. The tale is told, between shots of whiskey, that Kevin:

- ☺ Cured an epileptic by forcing a willow tree to produce apples.
- ☺ Kept his monks fed through a drought by harvesting salmon brought him by a friendly otter.
- ☺ Stood in one place praying all through Lent, so that a blackbird laid an egg in his hand, which hatched by Easter.
- ☺ Lacking a cow, milked a deer to provide for a needy child. When a she-wolf ate the doe, he milked the wolf.

June 5

Boniface (680–754): St. Paul Bunyan

This Christian evangelist spread the Gospel through much of Germany. Instead of forcing people to convert, as the Emperor Charlemagne had done in violation of Church law, Boniface preferred to use persuasion. But since he was preaching to tribes of rough and ready Teutonic warriors, he knew that devotional tea-cozies and little Infant of Prague dolls wouldn't do the trick. Instead, he relied on fierce, emo-

tional preaching and dramatic gestures. When he came across a band of backsliding pagans who'd revived the favorite local custom of sacrificing human beings before the "sacred Tree of Thor," Boniface decided to teach the warrior god a lesson. He pulled off his shirt, pulled out an ax and hacked his way through the ancient, mighty tree—sneering as it fell, "How stands your mighty god? My God is stronger than he." Then he stuck out his tongue and made the ancient "L" sign for loser, taunting the puzzled pagans by dancing about and slapping their knees—thereby inventing what was to become the classic German folk dance. Boniface went on, it's said, to build a church out of Thor's wood, later dying as a martyr at the hands of medieval environmentalists.

....

June 12

Onuphrius (+440): Hermits at Houlihan's

This Egyptian monk lived for years with other austere penitents, but eventually he felt called to emulate St. John the Baptist and dwell alone in the desert. He moved off by himself and lived as a hermit for seventy years, where he lived only on the food that appeared mysteriously on his table every day and clad himself only in his long, unwashed hair and a loincloth made of leaves.

CELEBRATE: Take the family out to a meal at the local mall, honoring St. Onuphrius by wearing only long hair (or wigs) and strategically located leaves. If the restaurant seats you for dinner, it will be a miracle.

June 13

Anthony of Padua (1195–1231):
The Celestial Lost and Found

This Franciscan friar was known in his lifetime for his amazing eloquence. Early in life he sought out a holy death, volunteering to preach in Moslem North Africa in what would surely have been a kamikaze mission. Our Lord suggested a change of plan by wrecking Anthony's ship and making him good and sick. Back in Italy, Anthony was soon discovered as a major talent and sent out to preach to stubborn heretics (Albigensians) who believed that the material world was evil, and crowds of lukewarm Catholics who thought it was just dandy. Anthony made himself famous by performing miracles like appearing in more than one place at a time, healing the sick, and convincing feuding Italians to put away their switchblades and embrace. Because the infant Jesus appeared to him and nestled in his arms, Anthony is a patron saint of children.

Anthony's popularity today stems from his posthumous generosity. St. Therese of Lisieux once said that she would spend her time in heaven doing good on earth. But she had big things in mind—like promoting the missions (of which this cloistered nun is patron saint). Anthony seems to have chosen an even humbler task: to mar his eternity of bliss in heaven and busy himself finding our car keys, tax receipts, ATM passwords, and bar napkins with telephone numbers.

....

June 16

Cyriacus of Iconium (+304): Baby Got Boar

This child saint, it's said, was killed along with his mother by Romans during the persecutions of Diocletian—the most comprehensive attempt ever made (until the French Revolution) to wipe out the Church. Desperate to hold together a crumbling empire, Diocletian imposed a fourth-century version of totalitarianism on the Mediterranean, decreeing that no one could change jobs, move from place to place, or generally break wind without express permission. A Church that insisted on spiritual freedom didn't fit into this plan.

We don't know much more about Cyriacus, except that the Emperor Charlemagne had a dream in which the saint appeared and saved him from death at the hands of the wild boars he was hunting. The little martyr rode naked on one of the boars and waved cheerfully to the grateful Kaiser—inspiring him upon waking to fix the roof of the cathedral of St. Cyr.

CELEBRATE: Take your children to the local petting zoo for the naked pig rides. Try to go at off-peak hours to avoid the lines.

Then, in gratitude to the pig who built St. Cyr, roast up a delicious piece of pork, and tell your kids the story between bites.

Roast Pork

Make the centerpiece this sumptuous roast. Have your butcher tie the meat for you, and then this recipe will be a cinch.

1 pork butt (about 5 pounds)	Freshly ground pepper
1 tablespoon butter	6 bay leaves
1 teaspoon vegetable oil	1 cup red wine vinegar
Salt	

Preheat oven to 400 degrees. Heat a cast-iron skillet to smoking. Add oil and butter. Add pork and sear in pan, turning until all sides are deep brown. Season with salt and pepper. Place bay leaves under string and in crevices of meat. Pour 1/2 cup vinegar over pork.

Place pork in roasting pan and roast for 45 minutes. Add remaining vinegar. Roast for another 45 minutes.

Makes 4–6 servings

Sacramental Executive Summary #3: Confession

This is a tough sacrament. Once enormously popular—older Catholics will recall that Confession lines on Saturdays used to approximate Communion lines on Sundays—it has fallen out of favor among most churchgoers. Instead, even blue-collar Catholics seem to favor going to therapy to face their personal failings. Which gives us an idea: perhaps confessors should start charging $100 a visit, keeping people there for 50 minutes, and sending them home with self-help books but no absolution; then we'll mistake it for therapy and come back every week for years. It's just a thought.

Here's another: in our parents' day, most parishes offered Confession just before Sunday Mass. This showed concern for those who'd had an interesting Saturday night, but it also displayed good retail sense: you've already got them in the door, now it's time to *upsell.* Don't expect everyone to make a special trip: create a one-stop shopping experience. The availability of priests to hear confessions tells you something about the priorities in your parish. Few pastors schedule the weekly collection for fifteen minutes on a Saturday afternoon.

In case you have a hard time getting your kids, your spouse, or yourself to Confession, may we suggest a way of making things easier? Why not throw open your home to family and friends in the form of a "Confession Party"?

Cook up a nice but simple dinner, say, red beans and rice or pasta with sauce, with a salad and a tub of ice cream for dessert. Remind your guests to come on time, and invite the priest to drop by a half hour later. Let the guests enjoy their dinner and have a few drinks before he shows up. Then install the fine fellow in the back with a pitcher of margaritas all his own to confess your guests.

You may encounter some resistance here. People are used to anonymous confessions—when they bother to go at all. (One of the most quixotic reforms in recent years was the push for "face-to-face" Confession—as if the one way to make it less embarrassing to tell a strange man all about your fondness for shoplifting, vicious gossip, and online porn were to stare him straight in the eye.[1]) It's understandable that your guests might be upset that you didn't warn them about this intrusively spiritual element in the festivities. So you should make it easier for each of them to comply with your hidden agenda. Here are a few ideas we've tried ourselves:

Introduce each guest to the priest personally, so they see he's not a judgmental scold but a tipsy Irishman who couldn't care less about anyone's personal life. Remind them that dentists are rarely fascinated by plaque. If any of your guests are no longer practicing Catholics, or you know their private lives to be particularly squalid, don't embarrass them. When you get to them, merely squint, shake your head in polite distress, and sigh, "Not you." Steer the curate gingerly to the next guest.

Make it clear that you and your kids will be going to Confession first, to break the ice. Hint broadly that your sins are so scarlet and overpowering that anything else the priest hears after that will sound rather tame. (This will almost certainly be a lie. Confess it, too.)

Most importantly, station the priest in the bathroom, where he's impossible to avoid. He can greet guests with a smile, "Anything you'd like to get out of your system?"

....

June 17
Hypatius (+450): Boycott the Olympics

This monk and theologian from Chalcedon is called a "thaumaturge" (wonderworker) for the many miracles he performed during his lifetime. Besides healing dozens of sick pilgrims who came to his monastery near Chalcedon, Hypatius became famous for defeating an enormous serpent that had crawled into the

---

1. A friend of the authors tells of his mother, a very active lay Catholic. She was upset when her pastor pulled out all the confessionals and refused to use a screen—denying her anonymity. So after a few complaints went unheeded, she showed up one Saturday afternoon in a Halloween mask, which she wore in to the "reconciliation room." The priest was aghast: "What are you doing?" She answered, coolly: "Retaining my canonical right to an anonymous Confession. And I'll be here like this every week, if I have to." The next day, one of the missing confessionals miraculously reappeared.

emperor's treasure vault, which he lured into an oven and roasted at 450 degrees for three hours and then served. His greatest miracle, however—at least to people like us who loathe professional sports—was that he singlehandedly put a stop to the Olympics. There was a movement in his day to revive the ancient games, which had once been enormously popular. Aware of their pagan origin, and annoyed at the prospect of product endorsements of jock-straps by pole-vaulters and contraceptives by gymnasts, Hypatius interceded with the emperor and shut down the games.

CELEBRATE: If you're a TV sports widow(er), invoke St. Hypatius's arguments against watching the Olympics, switching the TV to a thirteen-part series on relics of the saints aired by EWTN, alarmist ecological exposés on PBS, or four-hour musicals from Bollywood.

June 19

Juliana Falconieri (1270–1341): Little Miss Perfect

Some saints' tales are more appealing to modern readers than others. It's easy to enjoy the stories of St. Francis preaching to animals, St. Joan riding into battle, St. Rita licking the sores of lepers. But the legends surrounding Juliana Falconieri seem designed to make us queasy—which is only fitting, since Juliana had a lifelong problem with vomiting. This devout Florentine joined the Servite order and lived a life of profound, mystical holiness, serving the poor. No problems there. But she was also, if legend be true, the kind of prissy, pious girl who makes herself hated in Catholic schools around the world—sucking up to Sister, reminding teachers to assign homework, and turning in the altar boys for spiking the incense with hash.

Perhaps we digress. All that's really said about Juliana is that she had an ultra-tender conscience: apparently she spent her whole life without looking in a mirror or glancing at a man's face, started shaking if anyone even mentioned sin, and would respond to the sound of gossip by passing out cold on the floor. All this made her wildly popular.

CELEBRATE: Our imperfections are cleaned up (some would say "burned away") in purgatory, so this once-prim saint certainly wouldn't mind if we marked her feast with the traditional French dessert *pets de nonne*, or "nun's farts." These fried-dough treats are named for the particularly *gastrointestinal* sound they make while they are cooking. Serve them on her feast day and tell her story to your girls.

Nun's Farts

Adapted from John Thorne's classic *Simple Cooking*.

6 tablespoons butter	1 cup sifted flour
2 teaspoons sugar	1 teaspoon vanilla
Pinch salt	1 teaspoon dark rum (optional)
1 teaspoons grated lemon peel	Oil for deep frying
1 cup milk	Confectioner's sugar
4 eggs	

Combine butter, sugar, salt, and lemon rind with milk in a saucepan and bring slowly to a boil. When butter is completely melted, add the flour all at once, stirring vigorously until all of it is absorbed. When the flour has been absorbed into a paste, adjust heat to medium high and return the pan to it. Cook this mixture for 3–4 minutes, stirring constantly, scraping sides and bottom, until the batter clings together in a solid mass, and takes on a glossy look. Transfer to a bowl stand mixer.

Beat in the vanilla and rum and allow the batter to cool for a while. Add eggs one at a time, beating each until fully incorporated. The pastry should be "flexible and soft, firm enough to hold its shape and not at all runny." Set it aside and let it rest for 45 minutes.

Heat oil in a heavy pot to 360 degrees. Drop the batter into the hot oil a teaspoonful at a time. The farts will puff up to about four times their original size, so don't crowd them in the fryer. When golden brown, drain on paper towels and sprinkle with confectioner's sugar.

Makes 40 treats

June 24

The Birth of John the Baptist:
Charging Bulls and Naked Sambas

In Brazil, nearly any saint's feast day serves as an excuse to get a lot of tanned, beautifully toned people naked as quickly as possible, jiggling their stuff in the streets. You aren't either quite so tan or quite so toned, so we suggest making this a party where people stay dressed, bring the kids, and make themselves ridiculous in other ways. For instance, hire a samba instructor to come over and teach everyone how to dance; this is the most fun after a few too many capairinhas.

Brazil is different from the rest of Latin America because its colonial heritage is Portuguese rather than Spanish. The country also boasts a much richer ethnic blend than much of South America because of the large-scale importation of African slaves—whose descendants contributed the many musical and cultural traditions we associate with Bahia, among other regions. An ethnographically correct celebration of Brazilian folk ritual would take account of these differences, the careful study of which would undoubtedly enrich your children's appreciation of the wonderful diversity that makes our country so *yadda yadda yadda, blah blah blah*. We know you couldn't care less, and neither could we. You want instructions on how to decorate, and here they are: *Think South of the Border*. Think Carmen Miranda, Ricky Ricardo, Speedy Gonzalez. Put up palm trees alongside cacti, hang strings of paper bananas from posters of Don Quixote. Raid the dollar store in the nearest *barrio*. Nobody will notice the difference—unless they're Brazilian, in which case they certainly know better than to use a tipsy party as a teaching moment in cultural anthropology. Pick up some samba, bossa nova, Brazilian jazz, and other varieties. Then mix them up to keep the beat varied throughout the evening.

If you can't afford a Samba instructor, we understand. Not all of us care enough to give our friends the best, so here's how to give them second best: by turning a bizarre, thinly Christianized pagan ritual into party fun for the whole family.

It seems that one of the ancient rites of pre-Christian Europe featured the ritual execution of a bull by a crowd of religious initiates, who would then sprinkle themselves with his "sacred blood" and drink it to tap into his vital energies. This rite survived in Portugal right through its conversion to Christianity and came to be celebrated on the Feast of St. John the Baptist. Why? No one knows. It's still practiced in some villages there, and in the northern regions of Portugal's one-time colony, Brazil. It lives on in the states of Maranhao and Amazonas in a stylized form that is wildly popular: a huge, elaborately decorated bull made of carved wood is inhabited by a group of sturdy dancers, and it pretends to charge a crowd of partyers, who respond by banging wildly on drums to a steadily intensifying beat—until at the climactic moment the bull is "killed" and everyone breaks out the red wine to celebrate. The custom is called *bumba-meu-boi,* perhaps from the name of the Brazilian bass drum, the *zabumba.*

Instead of a carved wooden bull—assuming you don't have one—order or make a large bull-shaped piñata, stuffed with treats for the kids. Distribute to guests big and small toy drums, which your children have decorated in wild colors with finger paints. Put on any Samba CD to set the beat—or go ahead and obtain some of the music specifically written for this feast, such as *Tic Tic Tac,* by Carrapicho, or *Boi Bumbá,* by José Tobias. (Learn more about this tradition and its music at *www. allbrazilianmusic.com*). Get everyone good and tipsy—not the kids of course, who should instead drink lots of coffee. In a room that has been cleared of anything breakable, have the dads hoist the Bumba bull over their heads and charge the party-goers, trying their best to spill them onto the floor. In return, everybody pretends to attack the bull, until it retreats. Then they start drumming again. Repeat as needed, until everybody's good and tired; then let the kids attack the piñata bare-handed and rip it to shreds, fighting in good Darwinian fashion over the spoils. The whole event should serve as good preparation for life in the adult corporate world.

Red Wine Tapioca Pudding

1 cup large pearl tapioca
3 cups water to soak
3 cups Argentinian Cabernet
  Sauvignon

2–3 cups water
2 sticks Mexican cinnamon
2 cups sugar

Soak tapioca at least 3 hours, preferably overnight. Drain. In a spacious, heavy-bottomed pot, combine tapioca and wine. Heat slowly and stir frequently. Do not allow to come to a full boil.

As the mixture thickens, add water 1 cup at a time. Cook about 45 minutes, until pearls are clear. When tapioca is nearly done, add sugar. Stir well until dissolved.

The last few minutes of cooking can be completed off the stove. Pour into a shallow uncovered container and stir often until cooled. Refrigerate for 2–3 hours. Serve with fresh thick cream or good vanilla ice cream.

Makes 6 servings

The Feast of Pentecost:
Flaming Punch and Speaking in Tongues

This feast is one of our favorites, for a number of reasons. First, it marks the birthday of the Church, the day when the Holy Spirit came down on the Apostles and Mary and gave them all the nerve they needed to preach the risen Christ to a hostile mob.

Pentecost also reverses the story of the Tower of Babel, the Old Testament tale of a king so ambitious he wanted to reach heaven through technological means. God tweaked him by inventing that bane of American schoolchildren over the millennia: foreign languages. In what we might call multiculturalism's founding moment, God scattered the king's workforce into a squabble of hostile ethnic groups who couldn't communicate with each other. Then, at Pentecost, He reversed the process—giving the Apostles the gift enjoyed by *Star Trek* crew members ever since the very first episode: the ability to be understood by anyone, no matter his or her native language. The Holy Spirit provided this universal translator, which is called "the gift of tongues," to kick start the Church into universality. For just a few hours on Pentecost morning, the Apostles spoke Aramaic, but they were heard in Greek, Latin, Esperanto—you name it. They were so jumped up with joy that people assumed they must be drunk. This is what it means to "speak in tongues." When Texas-based televangelists lapse from prayers into gibberish, mumbling *"Hamana-shamana-freddigah-limina-bop-bop-a-doowop . . ."* and then ask you to send in a check. . . . Well, that's something else.

In the Old Testament, Pentecost made its first appearance as a harvest festival, marking fifty days after Passover, under the title the "Feast of First Fruits." Carry on this part of the tradition by providing lots of tasty fresh edibles, from kiwis to kumquats, arrayed around the house in bowls. It will help the guests' digestion—since the meal doesn't include the ordinary quantities of greens. (They'd clash with the red; we're not going for a Christmas theme.) The Israelites also hung the home with garlands and flowers, a custom that in the Christian East meant roses throughout the house. (The Greeks called Pentecost "the feast of roses.") If you can afford the expense, collect a few dozen red roses or other flowers, and plant them all over the house. In Italy, rose petals were traditionally scattered from the church ceiling on this feast; in France, trumpets were blown to sound forth the Holy Spirit. Before the Reformation, English priests released a dove inside the church during Mass. Any variation on these customs would be most festive—until you have to clean up after the bird.

Many curious activities have arisen to mark this feast, perhaps the strangest in Merrie Old England. Some villages in Gloucester still keep alive these customs, which include a cheese-rolling contest that pits country folk against each other in a race with enormous cheeses down the nearest hill. The winner gets to keep, and presumably eat, the giant, dusty cheese. In St. Braivels, the villagers celebrate the day after Pentecost by hurling baskets full of bread and cheese from a castle wall for the common folk to scramble and fight over on the ground.

The most exotic Pentecost activity arose on the tropical island named for the feast, near the Pacific tax haven of Vanuatu—the home of the original "Cargo Cults," where cannibalism, we must insist, *is no longer legal.* On the Catholic half of religiously divided Pentecost Island, the natives practice a perilous sport they call "Nagol," or land-diving.[2] As soon as the yam crop is ready, the island's

2. On the Anglican half, they practice golf.

Catholics start to build enormous towers out of wood cut from the forest, tied together with liana branches, standing forty to fifty feet high. Any male old enough to be circumcised is expected to climb the tower, have his ankles tied with vines, and leap to the ground, bungee-style. If the vine is even a foot too long, he splats on the ground in an ex-Pentecostal heap, so divers pay close attention to the art of measurement. Missionaries say that this leap of faith is meant to evoke the descent of the Holy Spirit on His feast day. Locals know better: the diving is what ensures the next year's yam harvest.

CELEBRATE: The very best thing about Pentecost is fire. *Fire is cool.* Setting fires is cool—except that it's usually illegal. Well, Pentecost gives us a marvelous excuse to set lots of fires, all around the house, in the form of a flambé dinner party. Since the theme of the feast is universality, fill up the house with foreigners, and watch the Holy Spirit (and other spirits) break down those cultural barriers. When decorating, think red. Hang bolts of scarlet silk in place of your curtains, and fill the house with glimmering red candles—you know, like in *Rosemary's Baby*. Get hold of as many silver platters as you can, and this time remember to polish them. No, the tarnish isn't quaint, no matter what your husband says. Dim the lights, maybe burn some incense to get the room fragrant and smoky. It's that simple.

If you don't have the nerve for Nagol, there's a simpler game you can play at the Pentecost party: speaking in tongues. After everyone has adequately been washed in the spirits, as the hostess emerges with dessert, have the host lead everyone at the party in a chorus of polysyllabic flim-flam, waving their arms, rolling on the floor—even handling rubber snakes (which you'll discreetly provide each guest upon arrival). Nothing brings a group of friends closer than a few minutes spent babbling and writhing before a platter of flaming pineapples.

Kava "blong" Pentecost
A mudlike drink made from the root of a pepper plant,
popular on Pentecost Island.
Kava drinks are available online from *www.kavaking.com*.
To keep in the fiery spirit, be sure to add some pepper vodka to the mix.

Whitsun (Pentecost) Ale
A light fruity traditional ale available
from *www.arcadiabrewingcompany.com*.

Polish Fire Vodka (Krupnik)
This hot, mulled vodka drink combines the tastes
of honey, cinnamon, nutmeg, and cloves.

Flaming Spinach Salad
The last thing your guests expect to see on fire. (See recipe)

Saganaki
A beloved appetizer of flaming
Greek sheep's milk cheese. (See recipe)

Flambéed Mushrooms in Sherry
A sweet and satisfying Spanish tapa.

Flaming Chicken Brochettes
Easy to serve, delicious, decorative and light.

Sizzling Steak au Poivre
One of the richest, most satisfying concoctions we know about.

Catalonian Cornish Hens
Tender little birds roasted with sherry and Seville orange glaze.

Caramelized Pineapple
A simple, explosively enjoyable dessert.

Flaming Strawberry Shortcake
A spirited variation on the traditional summer favorite.

Flaming Spinach Salad

This is particularly fun flambé to serve—burning salad is always such a nice surprise!

4 bunches spinach, washed and dried

4 hard boiled eggs, sliced

1/4 teaspoon salt

Freshly ground black pepper

DRESSING:

1/2 cup bacon drippings

2 tablespoons grapeseed oil

2 tablespoons walnut oil

1/2 cup malt vinegar

1/4 cup lemon juice

4 teaspoons sugar

1 teaspoon Worcestershire sauce

1 1/2 ounces brandy

Toss spinach, eggs, salt and pepper.

Combine dressing ingredients in a saucepan. Warm dressing and cook for a few minutes to balance flavors. Adjust seasoning. Heat brandy, add to dressing, and ignite.

Toss salad as it flames, before guests. Serve on warm plates.

Makes 8 servings

Saganaki (Greek Flaming Cheese)

2 pounds Kasseri or Halloumi cheese

Flour, for dredging

Butter

3 lemons, cut in quarters

Cognac

If the recommended cheese is not available, ask your cheesemonger for a recommendation or search out a Greek purveyor. They will be sure to have an opinion about the best cheese as well as how it should be cut. Of course, "the only way it should be done" will differ from vendor to vendor.

Slice cheese into 1/2 inch thick rectangles. Keep cold at all times when not working with it.

Heat a medium size sauté pan and melt 1 tablespoon butter.

Dust cheese with flour in a shallow plate, lightly tapping to remove excess.

Gently lay 2–3 slices at a time in pan and cook until golden on each side.

Remove to serving dish and cook remaining slices, adding butter as needed. As cheese comes out of pan, squeeze lemon over slices. (Work quickly as the cheese is best eaten hot.)

Heat a few tablespoon of cognac. This can be done by holding it in a large spoon over a flame. Pour over the cheese and ignite in front of your guests. Serve with lemon quarters.

Makes 8 servings

July 4

Independence Day: Dress Your Kids as Kennedys

From the very beginning, Catholics have struggled to find their place in America—with mixed success. Both the Plymouth and the Jamestown colonies were officially, intolerantly Protestant (as Spain and France were intolerantly Catholic). Early Puritan stories of women kidnapped by Indians dwelt equally on the fear that these colonists would be raped and that they might be converted to Catholicism. (For all their flaws, the French and Spanish believed in evangelizing the natives, rather than labeling them "children of the devil," as the Puritans did, and trying to exterminate them.) The single British colony, Maryland, founded as a haven for persecuted English Catholics, was taken over by a Protestant coup in 1689. It soon seized all Catholic churches and forbade the faith. One of the grievances Thomas Jefferson put into the Declaration of Independence was King George's generous treatment of Catholics in Quebec. Not surprisingly, almost all the Catholic clergy in the colonies in 1776 opposed the American Revolution.

But some elite Catholics did take part in the founding; Charles Carroll, cousin of Baltimore Archbishop John Carroll, signed the Declaration of Independence. In time, as states abolished their established Protestant churches, Catholics gained new rights. However, they were still treated with profound suspicion by many Americans, who saw them as agents of a sinister, worldwide plot for papal domination—which very few of them were. Okay, *maybe* the Jesuits. . . .

An entire political party, the Know-Nothings, was organized to oppose Catholic influence; its members helped form the Republican party, which after the Civil War would promise to fight "Rum, Romanism, and Rebellion." Having crushed the rebellion, Republicans addressed the next two together when they successfully imposed Prohibition—which was largely aimed at "Americanizing" (i.e., Protestantizing) the beer-drinking Irish and German immigrants and the wine-loving Italians. The American bishops, in a great moment for the Church, declared Prohibition an unjust law, which Catholics could rightly violate. And we did so with gusto, with help from an informal network of community resistance leaders, such as Chicago's Al Capone, New York's Owney "The Killer" Madden, and Boston's Joseph Kennedy.

It's no great mystery why most Catholics became Democrats—sticking with the party even when the "solid South" turned against candidate Al Smith in 1928, with six states voting Republican for the first time since Reconstruction in order to reject a Catholic candidate for president. In the 1932 election, Catholics gleefully joined Franklin Roosevelt's coalition—which promised to repeal Prohibition, and which depended on the political machine Joseph Kennedy had built in the wards of Boston. In return, Kennedy demanded (and got) the post of ambassador to Great Britain; in the job, he supported the appeasement of Germany, opposed U.S. aid to England, and generally did all he could to repay the British for the past six hundred years. But once America was at war, three Kennedy sons served faithfully in the military (one died), and after the war the family political machine revved up again. John Kennedy, the hero of PT-109, was elected to the Senate, while Robert Kennedy served on the staff of Senator Joseph McCarthy.

It was in the election campaign of 1960 that American Catholics finally "arrived," politically. With a single address by Sen. John F. Kennedy to an audience of Texas ministers, that statesman showed the American Protestant majority that we are, and will remain, forever harmless. In his address, JFK promised that his deepest personal beliefs—on display when he campaigned with priests and nuns in Boston—would never, *never* influence his official actions "directly or indirectly." It is a promise that most American Catholics have faithfully kept ever since.

CELEBRATE: As you grill steaks and shrimp and violate another unjust law by shooting off fireworks, why not turn today into a pageant of American Catholic history? We suggest you celebrate the family that brought Catholicism into the mainstream of American life, the Kennedys. First of all, there were so many of them, it offers lots of opportunities.

Dress some of the boys as young Joseph Kennedy and his "associates," complete with gangster suits and tommy guns. Invite Grandma (or an elderly neighbor) to play Rose Kennedy. Take your prettiest daughter (come on, you know which is which) shopping at a thrift store for 1960s outfits, complete with pillbox hat, to play Jacqueline Kennedy. Get a girl done up in tight, pink halter dress like Marilyn Monroe, and teach her to croon "Happy Birthday, Mr. President" before the boy playing JFK, while "Jackie" silently seethes. (Important: Do not have a brother and sister play these roles; your kids have enough psychological problems.) Dress the frailest-looking boy as Robert Kennedy, while your teenager who already drinks too much and totals cars will have to play Teddy.

Have the party outside around the pool; whenever anyone shouts the "codeword," everyone has to jump in. The codeword is "Chappaquiddick."

Benedict of Nursia (480–547): Enjoy a Dominican with Your Benedictine

Here we come to the namesake chosen by the recently elected Pope Benedict XVI, who picked this name in part to honor one of the great evangelizers of the European continent.

When the young Italian student Benedict decided to take up the life of a monk, his parents can't have been pleased: for centuries, the Christian ascetics of Egypt and Syria had been making a nuisance of themselves—eating locusts in the desert, living on top of pillars, and lashing themselves with whips to quell their hallucinations.

Now and then they might pen a worthy spiritual book, but generally they stayed out of sight and made themselves useless—waiting for pilgrims to come pray at the foot of their pillars and empty their Port-a-Potties. When they did live in communities, these tended to be fractious and filthy, like an Ivy League fraternity house.

Somewhere along the line, Benedict got a better idea: Why not put all that learning and spare time to work and harness the work to prayer? Attracting a group of followers, Benedict drew up his own monastic Rule, which dictated that certain parts of every monk's day must include useful labor, which itself would be dedicated to God. The monks would hoe their gardens, jar apricots, make beer, or copy ancient manuscripts, and they'd gather, when summoned by a bell, to chapel to sing the Liturgy of the Hours.

Although Benedict's first followers resisted the "useful labor" part of the rule— for instance, they poisoned him—it soon caught on, and he survived to found some twelve monasteries. Many hundreds more, both male and female, sprang up around Europe over succeeding centuries, of which a great number still survive. Western monastic houses inspired by Benedict's Rule helped preserve the ancient learning that would otherwise have disappeared from the Continent, opened schools that created Europe's educated class, developed the exquisite music we know as Gregorian Chant, and—most importantly—created a wide variety of beers, wines, and liqueurs we still enjoy today: Riesling, Trollinger, Scottish Ale, Belgian Trappist Ale, Benedictine, and the sublime Chartreuse, among many others. Without St. Benedict, we would indeed live in a different America today—one in which no one read the classics of ancient literature, understood Latin or archaic Greek, prayed the liturgical hours, fasted for Lent, or drank Chimay with dinner. And our beloved new pope might have taken the name "John Paul III." Or maybe "Ringo." All sobering thoughts.

July 14

Bastille Day: Vive le Roi!

Today marks the beginning of the French Revolution, and is celebrated as the country's founding feast throughout most of France—with a few exceptions. The people of Brittany, Normandy, and especially the Vendée show a little less enthusiasm—since for them today recalls the virtual genocide committed in those regions by the new French Republic. We don't have space here to address the whole question of whether it was necessary—in order to correct the fiscal ineffi-ciencies and backward laws of the French monarchy—to launch a bloody revolu-tion, create the world's first police state, persecute the Church, decapitate thousands of dissidents and immigrants and then wage war on the rest of Europe for twenty years. You decide.

But we do like to take this opportunity to honor the memories of all the inno-cents who died during the Revolution, particularly those who were killed primarily for clinging to their Catholic faith. (Some argue that this includes King Louis XVI and Queen Marie Antoinette, who could have saved their lives by endorsing the Revolution's attack on the Church.) In the Vendée region, for instance, pious peas-ants were horrified at the news that their king and queen had been beheaded and their young son (Louis XVII) left to die in a filthy prison. Matters got worse when the Vendéens learned that the revolutionary regime—controlled by wealthy Paris burghers—intended to draft 300,000 men from their region to fight for the Revolu-tion. When churches were closed because their priests would not renounce the pope, the people of the Vendée and neighboring provinces went into open revolt. Under crudely drawn banners bearing the Sacred Heart and the slogan "For God and King!" they began a guerilla war. The rebels called themselves "Chouans," after the screech-owl sound which they used as their rebel yell.

The fighting raged for almost two years, requiring a full-scale invasion by the Republic's professional armies to defeat them—and even then, the region was seething with resistance. As historian Sophie Masson (a descendant of Vendée sur-vivors) has written,[1] the revolutionaries in Paris decided to make an example of the Vendée. In 1794, revolutionary leaders decided to exterminate the entire population of the region, issuing decrees such as:

"Fire, blood, death are needed to preserve liberty."
"Not one is to be left alive."
"Women are reproductive furrows who must be ploughed under."
"Only wolves must be left to roam that land."

Vive la République!

The revolutionaries ordered, Masson reports, "the mass drownings of naked men, women, and children, often tied together in what [they] called 'republican marriages,' off specially constructed boats towed out to the middle of the Loire and then sunk." Historians estimate that several hundred thousand died, most of them civilians, many of them martyrs.

The rebellion was crushed—but not defeated. The sheer devotion the Vendéens and other peasants showed to the faith forced Napoleon, now in control of France, to suspend the persecution of the Church and allow priests once again to distribute the sacraments freely. Catholic apologist Michael Davies has called this "the vic-tory of the Vendée."[2] In 1993, Alexander Solzhenitsyn spoke as guest of honor at the opening of the Vendée Memorial.

---

1. "Remembering the Vendée," (*www.godspy.com/culture/Remembering-The-Vendee.cfm*).
2. Michael Davies, *For Altar and Throne: The Rising in the Vendée* (St. Paul, Minn.: Remnant Press, 1997).

CELEBRATE: On July 14, 1989, the authors decided to mark the bicentennial of Bastille Day by helping to organize a Requiem Mass for the victims of the Revolution. We invited the French consul in New York, but he claimed a prior engagement. More recently, we threw a Vendée Party, featuring the food, wines, and songs of the region. Why not surprise your friends (especially those of French descent) by doing the same?

Download the patriotic songs these Catholic guerrillas raised while marching into battle (*http://chants.royalistes.free.fr/*) and plaster your walls with pictures of Louis, Marie, and the heroes of the revolt (Charrette, Stofflet, Cathelineau, La Rochejacquelein), and the royal *fleur-de-lis*. You might begin the evening by recounting the Vendée story to your guests—or perhaps by reading aloud the last will and testament of Louis XVI (*www.chivalricorders.org/royalty/bourbon/france/louistst.htm*), a profoundly Christian document in which the king, expecting death, both begs for and offers forgiveness to all involved. Have your hankies ready; there won't be a dry eye in the place.

By way of entertainment, you might show the film that depicts the revolt, *Chouans!* (1988), or Eric Rohmer's exquisite portrait of Revolutionary Paris, *The Lady and the Duke* (2001). But since this is a French celebration, the central event really should be dinner. Here's a menu made up entirely of specialties from the Vendée region, and wine from the Valley of the Loire, which runs through it:

APPETIZERS

Cockles Steamed in White Wine, with Cream Sauce

Sautéed Radishes with Wilted Watercress

Green Beans with Toasted Walnuts and Chives and Sheep's Milk Yogurt

Roasted Asparagus and Mushrooms

Cauliflower and Roasted Peppers

Nicoise Olives and Capers

ENTREES

Bay Scallops with Cherry Tomatoes (See recipe)

Poached Salmon

Stuffed with herbs, arugula, chives, and parsley,
in a Dijon mustard sauce with tarragon.

Bay Scallops with Cherry Tomatoes

1 pound bay scallops
1 tablespoon butter
1 teaspoon olive oil
1/2 pint cherry tomatoes
sea salt and freshly ground pepper

1 sprig fresh thyme
2 sprigs fresh parsley
1 sprig fresh oregano
1/4–1/2 cup Vouvray

Rinse and pat dry scallops. Set aside.

Heat pan and add oil and 2 teaspoons butter. Add tomatoes and herbs to pan. Shake occasionally. Tomatoes will swell slightly. Slide out of pan and set aside. Without cleaning pan add scallops. Turn after 1 minute. Cook for 30 seconds. Return tomatoes to pan and shake lightly. Pour in wine and reduce quickly.

Swirl in reserved butter, adjust seasoning, and serve.

Makes 4 servings

DESSERT

Of course your guests must eat cake! Not that Marie Antoinette ever said such a thing; this nasty slur about a queen mocking the hungry was already a hundred years old when Marie took the throne, and had been made up to slander a previous royal wife whom the French hated because (like Marie) she was foreign. But don't let that stop you from making a really marvelous cake for dessert, from a classic Vendée recipe:

Cheesecake with Chèvre and Nectarines

1/4 cup graham cracker crumbs,
  toasted
5 ounces chèvre
5 ounces fresh ricotta
1/2 cup superfine sugar

Pinch of salt
5 eggs, separated
1 tablespoon corn starch
1 tablespoon orange blossom water

Preheat oven to 400 degrees.

Prepare pan by lightly buttering. Coat bottom of pan with toasted graham cracker crumbs. Set aside.

Mix together cheeses, sugar, and salt. Add egg yolks one at a time, mixing in thoroughly. Mix in corn starch, followed by orange blossom water.

Whip egg whites to stiff peak and gently fold into cheese mixture. Pour into pan and bake on middle rack of oven for 50 minutes.

Allow to cool before unmolding onto a serving plate. Arrange nectarines on top of cake and serve remaining fruit in a bowl alongside.

Makes 12–16 servings

July 20

Margaret of Antioch (fourth century) and Wilgefortis (dates unknown): The Dragon Lady and the Bearded Nun

Today we celebrate two popular martyrs whose stories remind us of the Church's sense of humor.

According to the stories that survive, Margaret was a young convert to Christianity during the persecutions of Diocletian; she made a private vow of virginity and died rather than submit to a forced marriage with a powerful Roman. There are so many such tales extant from the early Church (see St. Agatha, February 5) that they must have some basis in reality: Christian women, in great numbers, died to assert their religious liberty against a wickedly patriarchal system that insisted on treating them as commodities. But the best part of Margaret's tale reads more like a modern alien-abduction account. Legend tells that at some point before her martyrdom, Margaret was swallowed whole by the devil himself, who appeared in the form of an enormous dragon. But the large wooden cross she carried around appears to have stuck in the creature's throat like a fishbone, since the monster eventually coughed her up, alive and intact. As a result, this girl who died rather than give up her virginity is a patron of childbirth. She was also one of the saints who appeared to Joan of Arc.

St. Wilgefortis, legend insists, was the daughter of a pagan Portuguese king who wished to force her into marriage rather than allow her to enter the convent which she'd chosen. To repel her suitor, she prayed that God would make him change his mind; it's said that Our Lord granted her wish in the form of a long flowing beard, which sprouted from her virginal chin. She is the rightful patroness of bearded nuns (we've all seen them, admit it!).

Mary Magdalene (first century): Toot-toot, hey, beep-beep!

There's not much known for sure about Mary Magdalene, except that she was exorcised of seven, count 'em seven, demons by Jesus and became one of His disciples—one of the three privileged to be the first witnesses of the Resurrection. St. Gregory the Great, perhaps incorrectly, identified her as the adulterous woman whom Christ saved from stoning, and again as the penitent who washed His feet with her tears and hair—a beautiful scene that has found its way into countless paintings, such as "Mary Anointing Jesus's Feet" by Rubens. The notion that Mary Magdalene was a repentant prostitute became quite popular in ages

when countless indigent women were driven into that profession as the only alternative to starvation. She became their patron saint, and religious orders bearing her name were set up to rescue women from this grim lifestyle—a story told in Rumer Godden's classic novel *Five for Sorrow, Ten for Joy.*

A recent best-seller[3] pegs Mary Magdalene as the wife of Jesus, who traveled with him to Marseilles where he fulfilled His *real* earthly mission: founding the Merovingian dynasty that ruled France during the Dark Ages. How inscrutable the works of God—to send the Jews a Messiah so that he could bugger off to the Côte d'Azur and father a race of incompetent, virtually incontinent petty kings. It sounds so much like the plot of a made-for-TV movie, albeit a French one. Why would Leonardo da Vinci have bothered to tell such a story in code? It sounds more like the screenplay that Judas was working on before he got that 30,000 denarii Macarthur Genius Grant. . . .

....

3. Called *What Da Vinci Left Behind* or *The Protocols of the Elders of the Vatican* or something.

Christina of Bolsena (+250), Christina of Tyre (dates unknown), and Christina the Astonishing (1150–1224): The Terminator Saints

The three impressive Christinas we honor today fit into a category we might call Terminator saints. Each one proved as hard to kill as a cybernetic assassin sent back in time to make Arnold Schwarzenegger governor.

Christina of Bolsena was an early convert whom the Romans threw in a lake with an anchor, tossed in a furnace, deprived of her tongue—but managed only to kill with a volley of arrows.

Christina of Tyre seemed determined to do her one better (*St. Christina II:* She's back and this time she's *pissed*). This Christina was tied over a bonfire—which didn't harm her but killed the pagan onlookers instead. Soldiers cut off her breasts; they continued, creepily, to lactate. Her tongue was cut out, but she kept preaching anyway and threw the tongue at her tormentor, blinding him. She survived a drowning attempt, and succumbed only when an arrow pierced her heart.

The medieval Christina the Astonishing was not a martyr, but she proved herself mighty durable anyway. Sleeping always outdoors in rags, she would roll in bonfires, stand praying in freezing lakes, live in tombs and allow herself to be submerged for long periods, all without coming to any harm. Christina claimed she couldn't stand being around other people, because she could *smell* their sins. No wonder her neighbors kept testing out how indestructible she really was.

....

Sacramental Executive Summary #4: Confirmation

If Baptism undoes the effects of Adam's sin against God the Father, and Penance and the Eucharist unite us to Jesus the Son, this sacrament confers upon us the gifts of the Trinity's third person—the one who functions incognito, often unnoticed: the Holy Spirit. As the bishop prays over those he's about to confirm:

> All-powerful God, Father of our Lord Jesus Christ, by water and the Holy Spirit you freed your sons and daughters from sin and gave them new life. Send your Holy Spirit upon them to be their helper and guide. Give them the spirit of *wisdom* and *understanding,* the spirit of *right judgment* and *courage,* the spirit of *knowledge* and *reverence.* Fill them with the spirit of wonder and *awe* in your presence. We ask this through Christ our Lord.

It's like a little Pentecost in the life of every teenager; at least, that's the idea. But not everyone receives, for instance, the gift of speaking in tongues at his Confirmation service. And those who do are often escorted out by the ushers.

Still, Confirmation is a very special sacrament in any Catholic's life, since it's the first one to which we're likely old enough to object to, or get excited about. More likely—since it's usually given to adolescents—it's some hormonally muddled, psycho-sexual mishmash of the two. Remember your quest for a Confirmation sponsor, as you tried to decide between the adults you most admired, and those who could afford the coolest gift? And the anxious thought about which new name to choose: one that signified a future career? the name you'd always wished you had? something really cool and dark, from a rock album or fantasy novel?[4] Of course the preparation for this sacrament is quite extensive in most parish schools; there are lessons in doctrine, ritual, and, most importantly, penmanship. Part of Confirmation in many dioceses entails writing a letter to the bishop explaining why you wish to be confirmed. And the critical element in such a letter is neatness. How many of us stayed after school, day after day, sometimes for weeks, rewriting the very same words, until we got it right. Like the movie *Groundhog Day,* this experience was a Dantesque glimpse of purgatory.

CELEBRATE: Instead of a lame family dinner that will make your young teens roll their eyes, why not throw a party they will genuinely enjoy? Let them invite their friends of both sexes and make the food they really want to eat—home-style pizza, mildly alcoholic punch, cartons of Chunky Monkey—to eat with music they actually want to hear. Absent yourself, with all the adults and clingy relatives, from the basement where the teens are celebrating, perhaps with the traditional post-Confirmation game of "Spin-the-Holy-Water-Bottle."

4. The good sisters took pains to explain to us that "Lucifer" was *not* acceptable, and *no* it didn't matter, as some stoners insisted, that "Dude, he was an angel, too. That's discrimination!" No, you can't take "Frodo." Or "Cobain." Canonized saints only, please.

Anne (first century): God's Grandma, the Yenta

The mother of the Blessed Virgin Mary is one of the Church's most beloved saints. But what we know about her comes mostly from charming legends, such as the second-century "Protoevangelium of St. James." This story reports that Anne and her husband, Joachim, had been childless for many years, despite their fervent prayers for offspring. Other pious Israelites would taunt Joachim as he entered the Temple, accusing him of having somehow offended God, and pelting him with empty Viagra bottles. Outraged, Joachim went off kayaking in the wilderness for forty days on a masculine spirituality retreat, leaving Anne to sit and pray for answers to her infertility issues. She pointed to the pigeons of the air, the rats of the field, the mosquito larvae in the cistern—all nature was richly, even repulsively fertile. Why was she alone left out? In fact, she began to think, it was about time she called the exterminator. At that moment, an angel appeared to Anne and bade her to spare the local vermin: her prayer would be answered, and she would be blessed with a very special child. The same angel paged Joachim, who floored it and met Anne back at the city gate. There he and Anne embraced, overjoyed, whispering sweet nothings in each other's ears and bickering amiably over the choice of Montessori schools.

In the retelling over the centuries, this sweet story got a little weird. As the Church clarified its teaching that Mary was conceived "without sin," some theologians decided that this also meant "without sex." So they began to teach that Mary was procreated right there, at the city gate, through a chaste kiss, or maybe—during all that whispering—*through the ear*. The Church in 1677 formally declared this notion mistaken, heretical, and creepy, affirming that Mary was conceived without sin, but not without sperm. Yes, Virginia, there is a difference.

CELEBRATE: In another twist of the St. Anne legends, it's said that she was twice widowed and twice remarried. Since she'd been able to attract three husbands, young women have been inspired ever since to invoke her help finding just one. The popular prayer went: "I beg you, holy mother Anne / Send me a good and loving man." Employ this prayer for a bachelorette whom you consider needy. But not *too* needy, okay?

August 4

Jean Baptiste Marie Vianney (1786–1859): The Penance Express

This beloved French saint is the patron of parish priests. He's well known for having barely gotten ordained, since he couldn't pass his seminary exams. But what he lacked in academic skill he made up in zeal and ferocity, and he was given a tiny parish in a town of 230 people called Ars. Seeing the lukewarmness of his congregation, who'd been exhausted by the persecutions of the Revolution, he took to giving the kind of sermons that nowadays would get him moved to a funeral chapel: he preached against everyone's favorite sins, denouncing these rural Frenchmen for drunkenness, gluttony, adultery, and pride. He once told a congregation: "Away with you, reprobate fathers and mothers, down with you to hell, where the anger of God awaits you and the good deeds you have done in letting your children go gallivanting. Away with you. They won't be long in joining you."

Jean soon gained a reputation as a most perceptive priest, and people from miles around began converging on his parish to hear his sermons and confess to him. He would spend sixteen to eighteen hours a day listening to penitents, serving as a kind of sewage reclamation plant for the region. In one year, 20,000 people came to his town—forcing railroad authorities to create a special stop for him on the train. Fr. Jean became ever more fervent, eventually waging a successful campaign for the suppression of taverns and public dancing in his town—which became a kind of inverted Las Vegas, the austerity and piety theme-park of France.

On some nights Jean would be tormented by bizarre occurrences, such as dishes flying from the wall and smashing themselves, and furniture moving around. After that he would be subject to diabolical attacks that kept him awake all night—not hard, since he slept wrapped in chains on a bare wooden board. On such nights, he said, he knew that the devil was angry with him because a great sinner would be coming to confess the very next day.

August 6

The Transfiguration: Trinkets on Mt. Tabor

This holiday, too little celebrated in the West, marks one of the most hopeful—and trippiest—moments in the New Testament, outside the positively psychedelic Apocalypse of St. John. According to Matthew 17:

> Jesus took with Him Peter and James and John his brother, and led them up on a high mountain by themselves. And His appearance underwent a change in their presence; and His face shone clear and bright like the sun, and His clothing became as white as light. And behold, there appeared to them Moses and Elijah, who kept talking with Him. Then Peter began to speak and said to Jesus, Lord, it is good and de-

lightful that we are here; if You approve, I will put up three booths here—one for You and one for Moses and one for Elijah. While he was still speaking, behold, a shining cloud overshadowed them, and a voice from the cloud said, "This is My Son, My Beloved, with Whom I am delighted. Listen to Him!"

Why did the Father perform this fireworks show for three apostles—particularly since Jesus told them not to talk about it until after His Resurrection? And what did it mean, anyway? Theologians don't agree, of course. But many suggest that the Father was offering Jesus's three most important followers a miraculous morale boost before they accompanied Jesus into Jerusalem for His capture, trial, and execution. Seeing their teacher elevated between Israel's great messianic prophet and the giver of the Ten Commandments, these apostles were left with no excuse for doubt. In case they missed the point, the Father spelled things out for the slow-witted, as if to ask, "What part of 'THIS IS MY SON' didn't you understand?"

But what does the Transfiguration offer us today? A lesson about the nature of the Church. Notice how Peter, the first pope, reacts to the miraculous theophany of the Second Person of the Blessed Trinity, flanked by two Hebrew prophets: he tries to open up "booths" for a gift shop. If Jesus had let him, within a few weeks Peter would doubtless have set up a "Feast of Elijah, Moses, and Jesus," complete with sausage and peppers, a Tilt-a-Whirl, zeppole, and three big, sticky statues for people to cover with money—all managed and "protected" by the Roman Mafia. If he'd given Pilate his cut, Jesus would still be alive today, serving as "capo" of the Galilee Family. But history is chock-full of such "What Ifs. . . ."

August 8
Dominic (1170–1221): Hound of Heaven

This great intellectual and evangelist was inspired to found the Order of Preachers (the Dominicans) in order to convert the stubborn heretics of southern France. Their "Albigensian" theology was a heady blend of science fiction, Bolshevism, and sodomy. It had resisted both persuasion and the blunt use of force. So Dominic decided to try a new strategy: holiness. He organized his preachers as mendicants, impoverished friars

who would wander from town to town, living as simply as the Apostles—in contrast to other, often corrupt clergymen. Dominic was astonishingly successful, in part through the "tool" of the Rosary, which he helped popularize. Soon the region experienced a massive religious revival, while troubadour poetry futures took a nose-dive and women put their bikini tops back on all along all the beaches of France.

According to his biographies, Dominic's mother, Blessed Joan of Aza, had a dream while she was pregnant, in which she gave birth to a dog carrying a torch. This emblem was soon adopted by the Dominicans as their symbol, which is still in use today; some say it puns on St. Dominic's name, since *Domini-canes* suggests "the Lord's dogs." That witticism became all the more piquant in 1233, after Dominic's death, when the pope asked his order to take charge of the Holy Inquisition.

CELEBRATE: In honor of the original heavenly hound, Dominic, we were tempted to offer up Albigensian Flambé. Then we took another look at the documents of Vatican II. So instead, we suggest you serve the classic French dessert *quatres mendiants* (four begging friars), a variety of chocolate that commemorates the four great mendicant orders of the Church—the Carmelites, Dominicans, Franciscans, and Capuchins.

Quatres Mendiants

1 pound high quality chocolate (we suggest Callebaut, Valhrona, or the chef's personal favorite, Scharffen Berger), tempered

1/4 cup dried figs, cut into small pieces
1/4 cup roasted hazelnuts
1/4 cup roasted almond slivers
1/4 cup raisins

Prepare parchment-covered baking sheets, or if you were foresighted enough to have purchased a marble slab, this is the time to use it.

Spoon chocolate by dipping from end of spoon to form circles of 1-1/2 inches. Do several; then add toppings. Continue until all toppings have been used.

Allow to set. Remove either by hand or small offset spatula. May be stored in airtight containers for several days.

Makes 50 treats

August 10

Lawrence (+258): Sanctity, Slow-Cooked

This early Church administrator is known both for his courage and his snarky sense of humor. When the increasingly intolerant Roman government demanded that Lawrence collect all the supposed "wealth" of the persecuted underground Church, Lawrence gathered all the widows, orphans, beggars, cripples, and lepers who lived on Catholic charity and presented them to the Emperor: "Here are the treasures of the Church." Charmed by his wit, Valerian condemned Lawrence to be slowly, agonizingly burned to death over a grill. As the Roman guards stoked the fires, Lawrence displayed the power of grace, and his irresistible comic timing, by telling the Roman: "I am done on this side, you may turn me over." Infuriated, they did just that (probably neglecting to baste). As he breathed his last, Lawrence whispered: "I am done. Now you may eat." Anticipating the publication of this book, the Church has named Lawrence the patron saint of chefs.[1]

On the same day, we also honor *St. Blane,* a sixth-century Scottish preacher and bishop, who according to legend had the power to make sparks between his fingers, starting fires. His Scottish thrift saved him the expense of flints, Aim-N-Flames, and lighter fluid, and endeared him to *St. Alexander the Charcoal Burner* (August 11).

CELEBRATE: Commemorate all three of these summer-themed saints tonight by hosting an old fashioned cookout on the grill. Pick up a nice brisket or goat to roast, in honor of St. Lawrence; use charcoal instead of gas, to honor St. Alexander; and in deference to St. Blane, don't bother with matches or butane. Have faith! Just keep downing beers and invoking the saint. If he doesn't show his favor and the coals remain unlit, order a pizza and distribute the uncooked meat to the poor.

1. No, we're not kidding.

Feast of the Assumption: The Vatican Space Program

This is one of the most cheerful feasts in the Church's calendar. Because it comes in high summer, the Assumption is a harvest festival. Throughout Eastern Europe, peasant girls collect bouquets and bring them to the church for blessings on this day. In Polish villages parishes organize parades, each led by a carefully vetted "virgin," carrying flowers through the streets to the church. In England, people used to take their medicinal herbs in "Assumption bundles" to the church for a special blessing, the medieval equivalent of getting F.D.A. approval. This marked their belief in a quaint legend—that all flowers had lost their scent and herbs their healing powers at Adam's fall, only to be restored after Mary's Assumption, when her tomb was found *without her body,* but full of flowers. Perhaps in honor of this legend, pious gardeners named hundreds of flowers after Our Lady. Some names, such as Ladyslippers (Our Lady's Slippers) and Marigolds (Mary's Gold) still survive in popular usage. Others are kept alive by enthusiasts, such the Mary Gardens movement (*www.mgardens.com*). Most edible flowers also bear Marian names.

Medieval theologians speculated that since Mary was spared Original Sin, we can see in her fate what would have happened to each of us if Adam had not fallen:

we'd have lived out a long, respectable life and then at the end been assumed into heaven—without a painful death, ugly decay, and a long prep baking in the divine microwave we call purgatory. (The other theory, that we would have just kept breeding and not dying until the whole planet was as thickly peopled as Hong Kong, does not bear thinking about.)

Although it does not appear in the Bible, we have evidence of belief in the Assumption of Mary dating back to the early Church: liturgies sung to commemorate it, icons depicting it, and, most persuasively of all, the fact that there's no place on earth that even claims to be Mary's tomb. No relics of Mary's body, real or spurious, are out there in church altars, museums, or e-bay bid rooms—unlike the countless pieces of lesser saints. This tells us something. If anyone, anywhere, had the slightest claim to knowing where Mary was buried, you can bet he would have published it to the skies—and set up a souvenir stand right beside it. It would be the most profitable pilgrimage site on earth. This very absence of lucrative tourist business is the most decisive argument that she wasn't buried at all.

The Assumption is not something invented by Pope Pius XII in 1950, the year when he infallibly declared it a dogma of the Catholic Church. Nor was he introducing some pious innovation to the core of the Catholic faith, indulging the excessive piety of Marian Catholics, or even—as C. G. Jung suggested—"restoring the feminine principle to the Godhead." No, the pope was doing something much more important: he was beating the Russians into space.

Think about it. Communism was not then the quaintly rusting (if blood-stained) hulk that collapsed in 1989. Ruling more than half the world—thanks to its victory in China—and commanding the sympathies of intellectuals throughout the West, the Communist regime in the Soviet Union possessed a new arsenal of nuclear weapons, a vast technical and research apparatus, and a widely accepted claim to being the most rational political philosophy. The slogan used throughout the Soviet Union for its practice of Marxist theory was "scientific Communism." Millions really believed that Communism, for all its flaws, marked the final liberation of man from all the superstitions and structures that had oppressed him—the crowning glory of the Western progressive tradition. As if to dramatize this superiority, the Soviet leaders were determined to lead the West in aerospace technology—to place the first satellites, and then the first men, into space.[2] By 1950, the technical apparatus was already in place for the Soviet's stunning 1957 Sputnik launch, which terrified Americans with the thought that Russian scientists and engineers were more advanced—and that weapons could not be far behind.

By contrast, the Church in 1950 was seen as a bulwark of reactionary politics,

2. When Yuri Gegarin, the first cosmonaut in space, returned to earth, Soviet journalists were quick to ask him if he had seen heaven or any evidence of God. His answer in the negative was widely used in Soviet antireligious propaganda.

The Miracle of the Vistula

The name of this feast day already rankled in Soviet ears, since it was on that day in 1919 that outnumbered Polish armies, on the verge of destruction, faced invading Bolsheviks who hoped to march straight through their territory to "liberate" Germany, and then the rest of Europe. On the Feast of the Assumption, the battle was joined—and thousands of Polish soldiers reported seeing a vision of Mary over the Vistula River, watching over the battlefield. The Poles were triumphant, the Bolsheviks driven back hundreds of miles, and the event dubbed "the Miracle of the Vistula."

bizarre beliefs, and backward practices, headed for the "dustbin of history." The Church appeared as an enemy of science, a negative force holding back human progress toward self-development and fulfillment (something to do with Galileo).

Pius XII was no idiot. In fact, he was an almost obsessive student of science. Whenever a group of beekeepers, opticians, or gynecologists held their convention in Rome—and swung by the Vatican to get an eyeful of art and a blessing—Pius wouldn't let them out until he'd given them a learned talk about the divine significance of pollen, glaucoma, or spermicides. So Pius knew his astronomy.

He could see the progress of Soviet technology, and the preliminary steps toward space exploration. It is our considered opinion—and we're breaking new theological ground here, so hold your breath—that Pius XII saw the Assumption as the Vatican space program.

What better way to trump the scientific pretensions of atheistic Communism than to demonstrate that the Vatican possessed a superior technology, a simpler and more elegant way to enter the heavens—and that its first pioneer in space[3] had ventured there nineteen hundred years before?

This interpretation of the mystery was inspired by meditation upon an image of the Assumption drawn by some well-meaning nun in the 1950s, which appeared in an encyclopedia of kitsch: it depicted a streamlined, aerodynamic Mary shooting up from the ground, leaving vapor trails as she passed. No doubt, the art critic dryly observed, this work was an attempt to make this curious ancient doctrine understandable by connecting it to the contemporary interest in space exploration. We think that nun was onto something. And Pius XII was way ahead of his time; he beat the Sputnik program by seven years!

---

3. Technically, Jesus was first, but since He was also divine, His ascent does not properly belong in the history of aerospace technology—but rather in Mel Brooks's long-awaited epic *Jews in Space*. The trailer appeared at the end of *History of the World Part I*.

CELEBRATE: To mark this new way of seeing the mystery of Mary's Assumption, we suggest you throw a NASA-themed party on the feast day. Combine some of the traditional trappings and treats of this summer holiday with the sleek, freeze-dried nutriments created by American scientists to feed our pioneers in space. Hang the house with flowers, yes, and pictures of Mary—but also with images of the various Apollo missions, space shuttles, and astronauts. See *www.the-spacestore.com* for a wide array of party favors and foods eminently suited to celebrating the Feast of the Assumption:

- space candles: an astronaut, stars, space shuttle, and planet, each about 2 inches tall
- NASA flags and decals to post around the house, beside images of the Blessed Mother
- astronaut balloon: a three-foot long inflatable spaceman. (If only there were helium-filled images of Our Lady—but give us time. . . .)
- party cups, napkins, and plates adorned with the space shuttle
- space party invitations
- party horns shaped like the shuttle

Add to the mix whatever movie posters and icons you have collected from *Star Trek, Star Wars,* and *2001: A Space Odyssey* and as many small, glow-in-the-dark statues of Mary as you can find. Plug in a few black light bulbs, and the effect is genuinely stunning.[4]

Assumption Tang Punch
Best served with dozens of tiny plastic statues of Mary floating,
as if in splash-down capsules.

NASA's Own Freeze-Dried Kosher Tomato Basil Soup
Make your first course easy—and ethnically appropriate—by serving up the
soup that NASA concocted under strict rabbinical supervision.

Rocket (Arugula) à la Virgin
The spicy vegetable sautéed in ever-virgin olive oil. What could be
more appropriate to the feast? Serve on NASA plates.

Yiouvetsi Lamb with Orzo Pasta
A savory, garlicky Greek dish that has been served
for centuries on this feast day. (See recipe)

Simnel Cake
This rich cake was traditionally made for medieval Mothers' Day. (See recipe)

NASA Ice Cream Sandwiches, Freeze Dried Strawberries,
and Freeze Dried Apple Wedges

---

4. Our pastor was stunned.

Yiouvetsi Lamb with Orzo Pasta

This recipe didn't fall from space. It comes from the lovely Greek islands and is served in the boites of the authors' neighborhood, Astoria, Queens, on the Feast of the Assumption. If you want to try it, you could move there. (No, the rents are already high enough. Please don't move there.) Instead, try this classic recipe.

4–5 pound boneless leg of lamb
5 garlic cloves, slivered
Salt and freshly ground pepper
Juice of 1 lemon
1 tablespoon olive oil
2 tablespoons dried Greek oregano
1/2 cup Greek red wine

1 cinnamon stick
1 28 ounce can imported Italian
  tomatoes
2 cups orzo pasta
2 cups chicken stock
1/4 cup feta cheese

Heat oven to 450 degrees.

Rinse and pat dry lamb. Make small slits all over roast using a sharp knife. Insert garlic into slits. Season liberally with salt and pepper. Rub all over with lemon, olive oil, and oregano. Place in roasting pan. Roast 20–30 minutes until meat begins to brown. Check every 15 minutes and baste with pan juices. If needed, add red wine. Reduce oven temperature to 350 degrees.

Add remaining red wine to pan, with cinnamon stick, tomatoes, and their juices. Roast about 40 minutes, testing regularly.

Bring stock to a boil; then add it and orzo pasta to roasting pan. Stir well and return to oven. Cook another 20 minutes or until orzo is done. Add water if more liquid is required. Sprinkle with feta cheese and return to oven just long enough to melt.

Remove meet to carving board and allow to rest 15–20 minutes covered in foil. Carve and serve on platter with orzo. The lamb should be medium rare.

Makes 6–8 servings

Simnel Cake

This cake was traditionally made for "Mothering Sunday," a holiday in mid-Lent when servants would be sent home to visit their families—bringing along this rich, satisfying dessert. It's perfect for any Marian holiday.

FRANGIPANE:
6 ounces sliced almonds
1 cup sugar
2 teaspoons almond extract

4 large eggs
1 stick unsalted butter, softened
1/2 cup flour

Pulse almonds and sugar in food processor until they form a fine powder. Add almond extract. Add 1 egg. Process until smooth.

Add butter in small pieces until completely mixed. Add remaining eggs, one at a time. Add flour. Process until just combined.

CAKE:

1/2 cup mixed, diced, candied
    fruits
1/2 cup golden raisins
1 teaspoon grated lemon rind
1 teaspoon vanilla extract
2 tablespoons cognac

5 large eggs
1/2 cup plus 2 tablespoons sugar
1 cup sifted flour
2 tablespoons unsalted butter,
    melted

SAUCE:

2 ounces rum   1 cup orange juice   1/3 cup powdered sugar

Combine candied fruit, raisins, lemon rind, vanilla and cognac in bowl. Allow to sit 20 minutes. Butter and flour an 8 inch springform pan. Preheat oven to 350 degrees.

Beat eggs with sugar in bowl. Set eggs and sugar over pot of warm water—not boiling—until mixture is slightly warmer than room temperature.

Whip egg mixture in mixer until cool and tripled in volume (the eggs will be at ribbon stage). Fold in flour in four additions, being careful not to deflate eggs. Gently fold in melted butter and fruit.

Pour three-quarters of frangipane into springform pan. Top with cake mixture. Cook for 20 minutes, and then add remaining frangipane. Cook 45 minutes. Then check to see if cake has browned. If so, cover with foil. Cook an additional 15–30 minutes, until an inserted toothpick comes out clean. Cool completely and remove from pan. Combine sauce ingredients; brush on cake. Serve garnished with fresh flowers.

Makes 12–16 servings

August 19

Sarah (Old Testament): The Power of Laughter

Not all Catholics realize that we have a long list of Hebrew saints—not just the apostles, but the heroes of the Old Testament. Abraham, Elijah, Moses, David, the Maccabees, even Adam and Eve: all of them have as much heavenly pull as any officially canonized saint. The Eastern churches make more of this, speaking of "St. Isaiah" and "St. Jeremiah" and featuring them prominently in icons. Along with these patriarchs and prophets of the Hebrew Bible, we also honor the matriarchs of God's chosen people, including Rachel, Judith, and, today, Sarah, the wife of Abraham.

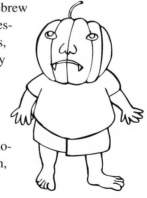

You might say that Sarah's greatest claim to fame is that she is the world's first Jewish mother. This is more impressive than it sounds, since she spent most of her married life bemoaning her apparent sterility. It wasn't until age 90 that she received a message from an angel that she would soon be pregnant—at which she fell over laughing. The joke kept on being funny; when her son was born she named him "Isaac," which means "laughter." It's said that Sarah lived to the ripe old age of 127—proof that if you laugh at your kids long and hard, it will extend your life.

> **CELEBRATE:** Today is an excellent pretext for mothers to amuse themselves by dressing up their kids and pets in ridiculous costumes and taking whole DVDs full of photos that will embarrass them in future years (particularly the dogs). Get together with a few other families and make this a group event—to maximize the mortification factor of your adolescent boys.

August 23

Rose of Lima (1586–1617) and Ebbe the Abbess (+879): Eternal Makeovers

These two female saints, who share a feast day, also had in common a fierce devotion to their vows of virginity—perhaps a tad too fierce. St. Rose was a beautiful young woman in colonial Peru who craved the life of a nun, but young men kept courting her and distracting her from her prayers. Legend says that she ruined her face with lye so they'd leave her alone. And leave her alone they did, ever after. She spent the rest of her life in solitary prayer in the family garden and became the first saint born in the Western Hemisphere.

When Ebbe ruled as abbess of a monastery in Coldingham, England, she responded to an attack by the Vikings by gathering all her nuns in the dining room and taking out a knife. These men, she warned them, were known for raping women before they killed them, but she knew a way to save herself from that humiliation: she sliced off her nose. Inspired, the other nuns did likewise and then trooped downstairs to confront the Vikings at the gate. The spectacle of dozens of bloody, noseless nuns was enough to frighten off the superstitious pagans, who left the convent in peace that day. Upon considering the matter further, the Vikings later did decide to burn the place down, with the holy nuns in it. The burnt offering was noseless, but the virginal nuns died knowing that they were spiritually intact.

The moral of this story is that nose jobs can be fatal. So we'd like to suggest

Saints Rose and Ebbe as the patronesses of plastic surgery in particular, and California in general. Actually, Rose is already patroness of Santa Rosa County, California.

August 25

Genesius (+286): Roman Snuff

If you think Hollywood is insensitive to Christian sensibilities now, you should have lived in late pagan Rome, when the theater consisted largely of pornographic skits that ended in orgasm, gladiatorial combats that ended in death, and creative combinations of the two. As soon as it could, the Church put a stop to these snuff shows, and for centuries thereafter, anyone associated with the theater was automatically excommunicated. Theatrics in the West began again very cautiously with liturgical plays, such as enactments of the Passion on Palm Sunday. Eventually, these playlets developed into full-blown pageants for Corpus Christi and other feasts, and those delightfully odd "Mystery Plays" you had to read first semester, freshman year. These Christian dramaturges adopted as their patron St. Genesius, a pagan actor who played a part in a bawdy spoof of Christianity. His legend tells that he had an epiphany of grace on stage and realized the truth of the faith. He proclaimed his change of heart before the emperor and was promptly executed—giving the audience precisely the kind of happy ending they were hoping for and increasing positive word of mouth for the production. Genesius is also the patron of lawyers, clowns, epileptics, and torture victims.

Monica (322–387) and Phanourios (dates unknown): Saintly Spam

These two saints share a feast day for a good reason; each one made reparation (and we can be pretty sure, made life hell) for a sinful relative. Monica was a Carthaginian Christian who married a pagan and raised a saint, Augustine. She was also a recovering alcoholic (she led the AA meetings in the cathedral basement), who suffered greatly through her son's long years of wild living. As Augustine's *Confessions* record, Monica prayed for him incessantly and did her best to remind him of his childhood faith. At last, at Monica's death Augustine rejoined the Church, to become a bishop and the West's first great theologian. But he was careful never to marry.

Phanourios was a Greek saint who spent his last days praying for the conversion of his famously immoral mother—which got him the reputation in the East as the saint of impossible causes.

CELEBRATE: Greeks make a cake in honor of St. Phanourios. Why not bake it for the member of your family whom you're most convinced is likely to go to hell? He might as well enjoy this life, you should explain, because the next one's going to be a doozy.

St. Phanourios Bread (Phanouropita)

1 cup freshly squeezed orange juice	1 clove
1/2 stick butter	3/4 cup brandy
1/2 teaspoon sea salt	2 cups all-purpose flour
2 cups raisins	2 teaspoons baking powder
1/2 cup sugar	1/2 teaspoon baking soda
1/2 cup honey	3/4 cup chopped walnuts
1 cinnamon stick	Zest of 2 oranges

Preheat oven to 350. Butter and flour a bundt pan.

Combine orange juice, butter, salt, raisins, sugar, honey, cinnamon, and clove. Heat to a small boil. Add 1/2 cup brandy and flame.

Remove cinnamon and clove and transfer to bowl of an electric mixer.

Beat on low until cooled.

Whisk together dry ingredients.

Combine in mixer and beat until smooth.

Fold in walnuts and zest of 1 orange.

Pour into pan and bake 55–60 minutes or until toothpick inserted comes out clean. Meanwhile combine remaining brandy and orange zest.

Using a toothpick poke holes all over the cake and pour brandy over evenly. Cool in pan.

Makes 10–11 servings

Raymond Nonnatus (1204–1240): Seen but Not Heard

This wealthy Spaniard gave up everything—his inheritance, his freedom, and finally his life—to ransom captives. In his day, Islamic pirates did a booming business selling as slaves the Europeans they captured at sea and in raids of coastal cities.[5] Raymond joined the Mercedarian Order, whose sole purpose was rescuing them. Each monk offered himself to serve as a slave instead of a captive; the Moslem owners, impressed by their sacrifice, would frequently free dozens of innocents to gain the services of one saint. But Raymond's new master was not so kind; he had the priest imprisoned and tortured. Raymond spent his time in jail preaching Christ to the guards, finally making so many converts that the authorities burned a hole through his lips and padlocked his mouth shut. St. Raymond is a suitable patron of laypeople who get involved in parish affairs.

---

5. To learn more, read Giles Milton's *White Gold: The Extraordinary Story of Thomas Pellow and North Africa's One Million European Slaves* (London: Hodder & Stoughton Ltd., 2004).

Sacramental Executive Summary #5: Matrimony

Single Catholics who understand Church teaching on sexuality develop a certain longing for the married state starting at, oh, about age eleven. But not all of us are really ready for the commitment—sixth grade being such a busy time. Those subsequent fifteen to twenty years or so when sexual fulfillment is both an urgent imperative and grave matter for mortal sin[6] lead one to wonder, sometimes, what God was thinking.

But as we grow in age, wisdom, and consumer debt, the prospect of marriage becomes more plausible. We begin to long for the comforts of human company, the pleasures of the flesh, the joys of children. We recall God's words to Adam in the Garden: "It is not good for man to be alone." We examine our collections of old magazines and aging vegetables, and realize God was right.

With time and maturity, adult Catholics of each sex look at partners with a different eye, with commitment in mind. Infused with the virtue of prudence, we start to wonder about possible spouses:

☺ "Would he make a good father?"
☺ "She's got a nice career. How will she feel about giving that up?"
☺ "Does he really put all his investments into Lotto tickets?"
☺ "How fat did her mother get?"

And so on.

Because the awkward thing about marriage—and we hate to be tactless here—is that it's meant to be permanent. As in: *Till one of you turns into fertilizer.*

The Christian faith was the first great world religion to suggest a number of nobly impractical ideas: offering up your suffering for the eternal good of strangers; praying for your enemies; taking vows of poverty, chastity, and obedience; giving young women the choice of whether and whom to wed. But perhaps the most quixotic element of our creed is the teaching that marriage is for life.

---

6. At Fatima, Our Lady offered the encouraging news that such sins cause souls to fall into hell like "leaves in the autumn." Thanks, Mom! On the other hand, Dante followed Thomas Aquinas in suggesting that the lustful dwell in the Inferno's least painful suite. It's not air-conditioned, exactly, but the folks in there simmer rather than roast.

Given all the data that have emerged since the 1970s on the devastating effects of divorce on children, one can appreciate anew the societal value of Church teaching—that is, unless you happen to be stuck in a marriage to someone who seemed just dandy ten years ago, but then somehow turned into another Donald Trump or Courtney Love. At that point, compromise starts sounding mighty tempting, and the children—well, kids are so *resilient,* aren't they?

The Church's elevated doctrine of marriage, which Jesus himself insisted upon,[7] was enough to make His apostles gasp. When He revoked Moses' permission to divorce, they answered: "If the case of the man be so with his wife, it is not good to marry" (Matt. 19:10).

Now you'd think at this point Jesus might have corrected them—offering encouragement, advice on how to improve marital communication, earthy suggestions on how to keep women happy (from the designer of the human body!). Instead, he *agreed with them*—and soothed their nerves by inventing clerical celibacy. He sugarcoated this idea by comparing it to castration:

> All cannot receive this word, but those to whom it has been given; for there are eunuchs which have been born thus from their mother's womb; and there are eunuchs who have been made eunuchs of men; and there are eunuchs who have made eunuchs of themselves for the sake of the kingdom of heaven. He that is able to receive it, let him receive it. (Matt. 19:11–12)

The apostles weren't quite ready to receive it; when some children clambered up to receive Jesus's blessing, they kept the kids away. They were still trying to figure out if maybe Jesus was nuts after all.

It's passages like this that stymie our attempts to read the New Testament and suggest that perhaps the medieval Church had the right idea: leave the Bible to the priests and professors, and we'll stick to those bullet point "action items" in the catechism.

One imagines lifelong marriage was an easier prospect before the Fall, which corrupted our wills, darkened our intellect, and drove us from blissful cooperation with God.

And before modern medicine, which made "for life" into a much more serious proposition. No longer can we count on plague, warfare, or malnutrition to claim us or an impossible spouse in a few short years. No, the average Westerner who marries today and doesn't divorce can expect to sit beside that person in Atlantic City forty years from now, counting liver spots and feeding the slots.

---

7. "Have ye not read that he who made [them], from the beginning made them male and female, and said, On account of this a man shall leave father and mother, and shall be united to his wife, and the two shall be one flesh? so that they are no longer two, but one flesh. What therefore God has joined together, let not man separate." (Matt. 19: 4–6)

This isn't the place to examine the question of annulments, the Church process by which a divorced couple can discover if one or both of them—please *God!*—was too drunk, too crazy, or "psychologically immature" to contract a valid, sacramental marriage. These handy canonical declarations are a source of great controversy among Catholics. Some believe that the annulment process is terribly abused in Western countries—especially the United States, where it's easier to get an annulment than permission to hold a Latin Mass. Others respond that the discoveries of modern psychology have taught us to reexamine the meaning of "free consent" in the marriage bond and ease the consciences of well-meaning Catholics who wish to marry. Some acute observers have suggested that most people who grow up in America today have deeply assimilated the idea that marriage is provisional, with divorce and remarriage always an option. With this in the back of their minds, they really *can't* contract a sacramental marriage. (Of course, this raises questions about your impending, festive second wedding to that hot young trophy bride or pool boy.)

To all this we answer: *Whatever.*

If you're married, make a heroic effort to stay that way. If things go really wrong, and ordinary unhappiness turns into hysterical misery, find a therapist who shares your faith.[8] Drag yourself and spouse into the therapist's office every week. You'll hate it, but not as much as you hated dating. It's probably easier to cut the mold off your own half-loaf of happiness than to build a new bakery out of straw. Let's face facts: you're getting a bit old for chat rooms, singles events, and those Speedos, come to think of it.

If your union has broken up and can't be reconciled, then to marry in the Church you'll need an annulment. If you think you might have grounds, bring your case to the diocese and leave it to the professionals. Your second marriage, like the state of the seminary, will be on the bishop's conscience.

CELEBRATE: What do we know about marriage? We're both single—and if we keep up this kind of "attitude," likely to stay that way. But we do know something about weddings—particularly those blue-collar, ethnic extravaganzas that begin in charming old Gothic churches and finish in places like "Tony's Matrimonial Chateau of Sunnyside, Queens, Inc., Ltd." You know the places we mean: most of them seem to have been inspired by the wedding scene in *The Godfather:* Red velvet, gold leaf, balsa wood furniture designed to resemble a Venetian palace in Vegas. The customs at such weddings differ according to ethnic group, of course. Among the Slovaks of Pennsylvania, if a younger sibling marries before an elder, the unlucky bachelor or spinster must do a ritual

---

8. Two really great resources for enhancing, or rescuing, relationships are Worldwide Marriage Encounter (*www.wwme.org*) and Retrouvaille (*www.retrouvaille.org*).

"pig-trough" dance before all the guests. At Cajun and Filipino weddings, people rent the bride for dances by pinning money to her dress. Italian-American nuptials feature the bride's mother holding an enormous handbag, into which you're expected to drop hefty checks between the servings of ziti and garlic-drenched chicken. Irish weddings, of course, are never complete until the fistfights have broken out and been broken up, with ushers dragged out into the parking lot by their sobbing, bedraggled dates.

But the most universal Catholic wedding customs in America are deeply rooted in the theology of the sacrament:

☺ The bride stuffing the largest serving of cake she can lift into the groom's mouth.

☺ The bride's father warning his new son-in-law, "If you ever lay a hand on my daughter to hurt her, I'll saw it off personally."

☺ The guy who catches the garter kneeling before the girl who caught the bouquet, and running it all the way up to her ears.

And:

☺ The band leader teaching the senior citizens how to dance along and spell out the words to the Village People's "YMCA."

It's hard to imagine a more fitting way to mark the sacramental union of man and wife than this joyful, nostalgic tribute to anonymous, all-male sex in public gymnasiums. It sets the tone for the whole relationship, from the wedding night right up through the annulment proceedings.

September

September 1

Giles (eighth century): Gather the Rams

This early medieval saint came from a wealthy family in Athens. Aspiring to live as a monk, he found that his relatives were interfering, so he moved across the continent, all the way to the Rhone Valley, where he tried to live as a hermit. This being France, crowds of people soon flocked to meet the holy man, and he was forced to hide in the woods from his would-be disciples. Don't you hate when that happens? Eventually Giles accepted some followers and organized them into a Benedictine monastery. Because he lived out among the beasts, Giles was taken up as a patron saint by shepherds. In the Basque country, shepherds gather on his day in native costume, collect their rams and dye their wool, tie lit candles to their horns, and bring them along to Mass to be blessed.

CELEBRATE: Dress in a festive Basque costume, gather your rams, color their wool a bright shade, and lead them into your parish church. Your pastor will understand.

September 3

Marinus (fifth century): The Saint of Restraining Orders

Marinus was a stonemason who worked on the Italian peninsula. He was ordained a deacon to serve the Christians who'd been sent to work in the mines; hey, it beat feeding the lions. Marinus wandered among the enslaved Christian miners, preaching the Gospel and trying to lift everyone's spirits, organizing sing-alongs, campfire pow-wows, and classes in how to make leather wallets. Not everyone appreciated his relentless good cheer, but they knew he meant well, so his fellow Christians tolerated him.

Legend says that Marinus was a "confirmed, lifelong bachelor" (like Liberace), but this may just be a fairy tale. It's said that a local woman lost her wits, became convinced Marinus was her long-lost spouse, and began to follow him everywhere, like poor David Letterman. It's possible that the miners put her up to it, to get out of Wednesday "Crafts Night." Horrified, Marinus fled to the isolated Monte Titano and lived chastely as a hermit in a tastefully decorated cave, composing operettas. On the site of his old monastery, Italians founded a delightful little country and named it for him, San Marino. This enclave still exists and is known for its buff military uniforms and ele-

gantly understated stamps. Marinus is a suitable patron for stalking victims, devoted bachelors, and church musicians—particularly the Fellowship of the American Guild of Organists (FAGO).

....

September 6

Magnus of Füssen (700–750):
Bear-Claws for the Bears' Claws

This early medieval missionary left the famous Swiss monastery of St. Gallen to preach around the city of Bregenz. He founded the famous monastery of Füssen, near the site of the nineteenth-century "fantasy castle" of Neueschwanstein. This enormous structure—built by the great Catholic statesman King Ludwig of Bavaria—was the model for the castle at Disneyworld. But 1200 years before, when Mickey was not yet a gleam in Walt Disney's eye, Magnus conducted a one-man war against cartoon vermin. The monk busied himself chasing out poisonous snakes, banishing destructive caterpillars (of which he is, no kidding, the patron saint), and slaying dragons. According to the delightfully unreliable, plagiarized, forged, and mutilated account of his life—which is energetically disavowed by no less an authority than the 1917 *Catholic Encyclopedia*[1]—he left one baby dragon alive, after it promised to eat only rats and mice.

Best of all, Magnus made a habit of feeding the bears, trading them chunks of cake in return for leads about promising local mines. Using only these ursine geologists, Magnus mapped the iron deposits in the area and laid the groundwork for the region's still-thriving mining industry.

CELEBRATE: Take the family to a local national park. (For an online guide, see *www.nps.gov/parks.html*.) Bring along plenty of honey cakes to feed the grizzlies—who will gladly lead you to valuable mineral deposits. Don't worry about what the park rangers say: they're just trying to keep the mining concessions to themselves. But watch out for those dragons.

German Honey-Cakes for Bears

1/2 cup sugar	2 1/2 cups flour
1/4 cup turbinado	1 cup pink grapefruit juice
1 cup honey	3 teaspoons baking powder
1/2 cup oil	1/2 teaspoon baking soda
4 eggs	1/2 teaspoon salt
1 teaspoon grated orange peel	1/2 cup ground almonds

Preheat oven to 350 degrees. Grease and flour a 13 × 9 inch pan and set aside. Mix together the flour, baking powder, baking soda, salt, and cinnamon and stir with a whisk to blend.

In large bowl, combine sugar, honey, oil, eggs, and orange zest and beat well until combined. Alternately add the flour mixture and orange juice, mixing well after each addition, beginning and ending with dry ingredients. Fold in almonds. Pour batter into prepared pan.

Bake at 350 degrees for 45–50 minutes or until top springs back when lightly touched in center and edges begin to pull away from sides of pan. Cool on wire rack. Serve by cutting into squares and drizzling with warmed honey.

Serve to bears in national parks.

Makes 10–12 servings

---

1. Our ultimate authority, which we have found scholarly, judicious, and entirely copyright-free.

September 14

Exaltation of the Holy Cross: Sacred Splinters

This day commemorates the achievements of one of the Church's most remarkable women, St. Helena. This daughter of an innkeeper married an emperor, Constantius Chlorus, and gave birth to another: Constantine the Great, the man who at last freed the Church from persecution and laid the groundwork for a thousand years of Christendom.[2] Jilted by her husband for a trophy wife, she returned to royal honors when her son took the throne. Herself a Christian, she personally led an expedition to the Holy Land in search of the True Cross. She found several likely candidates, and subjected them to a clinical study: she offered each one to an incurably sick person to kiss, to see if anything happened. For two of them, nothing did. The third cross effected a miraculous healing. Helen had her answer and published it widely. This feast celebrates her discovery.

It's thanks to Helen that we have those tiny splinters of wood encased in crystal that reside in churches around the world, sometimes in altar stones, which pious folk are honored to venerate and kiss. Of course, with so many relics scattered about, it's hard to believe that all of them are real. Clever skeptics have quipped that if you gathered all the pieces of the so-called True Cross together, you could dam the Mississippi River with them, or rebuild London, or build a bridge all the way to the moon.

We wouldn't put it past some pastors to accept dubious relics; in the Middle Ages, churches claimed to hold the milk from Mary's breast, the nail clippings of Christ, even His foreskin (how thoughtful of those rabbis to save it all these years!). It would be just like God to multiply the True Cross[3] as he did the loaves and fishes, so nobody had to be left out. It's exactly what he does with His Body, in the form of the Eucharist.

But here it isn't true. One archaeologist with a very strong interest in the subject, and the patience of a man obsessed, spent much of his life tracking down every known relic of the True Cross. Rohault de Fleury weighed or measured each fragment ever authenticated by the Church, and announced his results in 1870. A cross on which a man could hang would contain at least 178 million cubic millimeters of wood. How many fragments of the True Cross now exist? Around 40 million cubic millimeters—or less than 1/3 the size of the whole cross.

---

2. There are Christians who say that the Church was purer before Constantine "corrupted" it by giving it freedom and legal support. We invite them cordially to move to Saudi Arabia and report back in a few years.
3. St. Cyril of Alexandria believed that this had actually happened.

CELEBRATE: If you're married, today's the day to make your bedroom more like your parents' and hang a big, heavy crucifix over the bed. Not one of those empty crosses, or those demure silver-plated models. The larger and bloodier the better—preferably one where Jesus's eyes are open, and looking down at you. Nail it up today, with a prayer to St. Helena, and see what happens tonight. If you can't stand to get undressed with Jesus watching, it's time for counseling.

September 17

Hildegard of Bingen (1098–1179): Polyphony for Bikers

This medieval hermit is a saint for all seasons. While she may never have learned to read, this German nun conducted advanced scientific research, a hundred years before Albert the Great, the first man in medieval Christendom to take biology and botany seriously. Hildegard tested and compiled herbal cures and pioneered what we call holistic medicine. For instance, she offered an innovative treatment for arthritis:

"Great strength is in the badger fur. Make a belt out of it and put it on the naked skin and all sickness. Make shoes out of the badger fur also and put them on and you will have healthy legs and feet." Who knew?

Because she was child number ten, her noble parents declared her a "tithe" and dropped off at a hermit's chamber at the age of eight. Since such "anchorites" were henceforth "dead" to the world, they were given funeral rites before entering their cells, with an anchor standing in for their corpse—a charming custom that persists in Catholic boarding schools today.

Hildegard was a sickly girl who spent much of her time in contemplative prayer. As years went on, she was flooded with mystical revelations about the profound connections among mind, body, and spirit that anticipated the insights of Aquinas, Bacon, and Deepak Chopra. Hildegard's visions, which she dictated to her followers, described a quality called "greenness" that united all living things with divine energy. She asserted the profound goodness of Creation in an age when popular heresies such as that of the Albigensians declared the material world an evil snare crafted by the devil. Hildegard's wisdom, holiness, and charisma radiated throughout medieval Germany, attracting dozens of followers to her lonely monastery in Rupertsberg.

To liven up the prayer services conducted among these solitary souls, Hildegard wrote dozens of pieces of exquisite liturgical music, becoming one of the most prolific composers of her age. Her ethereal hymns and settings of the Mass are rarely heard in churches nowadays, but they grace the iPods of aromatherapists, pet psychologists, and psychic surgeons around the world. While the thrifty, entrepreneurial nun would be pleased by the royalties, she can't be as happy that her achievements have been co-opted by New Agers. In her day, Hildegard was a fierce heresy-hunter, writing to the pope to denounce him for laxity toward contemporary compromisers: "Why do you put up with depraved people who are blinded by foolishness and who delight in harmful things, like a hen which cackles in the night and terrifies herself? Such people are completely useless." Hildegard sounds more like the crotchety Mother Angelica than Sister Mary Moonbeam over at the Jungian Grail Research Center.

But as we say, Hildegard had her wacky, fun-loving side. She encouraged the nuns to play dress-up on major feast days, filled the convent with highly educated noblewomen so fanatical peasants wouldn't spoil her fun, and made up her own private language called *Lingua ignota,* an early form of Tolkien's Elvish.

Hildegard is considered a national hero in Germany: her face has adorned the Deutschmark, tourist groups wander her hometown of Ruedesheim in search of signs reading "Hildegard Meditated Here," and each year (no kidding) the town's denizens are disturbed by the gunning engines of the nun's own biker band, the Hildegard Motorcycle Tour. Only in Deutschland. . . .

··

September 18

Joseph of Cupertino (1603–1663): The Flying Piñata

This Italian saint made a huge impression in his day and has remained a favorite ever since, for his simplicity, sanctity, and sheer oddity. If God usually confers holiness through the ordinary things of life, sometimes He also lets slip the mask and reveals His bizarre sense of cosmic humor. Just think of the dodo, the platypus, the Australians—and Joseph of Cupertino. This friar was once portrayed on film by Maximilian Schell (*The Reluctant Saint,* 1962), but from reading his life we think that Joseph should really be played by Jim Carrey.

Born in a stable, Joseph was given to long, ecstatic visions during class time. He'd get lost in a mystic rapture and stare with gaping mouth at the mysteries of grace enacted before his eyes— while his classmates backed away nervously and reported him to the teacher. He was soon declared a "special needs" child and expelled. His exasperated mother and embarrassed uncles found a task they thought even Joseph could perform: they packed him off to be a cobbler's apprentice.

Joseph dutifully crafted hundreds of beautiful left shoes, all size twelve, and then applied to the Franciscans, an order that valued simplicity. But he was too ignorant even for them. Capuchin monks took him on as a lay-brother—basically a warm body who could do the cleaning up—but even that was too taxing for Joseph. He'd be found, standing still for hours at a time, mop in hand, watching sacred dramas that only he could see. The creeped-out friars showed him the door. In time, through the magic combination of prayer and pestering, he won the right to mop up the stables of a Franciscan convent near Cupertino. There the brothers finally began to recognize his holiness and just leave him alone while he was in "the Zone." Within a few years, they ordained him a priest and began turning to him for answers to tricky theological questions—the kind that could get you in trouble with the Inquisition. (Eventually, Joseph would find himself hauled up before this tribunal, which judged him too dumb to be dangerous.) While Joseph hadn't learned enough in school to think his way out of a wet paper sack, he received supernatural answers that stunned the order's scholars and won him acclaim. His rigorous, self-punishing penances—he would eat only twice a week—convinced folks he must be sincere.

But that didn't make him any easier to live with. Joseph's "ecstasies" began to happen more often—and mischievous friars figured out how to trigger them. As the *Catholic Encyclopedia* reports:

> Everything that in any way had reference to God or holy things would bring on an ecstatic state: the sound of a bell or of church music, the mention of the name of God or of the Blessed Virgin or of a saint, any event in the life of Christ, the sacred Passion, a holy picture, the thought of the glory in heaven, all would put Joseph into contemplation. Neither dragging him about, buffeting, piercing with needles, nor even burning his flesh with candles would have any effect on him— only the voice of his superior would make him obey. These conditions would occur at any time or place, especially at Mass or during Divine Service. Frequently he would be raised from his feet and *remain suspended in the air.*

You can imagine it might be hard to pay attention to the Mass with Jim Carrey floating over your head. Flocks of groupies began to invade the convent to see the "show." The friars decided to lock Joseph up out of sight. So the poor mystic spent most of his remaining years in his cell, which he turned into a chapel. Through it all, he stayed simple and happy, never complaining, absorbed in the programming that came in on his personal satellite dish. Because he spent so much of his time airborne, the Church has made Joseph the patron saint of aviators.

For those of you who fear flying, beat your anxiety the next time you're up in the air by imagining your pilot as a semiliterate, fanatically religious Mediterranean mystic who rarely eats, goes into frequent trances, and relies exclusively on divine inspiration. If that doesn't reassure you, nothing will.

Gennaro (+305): Take His Head to the Volcano

Here's another saint whose life, legend, and posthumous cult delightfully combine the sublime and the ridiculous. As a bishop under the proto-fascist emperor Diocletian, Gennaro (or Januarius) won fame as a heroic Christian bishop by risking his life to visit those imprisoned for their faith. He was tortured, beaten, and thrown into a fire, but nothing harmed him. At last, the Romans decided to try beheading. This seemed to work. (Of all the Church's many nearly indestructible saints, very few appear to have survived decapitation—the last resort, it seems, when dealing with brain-eating movie zombies and saints.)

But Gennaro would live on long after his death in the hearts of the common people of Naples and Bensonhurst. A pious old man thoughtfully scooped up Gennaro's body and bleeding head and kept them safe in an ice chest or something—because they are still preserved in his church at Naples, of which he is patron saint. Best of all, we still have two vials of Gennaro's blood, which provide an annual miracle for the faithful of the region.

Every year, on the major feast days of the saint, these vials of blood change from a dry, red powder into a bubbling, boiling liquid. This usually happens during the procession of Gennaro's relics through the public square—and when it does, it sets off a wave of happiness and relief. Because when the blood does not liquefy, it invariably signals disaster. The last time St. Gennaro didn't come through, in 1941, Vesuvius erupted in the middle of World War II. Mindful of this theological terror alert, Neapolitans watch the blood as carefully as fishermen checking the Weather Channel. One year, when the blood stayed dry and the crater began to erupt, the king of Naples 20,000 of his subjects on a pilgrimage up the volcano—holding aloft the skull of St. Gennaro to calm the lava flow. It worked. We *love* this religion.

CELEBRATE: Of course, no account of St. Gennaro would be complete without mention of the delightful, noisy, greasy, Mafia-dominated feast that explodes in Manhattan's Little Italy every year on his day. Where else can you win posters of greased, half-naked NYC firemen by dropping ping-pong balls in a goldfish bowl, or gain a partial indulgence for taking part in a cannoli-eating contest? For an inside look at this event, rent *Godfather III,* which stages one awesome shoot-out at the feast, featuring Andy Garcia.

September 20

Andrew Kim Taegon (+1846): Of Martyrs and Rotting Cabbage

This Korean convert, who died as a martyr, was the first native-born Catholic priest in his country and the leader of its heroic, persecuted Church. The story of Christianity in Korea is a curious one, because it started not with missionaries preaching the Gospel, but with intellectuals forming a book club. Seriously. In the 1600s, a group of Korean poets and philosophers who'd become disillusioned with court Confucianism heard about this new "Christian faith" from contacts in China and Japan, and their curiosity was piqued. This religion, they learned, had the power to keep young women virgins and wives faithful—*voluntarily*. No Chinese footbinding required.

They had to learn more. So these literati ordered Christian books from China, read them as a group, talked the whole thing over, and decided to found a church. They baptized each other, made their own vestments, and started holding liturgies and hearing confessions—all without ever having met a real-life Christian. Eventually they wrote to the missionary bishop in Beijing, China, to inform him that they'd founded their own church. He wrote them a tactful letter explaining that to have all the sacraments, they really did need an actual priest with valid orders—which he would be happy to send them.

This sudden interest in a foreign religion that proclaimed the fundamental equality of all men and women struck the king and his court as a dangerous proposition, so they decided to obliterate it. Within a century, some 110,000 Korean Catholics were killed for their faith, including Andrew Kim Taegon. But the Church survived underground to flourish in the twentieth century. It even persists today in the garrison state of North Korea, despite fierce persecution. A majority of South Koreans now belong to some Christian church.

CELEBRATE: To honor the courage and fortitude of the Korean martyrs, today you might help develop these virtues among your family members, by serving them Kim-chee, the Korean national dish. It's made of cabbage that has been buried in a jar, in a sauce of extraordinarily hot pepper, to rot until it ferments. Served as a side dish at almost every Korean meal, it is decidedly an acquired taste (especially with your morning coffee). Force yourself, your spouse, and each one of your kids to eat a healthy portion. It will build character and prepare you for any kind of persecution. Whatever happens today, it won't be as painful as breakfast.

Martyrs of the Spanish Civil War (1936): Homage to Valencia

The official view of the Spanish Civil War is that it was a battle between the forces of democracy and those of tyranny. The chattering class spent approximately 61 percent of the twentieth century mourning the defeat of the Spanish Republic. Great writers such as Hemingway and Orwell enlisted to fight on the side of the Republicans. The American Communist Party, under orders from Moscow, gathered the members it didn't trust—particularly those with unconventional sexual practices—into the "Abraham Lincoln Brigade," and sent them off to Spain, where Stalin hoped they would get themselves killed.[4]

Meanwhile, Mussolini and Hitler supported the Nationalists, mistakenly believing that, once in power, their leader Francisco Franco would join the Axis and let German armies march through Spain to take Gibraltar. (Military historians suggest that this would have given Hitler the Mediterranean, the Middle East's oil, and victory.) As it happened, Franco spent World War II fobbing Hitler off with hollow promises and sheltering some 30,000 Jewish refugees—to whom he issued false passports so they could escape Nazi territory.

This isn't the place to recount the bloody history of the Spanish Civil War. There were good Catholics on both sides: the clergy and laity in the Basque country backed the Republic, vainly hoping to gain autonomy, while most other Church-goers supported the Nationalists, who said they were waging a "crusade for Christendom." Prominent Catholics such as Jacques Maritain and George Bernanos disagreed.

This feast day is designated by the Church as the feast of the Martyrs of Valencia to mark one incontrovertible fact: the mass murder of Catholic clergy, religious,

---

4. The Soviet dictator had just completed the Ukrainian famine and was busily conducting one of his mass-purges, sending thousands to be shot and millions to Siberian prison camps. But he took time to stand up for "democracy" in Spain. That's just the kind of guy he was.

and laity by supporters of the Spanish Republic. As Robert Royal, author of *Catholic Martyrs of the Twentieth Century,* recounts, "At least 6,832 priests and religious were martyred, including 13 bishops." He notes that some priests "were killed and had their ears cut off and passed around as trophies—as if they had been bulls killed in a bullfight." Several thousand churches were burned, and anarchists enjoyed themselves by opening up the tombs of nuns and profaning their corpses.

Progressive people didn't want to hear about this persecution—why confuse themselves with facts? Even the fair-minded C. S. Lewis dismissed such accounts, which the brave Catholic convert and poet Roy Campbell brought back with him from Spain. This enraged J. R. R. Tolkien, who accused his close friend Lewis of bigotry, of unconsciously believing that the Spanish clergy must have somehow deserved persecution. Even today, few outside Church circles acknowledge the wholesale slaughter, which anarchists and Communists committed against helpless, unarmed priests, elderly nuns, pious peasants, and dissident intellectuals in their territories.

But the Church remembers. In 2001 Pope John Paul II beatified hundreds of these martyrs. We mark their feast day today.

CELEBRATE: In honor of the martyrs of war-torn Valencia—the region where Catholics suffered the most—tonight cook up a tasty regional dish, a gleaming dish of Arroz Negre.

Arroz Negre

4 tablespoons olive oil
1-1/2 pounds squid, cleaned and
   bodies cut into 1/2 inch rings,
   tentacles chopped
1 medium onion, chopped
1 pimiento, chopped
2 tomatoes, peeled, seeded,
   chopped
2 cloves garlic, chopped
Salt and freshly ground pepper

4 cups fish stock
2 cups short grain rice
1 tablespoon sweet paprika
1/4 cup dry sherry
1 tablespoon squid ink
Garlic sauce
3 cloves garlic
1/2 cup olive oil
1 teaspoon lemon juice

Heat oil in large skillet. Add squid and cook about five minutes, till firm. Add onion, pimiento, tomatoes, and garlic and season with salt and pepper. Cover and simmer 15–20 minutes.

Meanwhile bring stock to a boil. Stir rice and paprika into sauce. Add broth gradually, stirring infrequently. Cook about 10 minutes until rice swells and absorbs some of the liquid. Combine the sherry and ink and add to rice.

Reduce heat to low and cook uncovered another 10 minutes. Adjust seasonings and cool loosely covered while preparing garlic sauce.

To prepare garlic sauce in blender place garlic jar with a bit of oil and purée. Add remainder of oil gradually and flavor with lemon. Pass separately.

Makes 6 servings

....

September 23

Padre Pio (1887–1968): Warning—Soul Reader!

This beloved, gentle-hearted Italian saint did the twentieth century a favor by serving as a one-man window into the Middle Ages. Many saints' lives are full of bizarre, implausible-sounding events: miraculous cures, self-punishing penances, outrageous miracles, and seemingly pointless wonders. Such lives have surely been embellished over the centuries by superstitious peasants and pious exaggerators, to the point where the truth is so encrusted with charming lies that it's impossible to know what really happened. Probably not much. Right?

We're not so sure. In the case of Padre Pio the same sorts of miracles found in medieval legend are attested by dozens, even hundreds of perfectly modern people—literate, educated Americans and Europeans who had TVs and radios, took penicillin, went to dentists, and everything. Yet they reported that Padre Pio:

☺ Appeared in two or more places at once, sometimes hundreds of miles apart, to heal the sick or hear confessions. He even visited the Vatican without leaving his remote village of San Giovanni Rotundo.

☺ Experienced the stigmata, the wounds of Christ, in his hands, feet, and side. Doctors could not explain these wounds, which went so deep that you could put your finger all the way through his hand, and which bled when he said Mass—but which healed instantly upon his death.

☺ Showed himself in the clouds during World War II, to warn aside Allied pilots trying to bomb his village.

☺ Could read the souls of those who came to him in Confession, telling them their sins before they opened their mouths.

This last aspect of Padre Pio's supernatural gifts is the most unsettling. A prominent Catholic journalist once went to Pio for Confession. He carried with him a long-time sin to which he was quite attached. The moment he met St. Pio, the priest looked up at him and smacked him, hard, across the face. "Cut it out!" said Pio. And the addiction departed, never to return. Impressive, but also a little creepy. Stay away from priests like this. To some of us, kneeling in that box and telling a weary stranger the most intimate, ludicrous details of our mediocre spiritual lives is a mortifying experience. Find confessors who understand English (so the whole thing's valid), but who speak it haltingly, if at all. This is a delicate balance to tread, but with the shortage of vocations in America, it's becoming ever easier to find such men. In major cities, African, Polish, and Vietnamese priests can usually be located and relied upon to listen compassionately, speak a few heavily accented words, and then give absolution. Beware of Filipinos! They're usually quite fluent.

September 27

Vincent de Paul (1580–1660): "Godfather of the Soul"

Today we celebrate a priest who achieved as much for the Church and for the poor as James Brown did for funk. Born a peasant, Vincent became an advisor to nobles, kings, and popes—and one of the world's first philanthropists. In his youth, Vincent was captured on a ship by Turkish pirates and enslaved in North Africa, along with thousands of other Christians. But Vincent had a salesman's tongue, and before long he'd convinced his guard to set him free. After closing that deal, Vincent managed to upsell him on the eternal warranty—converting the guard to Christianity. They escaped together to France.

In the course of his travels, Vincent saw that the local Church was in a wretched state: uneducated, apathetic priests who didn't know the Bible preaching to ignorant, superstitious peasants tempted by Protestantism; religious wars raging in several provinces, subjecting women to rape and robbery; petty criminals sentenced to decades chained up in galleys, rowing war ships; poor folk starving in the streets, sometimes mutilating their children to attract more alms from the rich; well-meaning prosperous ladies marching off into the ghettos in their Manolos to pass out snacks and then running away from the smell. It sounds like New York City in the 1980s. The upbeat, immensely practical Vincent decided to do something about it.

He cultivated female aristocrats and learned how to play their heart strings. Vincent made friends with powerful clerics of dubious morals (such as the ruthless Cardinal Mazarin) and gently induced in them an almost crippling guilt—which could only be assuaged by paying, handsomely, to feed and clothe the poor. He preached missions, inspiring wealthy people with new love for God—then hitting them up for contributions. In sum, Vincent turned the French church of his day into a vast Jerry Lewis Telethon, but without Liza Minnelli.

Vincent founded religious orders and congregations organized around providing useful services to the desperately poor; taught rich girls to swallow their gorge and wash the sores of neglected beggars; organized real seminaries that would teach priests, for instance, the correct formula for absolving sins and techniques for preaching simply but soundly. When the austere, miserable heresy of Jansenism arose, he fought it fiercely—using persuasion, not the police. One of the organizations that arose from his work, the St. Vincent de Paul Society, runs thrift stores and soup kitchens around the world today, catering exclusively to those whom Jesus called "the least of my brothers."

CELEBRATE: Clean out your clothes closet, book collection, and extra appliances and arrange to deliver the worthwhile stuff to the St. Vincent de Paul center nearest you. The volunteers there will pick through it and keep what's worthwhile, selling it cheap to the genuinely destitute (i.e., grad students), using the profits to benefit the working poor.

September 28

Bernardine of Feltre (1439–1494): Holy Pawnshop!

St. Bernadine was a Franciscan preacher who traveled Renaissance Italy, basically urging people to cut up their credit cards. This fiery friar saw how many people had gotten themselves into hopeless consumer debt and took it upon himself to change things. Besides condemning those who lent out money at outrageous rates of interest, he undertook to put them out of business. Bernadine organized the *monti di pietà,* a string of Catholic pawn shops that loaned money to the needy, interest-free.

If you're interested in how Church doctrine develops, the history of Catholic teaching about charging interest on loans shows how the whole process works. From the outside, it looks like a vast Rube Goldberg device: Church officials draw on the Old Testament, pagan philosophers, Roman law, early Church fathers, the input of economists, decrees passed at councils during the Dark Ages, dissertations

by medieval theologians, letters from popes. They borrow ideas from every source imaginable except Craig's List and *The Onion*. You'd expect the result to be hopelessly convoluted and useless. But it turns out that here, as elsewhere, the Church's doctrine holds up pretty darn well.

From the early Church up until the Renaissance, most Christians believed it was sinful to lend money at interest, at any rate whatsoever. Theologians explained that it was our duty in charity to lend to the needy and pointed to Old Testament prohibitions against exploiting the weak. What they didn't address was the question of investment. How "needy" was a man who planned to import a load of ivory from Ethiopia and sell it in Rome for 1000 percent profit—provided his ship wasn't sunk or stolen by pirates? Was it wrong to make a profit by lending capital to capitalists?

It took centuries of back and forth, during which the consciences of merchants were tormented by fear of hell (they bought a little peace of mind by endowing elaborate chapels and buying indulgences), but eventually Church teaching recognized that economic realities had changed since Aristotle's time. The Holy See issued clarifications, explaining: yes, usury is still a sin, but that term only describes excessive, exploitative interest rates—which differ according to circumstances. Over time, Catholic thinkers supported reforms such as bankruptcy laws, to offer hopeless borrowers a chance to start again—instead of a cell in debtor's prison. In the twentieth century, supporters of Church social teaching helped pioneer the credit-union movement; in the spirit of St. Bernadine, these institutions are mostly nonprofit co-ops designed to offer reasonable interest rates to ordinary people buying homes and cars.

Of course, most of us nowadays don't buy those things with low-rate loans from credit unions; we put them on our Visa cards, at 23 percent interest. Then when those credit lines max out we do a balance transfer to new cards—building thereby a house of cards, on which we've taken a second mortgage. Meanwhile, credit card companies are using their extra cash to buy up office space in hell, in the prestigious "Usurer's Circle." St. Bernadine, pray for us!

September 29

The Holy Archangels: Flying Two-Year Olds

Angels, as we all know from popular culture, are cuddly widdle things with the faces of sunless, obese white Victorian toddlers, banging away at harps and mandolins and generally making themselves harmless and cute, occasionally appearing to warn kids away from broken bridges and keep company with magical unicorns in suburban crystal boutiques. Which makes it all the more amazing what a sheer variety of *uses* God has found for these doughy-faced, bumbling boys. For instance, did you know that:

☺ By flapping his tiny wings and waving a pudgy hand, St. Michael cast Satan out of heaven.

☺ Raphael played matchmaker for pious Jews in the Old Testament and splashed around in the kiddie pool at Bethsaida in the New, occasionally healing people just to show off.

☺ Gabriel busies himself announcing miraculous births (such as John the Baptist's, and Jesus's), but also (being a messenger saint) takes time to serve as patron saint of stamp collectors, mailmen, and Argentinian ambassadors.

Given how helpful angels are, we're surprised to read in the Bible that any time an angel appears to someone, the person just about soils his shorts. ("Fear not, Mary!" Gabriel told Our Lady.) They say this every time, even when they haven't come to tell a virgin, "Hi. You're pregnant." Some theologians suggest that the cherubic image of angels we've inherited from the Renaissance might not be accurate—that these heavenly messengers are more like the winged warriors depicted in Byzantine icons than the airborne toddlers we know and love. To this we answer: can you think of anything scarier than a flying two-year-old?

Pope Leo XIII could. This great Catholic theologian and innovative pontiff was once subjected to a terrifying vision of the spiritual assaults to which the Church would be subject in modern times. He collapsed after the vision and was taken for dead. When he awoke, he told his advisors, "Oh what a horrible picture I was permitted to see!" Admittedly, the pope was quite old at the time, and he relied for strength on a then-popular tonic of red wine laced with cocaine.[5] But there's no reason to doubt his sincerity. Leo became convinced that only angelic intervention could save the Church from persecution, so he added to the end of every Mass the following prayer:

> St. Michael the Archangel, defend us in battle; be our safeguard against the wickedness and snares of the devil. May God rebuke him, we humbly pray. And do you, O prince of the heavenly host, by the power of God, cast into Hell Satan and all the evil spirits who prowl about the world seeking the ruin of souls. Amen.

This is an excellent prayer to teach your children. Tell them to recite it whenever they feel any vague, unspecified fear, and in times of special temptation—for instance, when someone offers them cocaine. It's also handy to know this prayer when you encounter traces of the occult: Ouija boards, Tarot cards, or poltergeists smashing dishes in your house. This prayer to our heavenly protector has been known, with a dash of holy water, to banish the devil.

However—and we cannot emphasize this strongly enough: If you start hearing voices coming out of the toilet telling you *"Get out. Get out!"* we suggest you heed their advice and *get out.* Have the house blessed. Then sell it.

---

5. The drink vin Mariani was widely prescribed at the time: Queen Victoria was also a fan. Leo swore by the stuff and minted a papal medal in honor of Signore Mariani. Coincidentally, Leo was the most prolific and perkiest pontiff the Church had seen in centuries.

CELEBRATE: After teaching your children the prayer, reinforce the message that there are angels on our side—and demons gunning for us—by serving a preternatural dinner:

Angels on Horseback (baked oysters wrapped in bacon)

Chicken alla Diavolo over Angel Hair Pasta

Devil's Food Cake (see recipe)

Devil's Food Cake

This recipe was inspired by a Charlie Trotter creation and has long been a celebration favorite.

2/3 cup grapeseed oil
1 tablespoon + 1 teaspoon ancho
   chili powder
2 teaspoons vanilla extract
1 cup sugar
2 eggs
1 cup pumpkin puree
1 cup + 2 tablespoons flour

1 teaspoon baking soda
1/4 teaspoon salt
2/3 cup cocoa
4 ounces bittersweet chocolate,
   melted
1/2 cup sour cream
Powdered sugar

Preheat oven to 350 degrees. Oil and coat 8 inch cake pan with cocoa. Heat oil and ancho together until pepper darkens. Allow to cool. Add vanilla. Strain into bowl with sugar. Beat 5 minutes. Add egg and pumpkin. Mix until thoroughly blended. Sift together dry ingredients and blend into sugar mixture. Add chocolate and sour cream. Mix well.

Pour into cake pan. Smooth top and bake approximately 35 minutes. Serve with dusting of powdered sugar.

Makes 8–10 servings

October

October 1

Therese of Lisieux (1873–1897): Carmel-Covered Corn

ST. THERESE
OF THE CHILD JESUS

Have you ever eaten a candied jalapeno pepper? We don't advise it, nor do we suggest that bad Catholics look too closely at the story of this simple, apparently unexceptional French country girl who died at age twenty-four. On the surface, her tale is sweet—almost cloyingly so. The immensely popular images depicting Therese transmute her sober, otherworldly expression into an insipid smile, and load her down with enough pretty pink roses that she seems like a nun who took a side job working for 1-800-FLOWERS. Indeed, her statues typically seem as if they should be made of marzipan. But this young girl from a large and loving family went on a spiritual safari that few of us could endure, which is harrowing even to read about.

Inspired by the examples of her older sisters, as a young teenager Therese aspired to join the austere Carmelites—a religious order devoted to constant prayer, little sleep, and less food. Frustrated by the order's age minimum, she went to Pope Leo XIII to pester him in person; he made a papal exception, allowing Therese to enter the convent at age fifteen. Once she'd locked herself up in the local Carmel of Lisieux, Therese devoted herself to what she called her "little way" of pleasing God. This sounds easy enough; instead of extraordinary penances and ambitious spiritual deeds, she looked for holiness in the thousand petty things of everyday life, trying to maintain a childlike dependency on Jesus at every moment of her life.

Look closer, and read some of the poems Therese penned in her short life, and you see how just plain terrifying such a program really is. How many teenagers do you know who could write: "I crave, indeed, my God, trials and sufferings," or "I thank You, O my God! for all the graces You have granted me, especially the grace of making me pass through the crucible of suffering." One night, in a burst of spiritual enthusiasm, Therese offered herself "as a sacrificial victim to the merciful love of God." The offer was accepted, and she was deathly sick within the year.

Therese's life in a peaceful French convent was a spiritual battleground; her superior was a sadist, who took pleasure in abusing little Therese; her health was poor from the beginning, and she died young of tuberculosis; worst of all, for most of her last years, Therese was tormented by a crushing fear that God did not exist, so she'd wasted her life pursuing a phantom. The devil was always at her elbow, whispering advice like this: "You dream of a land of light and fragrance, you believe that the Creator of these wonders will be forever yours, you think to escape one day from the mists in which you now languish. Hope on! Hope on! Look forward to death! It will give you not what you hope for, but a night darker still, the night of utter nothingness!" Meanwhile, God had withdrawn all "consolations," or evidence of His presence, as a way of testing and purifying her—an experience that John of the Cross called the "dark night of the soul."

Nice going, God. We have to agree with another Teresa here, St. Teresa of Avila, who wrote: "If this is how you treat your friends, O Lord, no wonder you have so few of them!"

CELEBRATE: St. Therese once promised to spend her time in heaven doing good works on earth, sending an unexpected shower or scent of roses to notify people that she was on the case. We think this is great. We suggest you ask Therese for help the next time a job falls through, the IRS investigates your "home office" deductions, or your spouse checks your Internet "history." Therese will usually come through—she was nothing if not reliable, toughing out a mystical road that earned her the title Doctor of the Church. But as for following her "little way" into heaven—we think we'll stay on the down escalator that leads to purgatory. We hope.

October 2

The Guardian Angels: Avon Calling!

If the spirits known as archangels spend their eternity defeating demons, appearing to virgins, and carrying celestial candygrams, another order of ghostly activists called "guardian angels" watches over each one of us, night and day, looking out for our well-being. And a good thing too.

Remember that time you took that '78 Dodge with dangling brake calipers and bald tires from Baton Rouge to New Orleans at 110 mph after two Sazeracs at four in the morning? Chances are, if you're reading this, you made it home alive. Did you ever wonder how? What about the time you asked for (and got) that sorority girl's phone number while her giant Cajun boyfriend was ordering a beer? Or went home with three Haitian dishwashers for "a quick game of Twister"? What mystic force intervened to keep your sorry name out of the Darwin awards, and your sodden soul out of hell? It was probably your guardian angel.

St. Thomas teaches that every human soul gets a guardian angel at conception, who stays by its side, coaxing it toward heaven; if you end up elsewhere he is quietly reprimanded and reassigned. Pious speculation asserts that these angels are try-

ing to save enough human souls to make up for the angels who fell with Lucifer. This heavenly recruitment drive reminds us of the sales structure employed by multilevel marketing companies such as Avon or Herbal Life; for each soul your angel signs up, he receives an "override" commission on each virtuous act you commit, and a bonus each time he pulls you back from the brink of doom. It's no accident that the ancient symbol of Divine Providence (which also appears on the dollar bill) mirrors the "org" charts of such companies: it's a pyramid, topped by a single, money-green eye.

This metaphor helps make sense of the whole celestial mystery. Your guardian angel is trying to recruit you for his team—much like those former friends of yours who tried to sign you up for Amway. Only you don't need to fill your garage with $3 rolls of toilet paper to please your guardian angel. Just invoke his help from time to time, and give him credit when it's due—for instance, when you find a twenty-dollar bill on the floor in time to pay for that round you ordered.

The classic American way to look at life is as an orderly progression of educating oneself and networking to attain a list of clearly defined priorities and goals. What a load of bunk. Catholics know better: our lives are much more like that of the nearsighted cartoon codger Mr. McGoo. We walk blindly out of a window, and an I-beam appears to lower us safely down to earth. Your guardian angel is that I-beam.

In sum, we suggest you attribute your life's disasters to yourself, and all successes to invisible, inexplicable forces working from another dimension. This productivity prescription, which we call "futilitarianism," is what makes Catholic lands like Sicily and the Philippines so much more inhabitable than such neopagan backwaters as the Upper West Side.

Francis of Assisi (1181–1226):
Flogging "Brother Ass"

Francis of Assisi is an easy saint to love, provided you are careful not to under-stand him. His story is full of romance, charm, and warmth. He was tender to wild animals—even wolves—and preached to little birds. He cared about the poor enough to join them, and organized a band of other well-meaning social workers devoted to serving them. Think of a genial, retired professor who has de-voted his afternoons to saving wetlands and his weekends to Habitat for Human-ity. Except that this green activist inspired painters such as Giotto to paint exquisite frescos on the roofs of magnificent Renaissance churches and countless brilliant writers to recount his life and works. At the height of the 1960s counter-culture, Francis was portrayed as a proto-hippie in *Brother Sun, Sister Moon,* a flower child who embraced the God we find in every leaf and bumble bee, to the warbling strains of folk hymns by Donovan. Soup kitchens and homeless shelters around the world have worked in Francis's name for centuries, and priests of his order are renowned as easygoing, gentle confessors. One of his spiritual sons, Fr. Mychal Judge, died on September 11—crushed by the rubble of the World Trade Center as he gave last rites to dying firemen. What's not to like?

But be careful. However appetizing the figure of Francis may seem, like a dish of authentic Mexican food, you have to eat around the peppers. As G.K.

Chesterton pointed out in his life of the saint, it was chockfull of disturbingly otherworldly elements unsuited to the modern American palate. When he famously renounced the wealth of his grasping capitalist father, stripping naked in the square before the bishop and clergy, Francis was not, we fear, striking a blow for nudity and naturalism. The truth is more disturbing: he was casting off the world, not as evil in itself but as a distraction. To us, this makes no sense at all—but there it is in the story, and there's no sense in Photoshopping it out.

Francis subjected himself and his followers to a poverty that appalled their fellow beggars, fasting frequently and sleeping on dirt (when perfectly good piles of filthy straw were available), taking all too literally Christ's eerie injunction, "Sell all you have, give it to the poor, and come follow me." When it comes to sex, Francis didn't just give up playing the field and settle down with a life partner; he embraced total celibacy and scourged his own flesh to remind it of its place. Naming his body "Brother Ass," he treated it as harshly as Italian peasants did their donkeys—rolling in snow or patches of thorns when tempted by lusty Italian maidens he saw along the road. (We can only imagine what they thought.) Inspired by his youth as a troubadour love poet who searched for an invisible, unattainable "lady love," Francis fixed his affections on "Lady Poverty" and tried his best to die of love for her—since she seemed to him the closest companion of Christ. To show his approval of all these undertakings, Jesus conferred the same stigmata (wounds). He bore on the cross to Francis, making him the very first saint documented as enjoying this painful privilege. One of the last things Francis did was to write a will forbidding his friars to accumulate possessions, build themselves elaborate churches, or try to introduce loopholes into his austere way of life. Of course, as soon as he died, that was precisely what they began to do.

But however comparatively corrupt one branch of the Franciscan order became, another would always spring up to reclaim its founder's original divine madness; even today, a band of men called the Franciscan Friars of the Renewal sleep on pallets on a gymnasium floor in the South Bronx, running a parish, and releasing Catholic rap albums with songs like "The Zipper Zone," preaching innocence and freedom to youths whom society has sloughed off like so much dead black skin. You can see the same friars on Saturday mornings, kneeling in silence and praying, eyes downcast, outside abortion clinics around New York. What rational motive could drive young men to throw their lives on such a bonfire? We don't pretend to know. We admire them, of course. But we wish they'd stand over there, on the other side of the church basement. We're trying to get to the donut table.

CELEBRATE: Looked at in its historical context, Francis's movement can be seen as a vigorous reaction against the effects of the newfound wealth of the Renaissance. As trade recovered after the Black Plague, new products flooded the market from the East ("globalization" anyone?), and the merchant classes got terrifically rich. They left the poor behind—as wretched as ever, in the midst of sudden prosperity. If you'd like to participate in Francis's spirit in a tiny way—and which of us aspires to much more than that?—why not keep him in mind the next time you go out shopping. As you get to the checkout counter, put just one item back. If every American would do this once a week, it would cut consumer spending, depress the economy, and bring on the sort of poverty that would make St. Francis smile.

The next time you go out to eat, don't supersize that meal. In fact, don't eat it. Take the time and forethought to cook at home. As an extra penance, do something really radical: gather every family member in the same room around a table to eat at the same time. We know; it will hurt. Offer it up. To ease the pain of socializing with relatives, we suggest serving a delicious dish that calls Francis to mind. Since he preached once to sparrows—admittedly, as a piece of sarcasm, since no people would listen—why not serve little potato spaetzles (German for "sparrows")? We suggest a sauce made from the tangy Czech sheep cheese called Bryndza, as served in our favorite Bohemian bistro, Koliba, in Astoria, New York. It goes great with a nice mug of pilsner!

October 5

Bartholomew Longo (1841–1926): Highway to Hell

Finally, after researching all these stories of saints from distant places and times whose lives are almost unimaginable to us, it's nice to come across a saintly, modern, almost ordinary man. Like most of us these days, the middle-class Bartholomew Longo attended college and went through his youthful phases: oratory, fencing, marching band, flute-playing, Satanism. At the University of Naples, he dabbled in the usual campus activist stuff, marching in protests against the Papal States (which of us hasn't?), holding mock church processions, and dabbling in the occult. He'd sit with his fraternity buddies playing quarters and contacting spirits, shifting furniture with unseen forces and making friends with the undead. By graduation, Bartholomew still hadn't decided on a career, so he snagged a fellowship to grad school, where he'd get his MBA (Master of Black Arts), en route to becoming a priest of Lucifer. Indulging in a series of bleak orgies and elaborate blasphemous rituals, he developed a following among the "Goth" teens of his region.

But Bart's clan was really, *really* unsupportive, preferring that he carry on the family religion. So they stormed heaven with prayers on his behalf—and sent him a series of vocational counselors, such as Professor Vincente Pepe and Rev. Alberto

Radente, to debate with him the merits of serving the Prince of Darkness. Eventually, they wore Bart down, and he agreed that invoking fallen angels for the corruption and damnation of human souls for all eternity might not be socially responsible. Besides, his student loans were piling up. He switched majors from Satanism to Theology, and joined E.A. (Evil Anonymous).

In time, Bartholomew would become a famous promoter of the Rosary, in 1871 joining the Third Order of the Dominican friars. He planted a shrine for the poor that in time grew into a vast basilica (the secret is not to overwater), built orphanages, and devoted himself to caring for the children of men in prison—this at a time when scientists had "proved" through the study of skull shapes that criminal "tendencies" were hereditary.

Bartholomew became a public opponent of the occult. He'd wander his old student haunts, handing out Marian medals, warning his former classmates to "just say no" to Satan, and promoting Christian heavy metal bands. All through his later years, his friends who weren't yet "in recovery" would greet Bartholomew by forming with their fingers the letter "L," which he cheerfully interpreted as "L" for "Longo." They'd just shake their heads, light a clove, and go back to their Ouija boards.

CELEBRATE: Quit that Satanist cult. Today. Acknowledge that you are powerless over the Lower Power to whom you have turned over your life, which has become unmanageable. Seek a Higher Power who can cancel out the Lower Power. Acknowledge your powerlessness. It's just that simple. Ask your Employee Assistance Program to refer you to the Evil Anonymous meeting nearest you, and get yourself a sponsor. The next time you find yourself walking into a séance or Black Mass, make a phone call instead. Find a meeting. Work the Steps. And keep coming back.

Lepanto Bowl Upset:
"Hail Mary" Helps BVM Pulverize Saracens 72–6

This feast marks the massive defeat of an invading Turkish navy by joint Christian forces (called the "Holy League," no less) off the coast of Greece in 1571. The pope of the day attributed the Christian victory to the rosaries said throughout Christendom on the day of the battle. We see no reason to doubt him, but we can't imagine how to work that variable into the computer strategy game version of the battle.

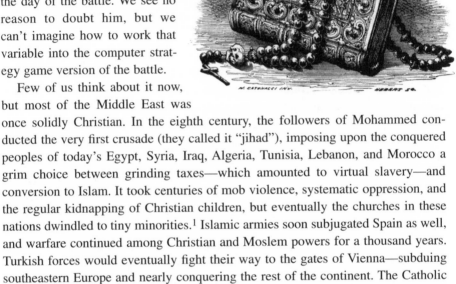

Few of us think about it now, but most of the Middle East was once solidly Christian. In the eighth century, the followers of Mohammed conducted the very first crusade (they called it "jihad"), imposing upon the conquered peoples of today's Egypt, Syria, Iraq, Algeria, Tunisia, Lebanon, and Morocco a grim choice between grinding taxes—which amounted to virtual slavery—and conversion to Islam. It took centuries of mob violence, systematic oppression, and the regular kidnapping of Christian children, but eventually the churches in these nations dwindled to tiny minorities.[1] Islamic armies soon subjugated Spain as well, and warfare continued among Christian and Moslem powers for a thousand years. Turkish forces would eventually fight their way to the gates of Vienna—subduing southeastern Europe and nearly conquering the rest of the continent. The Catholic Crusades were only one episode in this civilizational clash, which continues to this day—as the Vatican opposes Turkish entry into the European Union, fearing it would open up childless old Europe to a nearly unlimited influx from the burgeoning peoples of Islamic lands. Secular Western resistance to resurgent Islam today consists of periodic, futile invasions of oil-rich nations and the export of *Sex and the City* DVDs dubbed into Arabic.

One of the great battles fought by the old Christian powers against Islamic forces took place at sea, in the port of Lepanto near Corinth. The navies of the Ottoman sultan had just conquered Cyprus, and their army was busily leveling towns and arresting monks when a fleet launched by the "Christian coalition" of Spain, Venice, and the Papal States appeared. Indeed, St. Pius V had organized the expe-

---

1. See Bat Ye'or, *The Decline of Eastern Christianity under Islam* (Madison, N.J.: Fairleigh Dickinson University Press, 1996).

dition, desperate to keep Turkish fleets from landing in Rome—as they periodically threatened to do. The armada was led by the gallant royal bastard Don John of Austria. One soldier aboard the fleet was Miguel de Cervantes, later the author of *Don Quixote*. As the navies engaged, with the wind favoring the Turks, Pope Pius V knelt in his chapel at dawn in the Vatican with all his highest prelates, saying the Rosary for victory. When the news came back of a massive Christian success, the pope named this day the feast of Our Lady of the Most Holy Rosary.[2]

CELEBRATE: No, we're not going to suggest going out and sinking some Turkish guy's yacht today. There's a time and a place for everything. Instead, why not mark this feast by saying a Rosary—for a change—then reading aloud the whole of one of our favorite poems, "Lepanto" by G. K. Chesterton. Find it at *www.poetry-online.org/chesterton_lepanto.htm.*

October 11

Kenny (Canice) (515–600): Sacred Pest Control

The son of a tribal bard (or warrior poet), this Irish missionary studied for the priesthood under several monastic saints and traveled all the way to Rome to get a blessing from the pope. Given the state of the travel industry in the sixth century, that's roughly like going to the South Pole to pick up a snowcone. But Canice was intrepid and dedicated, and he made his way back through a Europe swarming with barbarians to found the monastery of Drumachose in Ireland and several places in Scotland. Since the natives liked to call him "Kenny" (when his back was turned), one county where he started a monastery was named for him, Kilkenny.

St. Kenny was what we call "handy." His legends report that while he sheltered on the island of Inish Ubdain, he found himself tormented by thousands of mice. According to Charles Plummer's *Vitae Sanctorum Hiberniae* (*Lives of the Hibernating Saints*): "One Sunday Saint [Kenny] was lodged on the island of Inish Ubdain; but the mice of that place gnawed his shoes and nibbled them and ate them. And the holy man, when he was aware of their naughtiness, cursed the mice, and cast them out of that island forever. For all the mice, assembling in a body,

---

2. We hate to seem unecumenical here. So we'd like to point out that no actual Ottomans were harmed in the writing of this entry.

according to the word of Saint [Kenny], precipitated themselves into the depths of the sea, and mice on that island have not been seen unto this day."

Another of St. Kenny's tricks involved the local birds. He found that when he preached sermons, their chirping and squawking distracted him to the point where he'd get lost in the midst of an anecdote and have to start again. So he called together the birds of the island and instructed them to keep silent throughout his services—and they did. Now, if he'd been able to manage that with his Irish parishioners, that would really have been a miracle.

CELEBRATE: Call in an Irish monk to take care of those "mice" in the basement about which your tenant has been complaining. You know, those foot-long "mice," with the thick brown tails, that can eat through cinderblocks—the kind you see scurrying down the subway tracks. No, buying a cat won't do. That breed of "mouse" would eat him.

October 16

Bertrand of Comminges (+1123): Imposing Celibacy on the French

This son of a military family entered the priesthood and rose to become the bishop of Comminges. But he was no less militant in a miter than his father had been in a helmet; somehow, wherever Bertrand went, trouble seemed to follow. Perhaps it has something to do with his zeal for reform. (Zealous reformers—don't you just love them? Name three of your favorites, right now.)

Bertrand helped impose monastic poverty and clerical celibacy on the local priests; you can imagine how popular this made him in France. He went on to work at a synod which excommunicated the king, and was stoned by a mob on his way out of the meeting. He opened and consecrated an extremely controversial cemetery (Hey, people had different priorities back then . . .), and was attacked by a band of angry monks who tried to burn down his church. On another occasion, Bertrand delivered a sermon so harsh that a riot erupted in the church. To soothe the townfolk, the mayor distributed free butter to the public—and promised that the town would do so every year during the week after Pentecost. This custom continued for some seven hundred years, until the Revolution.

CELEBRATE: Did you know that butter is much healthier than margarine, which is full of trans-fats—a substance designed by alien species who wish to depopulate the planet? It's true! We found it on the Internet! So celebrate the feast of St. Bertrand by tossing out those vile substitutes such as "I Totally Cannot Believe This Isn't Butter, Omigod!" and get some fresh, real butter—preferably from a family farmer at a market. In Bertrand's honor, deliver a few pounds to your local parish rectory. Explain to the puzzled secretary the story of St. Bertrand and promise that you'll be back every Pentecost unless you are attacked by French revolutionaries.

October 19

North American Martyrs (+1642–1649): Typhoid Mary and Jesus

Chances are that anywhere you live in North America, you're near some place with an Indian name. From Nachitotches, Louisiana, to the island of Manhattan, from Connecticut to Minnesota, this country is covered with names of tribes and nations—but oddly enough, it has very few Indians. This might have something to do with the attitudes of the earliest English settlers toward the native inhabitants. Conversely, for all the greed for gold displayed by the Spanish conquistadors, they still knew in the back of their minds that Indians were human and that they had some duty as Catholics—once they were finishing subjugating them—to convert the survivors. In case they forgot, the Church and even the Spanish crown reminded them regularly and sent missionaries by the thousands to preach to the new peoples. The kingdom of France did likewise, sending along with fur trappers and soldiers the intrepid evangelists whom we call the North American Martyrs.

From their name, you can tell that things didn't quite work out. Fervent Jesuit preachers like Isaac Jogues, René Goupil, and Jean LaLande set out from France throughout the seventeenth century to convert the hunter-gatherer tribes of New France (now Quebec) including the Hurons and Iroquois. Learning the local languages and adopting wholesome native customs (such as smoking), these "black robes" preached gentleness and peaceful coexistence to tribes who'd warred for centuries. They made converts such as St. Kateri Tekakwitha and enraged their fellow Frenchmen, who wished to sell the Indians liquor. They also made enemies of their Puritan neighbors—who shuddered to see Indians carrying rosaries along with their tomahawks.

But the missionaries carried something else with them along with the Catholic faith—European diseases, to which the Indians had no resistance. Wherever they went, large numbers of natives began to sicken and die; the Indians were perspicacious enough to see the connection. The Indians began to turn against the missionaries in subtle ways—for instance, by torturing them in elaborate public rituals, cutting off parts of their bodies, and burning them. This didn't scare the black robes—who impressed the warrior tribes by never flinching under torture—and a good part of the Huron tribe was converted. The site where three of these saints were martyred, Auriesville, New York, is now a major destination for pilgrims. And modern missionaries carry vaccines.

CELEBRATE: For a decade now, intrepid American Catholics have been trooping every September through the wilds of upstate New York, marching seventy-two miles in three days from the Lake of the Blessed Sacrament (now sadly renamed Lake George), to the North American Martyrs' Shrine in Auriesville, stopping along the way at the National Shrine of Blessed Kateri Tekakwitha. As they stumble ahead, they pray the Rosary, occasionally stopping to hold a chanted Latin Mass or sing traditional hymns. The presence of dozens of weary children, talkative seniors, and one's own family members reinforces the march's penitential theme. To enlist in this "Pilgrimage for Restoration," visit *www.national-coalition.org/pilgrim/index.html.*

Of course, not all of us bad Catholics are up to this challenge. Our idea of exercise is walking quickly between ethnic restaurants; a pilgrimage is making it to Saturday evening Mass. For the rest of us, a good way to mark this feast that celebrates the arrival of Christianity among the continent's native peoples would be to attend one of our country's many fine Indian casinos. The organizers of the pilgrimage suggest that for those who lack the fortitude for the trip, they may partake in it "spiritually," from a distance—for instance, from a gaming table at the Mohegan Sun casino in Uncasville, Connecticut.

Otherwise, honor these missionaries and the souls to whom they ministered by cooking up an authentic Native American treat.

Warm Indian Pudding with Ice Cream

4 cups milk	Pinch of salt
3 inch piece ginger peeled, sliced thin	1/2 cup dark molasses
1 stick Mexican cinnamon	Vanilla ice cream
1/2 cup corn meal	

Preheat oven to 350. Butter 1 quart baking dish.

Bring 2 cups of milk, ginger, and cinnamon to a boil. Turn off heat and cover with plastic wrap. Allow to steep 15–30 minutes.

Combine remaining milk, cornmeal and salt in heavy-bottomed saucepan. Stir until smooth and heat slowly. Bring to just below boiling point, stirring frequently. Strain milk and spice mixture, discarding spices. Blend into warm milk. Cook for about 30 minutes. Remove from heat. Stir in molasses.

Bake for an hour. Serve warm with vanilla ice cream.

Makes 6 servings

....

Sacramental Executive Summary #6: Holy Orders

Here's a sacrament that's all too little used; indeed, in some dioceses it seems as sadly obsolete as the coronation ritual for Holy Roman Emperor. But the role of the priest is absolutely central to Catholic life. While a layperon may in emergencies baptize, give out Holy Communion, even conduct a marriage, for confecting the Eucharist and hearing confessions, there really is no replacement for a priest. Accept no substitutes!

This makes the shortage of priests in the Western world a grave crisis for the Church. What's the root of the shortage? Observers disagree. Some point to the overall decline of spirituality and an unwillingness to make sacrifices among postmodern people. (That would be us.) Others suggest that the requirement of priestly celibacy is at fault—that the Church should consider revising its thousand-year-plus discipline requiring priests of the Western rites not to marry. And that might help—except, of course, then we'd have to start paying priests more than $11,000 a year (about what they make in New York City)—which might mean putting more than a buck in the collection every week. Nobody's going for that. It's much easier to wangle visas for Vietnamese, Lebanese, and African priests.

It's true that in the old days, when marriage really *was* for life, celibacy was a much easier sell. As for men who weren't, er, *attracted* to marriage, putting on

a cassock was a way to make your mother proud—much prouder than if you came home in a pink taffeta ball gown, for instance.

Whatever the reasons, chances are good that you probably don't know anyone who's considering the priesthood. If you do, the rarity of this vocation is all the more reason for you to be supportive and solicitous, to help him nurture his resolve to accept the countercultural life he will face. And what better way of doing that for a future priest than by throwing him a Seminarian's Bachelor Party.

Calm down, everybody. We're not suggesting anything obscene. We just think it's appropriate to offer a man who's about to give up the life of the flesh for that of the spirit a hearty farewell party.

Anyway, even for someone who's about to get married, there's something really disgusting about the way bachelor parties are thrown nowadays. Instead of gathering the groom's old friends for a night of male conversation, cigars, reminiscences, and bourbon, too many bachelor (and bachelorette!) parties now wallow in the sordid. Trips to strip clubs, rented "escorts," lap dances, and worse—is there any way to better prepare a man who's swearing faithfulness to a single woman for a lifetime of addiction to pornography? We can't think of one.

Instead, we'd like to suggest a return to older ways, with a mildly bawdy twist. Whether your "bachelor" is preparing for the priesthood or the marital bed, we propose the same sort of party: find the nearest Middle Eastern restaurant and gather the gent's best pals for night of male bonding, shish-kebab, hookah pipes, and belly dancers. That ancient Arabic art is plenty erotic to mark the occasion, without ever verging on pornography. Its practitioners can be any age, and (to put it gently) they vary widely in body type. They're not likely to tempt anyone who's used to R-rated movies into a wild erotic frenzy. But the experience of watching a self-possessed and skillful woman perform this ancient dance is enough to bring the men together in joint appreciation of the beauty of God's feminine creation and forge a memory that's fun to talk about over drinks some day—whether in a rec room or rectory. And that's the point, isn't it?

....

October 21

Karl I of Austria (1887–1922): Vote Habsburg!

The House of Habsburg, more than any other family in the history of the Church, is renowned for having supported and promoted the Catholic faith, endowing countless thousands of monasteries, schools, universities, and seminaries; defending Catholic regions from invasions by nonbelievers; colonizing and evangelizing whole continents (Asia, North and South America, for instance); and helpfully "reminding" errant countries (such as Bohemia and Poland) of the truths of the faith, with an occasional whiff of grapeshot. (Okay, nobody's perfect. But how many Catholic families can boast of having equipped the Spanish Armada? Not the Kennedys.)

In October 2004, Pope John Paul II declared Karl I, the last Habsburg emperor, "blessed"—which means that he is just one miracle away from becoming, like Louis IX of France, Edward of England, and Vladimir I of Russia—a royal saint. Karl died penniless at the age of thirty-four, in an exile as distant as Napoleon's, accompanied only by his disconsolate wife and children—whose birthright had drowned in blood. This well-meaning man was thrust into leadership of the crumbling Habsburg monarchy at the height of World War I—a war he strove mightily to end. But the last emperor is much more than a tragic figure. He is an icon of a world we've lost.

Karl is known for abolishing flogging, dueling, and other abuses in the army he briefly commanded, restricting the use of poison gas and civilian bombing, and attempting to decentralize power among the ethnic groups of his polyglot monarchy, which he came to rule in 1917. Karl insisted on eating the same rations as an ordinary civilian—refusing even white bread, which he handed out to his troops. His court photographer reported seeing the newly-crowned emperor visiting a battlefield full of corpses—and collapsing into tears. Karl murmured, audibly: "No man can any longer answer to God for this. As soon as possible I shall put a stop to it."

Almost immediately, Karl began attempts to negotiate a "peace without recriminations" to end the criminal slaughter of World War I. He was the only sovereign in Europe to attempt such a peace. Had he succeeded, the world might never have witnessed a Bolshevik or Nazi regime, a Holocaust, a Ukrainian famine, a Dresden or a Hiroshima.

Karl's clarity and charity, alas, were no match for the war parties that ruled in London and Berlin, Paris and Washington, from 1914 to 1918. President Woodrow Wilson insisted personally on the dismemberment of the Austrian monarchy, as one of America's war aims. Fighting dragged on another fateful year—giving Lenin the chance to seize power in Russia—before it ended with the collapse of Germany and Austria. The victors' peace imposed by the Allies sowed the bitterness that would someday bring the Nazis to prominence. The weak republics carved out of Austria's corpse would all, one day, fall first to Hitler's armies—and then to Stalin's. So went this world "made safe for democracy."

Exiled on the wintry island of Funchal with his young family, Karl soon succumbed to disease and died while still a young man. The night before he passed, he whispered to his wife, Zita: "All my aspiration has ever been to know as clearly as possible the will of God in all things and to follow it, and precisely in the most perfect manner." By the Church's infallible judgment, he succeeded.

The same Church seeks to incarnate divine goodness in earthly—including civic—life. This fact of faith was reasserted every time a Christian king or emperor was anointed by pope or bishop—in a conscious reenactment of the anointing King David underwent in ancient Israel. The last time a genuine monarch—something more than a figurehead—assumed a throne in the West was 1917, when Karl was crowned emperor of Austria and king of Hungary. It may never happen again. But we can always hope.[4]

....

Bonus Saint: Ursula (dates unknown): The Saint of Slasher Movies

If St. Expeditus (April 19) may owe his fame to a shipping label, here's a saint whose story could be entirely due to a typo. According to a disturbingly popular legend, Ursula was the daughter of a British king during the Dark Ages, who was promised in marriage to a royal pagan. Ursula was horrified; she'd taken a vow of virginity. So in return for obeying him, she asked him for just one favor before she left. The king agreed: "Whatever you want. Just go." She wanted ten companions to travel with her. He nodded impatiently. Oh, and *by the way*—each of her friends

---

4. The theological virtue of hope was perhaps best expressed in a scene featuring Charlton Heston from the original *Planet of the Apes*. Held in a bamboo cage, guarded by heavily armed gorillas, Heston asks the ape when he may hope to be released. The ape quips back: "You can *hope* any time you like."

had to take with her a thousand virgins. The king stared at Ursula long and hard, thought about refusing—then decided it was worth any price to get this woman out of the British Isles. Soon England was scoured for virgins to fill the quota, and when all ten thousand were packed on ships, Ursula said her farewell. Her father returned to his palace, eager to father some sons.

Ursula spent three years procrastinating, leading the ten ships on a merry chase around the sea, landing first at Cologne and then at Basle—impressive, since that lake city is in the midst of the Alps—then finally sailing, via Rome, back to Cologne. They arrived in that city triumphantly and told their story to the Huns who'd just conquered it. The king of the Huns listened carefully, thought things over, and decided to slaughter all the women—starting with Ursula.

Sadly (or perhaps happily) this whole tale seems to have been a clerical error. It all began with an ancient Roman inscription found by a monk, which spoke of a martyr named "Ursula" and "11 M." Instead of taking this to mean 11 martyrs, he thought it meant 11,000 (M being the Roman numeral for 1,000). From that "high concept," medieval screenwriters spun their very own slasher stories, inventing 10,011 different ways for Huns to torture and murder virgins. Their scripts (okay, their hagiographies) run hundreds of dark, disturbing pages, and ghastly pictures from it covered the walls of teenage boys' rooms throughout medieval Europe. St. Ursula was removed from the Church calendar in 1969 as unsuitable for children. But an entire religious order of moderately ferocious virgins, the Ursulines who teach in schools, still bears her name.

John of Capistrano (1386–1456): Homeland Security

No, he didn't breed swallows or found a mission in California. The exquisite church that bears his name was given it by his fellow Franciscan Fr. Junipero Serra, who founded this mission in 1776 among twenty others that dot the state. San Juan de Capistrano is the oldest building still in use in the state of California.

St. John was no swallow, but a tougher bird entirely—more like an imperial eagle. Born in Italy to a family of warriors, he ruled the city of Perugia on behalf of the king of Naples. Captured in a war he was trying to mediate, he discovered a call to the religious life and got permission (from his wife as well as the Church) to annul his marriage and join St. Francis's order as a priest. He walked up and down the length of Italy, preaching and attracting crowds—one as large as 126,000 people. We've been to TAFKAP concerts smaller than that.

John's preaching made him famous and got him appointed papal nuncio (ambassador) to Austria, where he led a movement against the popular, proto-Protestant heresy of Jan Hus. When Turkish forces invaded Serbia (are you seeing a pattern here?), the pope appointed John to preach and lead a crusade to turn them back. At age seventy, he personally led seventy thousand men into battle, defeating the Ottomans outside Belgrade in 1456. He is customarily pictured stomping on a turban—an image that now appears in the official seal of the U.S. Department of Homeland Security.[5]

---

5. You have to squint a little, but it's there. . . .

October 25

British Martyrs (1535–1679):
Atrocities? We've Got Atrocities. . . .

It doesn't happen as often now with the paucity of vocations to the priesthood, but Catholics of a certain age may well remember the phenomenon: a really handsome, dashing young man disappointing the prospective brides in his high school or college by announcing—sometimes tearfully, over a shaker of last-date martinis—that he had a higher calling and was off to the seminary. They were duly impressed, and sure he'd cut an excellent figure up on the altar some day, but once the women were together, they'd whisper to each other: "It's a crime."

Well, in England after Henry VIII, serving as a Catholic priest *was* a crime. In fact, Queen Elizabeth I had her parliament declare the very act of saying Mass an act of treason, punishable by death. Not a quick death, such as Thomas More was granted because he was a nobleman, but a slow, lingering torture, which usually entailed being disemboweled while still alive and then cut into pieces before a jeering crowd. The relatives of such "traitors" were also disinherited, which meant that the family lands of Catholics would end up in the royal treasury.

As historian Eamon Duffy documents in *The Stripping of the Altars,* the newly Protestant English state knew that a majority of Englishmen, for at least a generation after Henry VIII imposed the Reformation by force, clung to the Church as best they could.[6] They resented the seizure of monasteries (which had provided free education and medical care) by greedy aristocrats, the mutilation of the sacraments, and the forced imposition of a new religion by "priest-hunters" and government spies. Popular resistance took many forms, from abortive revolts to exile, but mostly amounted to people staying home—refusing to attend the new Protestant services. So the English crown ordered local sheriffs to keep attendance and imposed a series of increasingly heavy fines on people who didn't show up "faithfully" every Sunday at Anglican liturgies. Those who skipped these services were called "recusants," and they were gradually impoverished by these fines. Many Catholic families sheltered priests in their homes, constructing elaborate secret rooms (or "priest holes") where undercover clergymen could hide from the secret police. This feast day honors just 40 of the hundreds of martyrs slain by the English government in the name of the Reformation—from priests such as Henry Walpole to married laywomen such as Margaret Clitherow.

CELEBRATE: Learn the stories of some of these martyrs online (see the lovely Web site *www.tyburnconvent.org.uk* run by a convent located at the site where many of these martyrs died). Stuff your head with some of the goriest details, and the next time someone comes at you with vague allusions to how "intolerant" the Catholic Church has been over the centuries, reply by telling him about these little-reported English persecutions. Remind him that Catholics couldn't even attend university in England until the mid-nineteenth century. Here in America, the first Catholic professor wasn't hired at Harvard Divinity School until after World War II. This isn't meant to excuse the excesses committed by Catholic rulers, but simply to provide comparative perspective. If your descriptions get gruesome enough, it will make your friend change the subject or will ruin his dinner. And that's really all that Christ asks of us.

October 28

Jude (first century): A Saint for Your Brother-in-Law

It's puzzling but not surprising that one of the most popular saints in the Church is also one of those we know least about. This is pretty much perfect from our point of view, since it gives us someone to pray to without loading us down with all sorts of heroic, self-denying, and just plain weird devotions we might be ex-

---

6. Eamon Duffy, *The Stripping of the Altars: Traditional Religion in England, 1400–1580* (New Haven, Conn.: Yale University Press, 2005.).

pected to emulate. Pretty much all you can do here is light a candle—and even we can manage that.

We do know that Jude existed, since he wrote the next to last book of the Bible, the Epistle of St. Jude, and ID'd himself as the brother of Jesus's cousin James. The rest of what we have about Jude is pious speculation, uncertain tradition, and legend. And yet, he's renowned as one of the saints with the most heavenly "pull," whom we pray to when all other hope seems lost. Indeed, Jude is the patron of "hopeless causes." Like your brother-in-law. You know, the one who's living in his parents' basement at forty, playing "City of Heroes" as an ersatz Spiderman character, taking time out only for blind dates with green-card hungry Czechs and meetings of Debtors Anonymous. How about your Rubenesque (i.e., fat) niece who's still "into Goth" although she's in grad school and corresponding with serial killers in prison? Your sister who's addicted to dollar stores, gay male porn, and Botox injections? You know exactly who we mean—and no, it's not

"I WAS ONCE WORTH $40,000. I WAS ONCE RESPECTED AND RESPECTABLE. I ONCE MOVED IN GOOD SOCIETY. SUCH THINGS AS I AM NOW ARE MADE OUT OF SUCH MEN AS I ONCE WAS."

"uncharitable" to admit it. Each of us knows at least one "hopeless case"—some of us even know ourselves—in need of help from good St. Jude. And he's willing to pitch in; his batting average is higher than the average saint when it comes to intercession. There must be a celestial competition among SS. Anthony, Jude, and Therese of Lisieux—like the old rivalry between Willie Mays and Hank Aaron to see who would first surpass Babe Ruth's 714 career home runs.

It's funny that God believes in division of labor, assigning different tasks to various saints. It's clear why St. Mary of Egypt, a former "exotic dancer," became the patroness of penitent strippers, and how St. Lawrence, cooked alive, was hired as a celestial lobbyist for chefs. But how did St. Jude get saddled with losers like our cousin Rolf, the autistic cop? Some hagiographers speculate that the very name "Jude" won this saint that booby prize; since it so resembled "Judas," early Christians considered it "hopeless" to expect many people to pray to him. So only hopeless people did. He repaid them lavishly, and still does today—getting unpaid cable service reconnected, scoring a second chance for airport security guards who let terrorists onto planes, and keeping inside-trading executives out of federal prison so they can keep attending their Opus Dei prayer breakfasts. It's all good to us—and so is St. Jude.

CELEBRATE: Make a list, in order of sheer desperation, of the hopeless cases you know. Get each one a third-class relic of St. Jude from *www.shrineofsaintjude. com,* and send it along with a long letter full of heartfelt, clearly thought through advice about how to resolve his financial/pharmacological/legal troubles that it's hopeless to expect him to finish reading, much less heed. While this won't do much good, it will clear your conscience and perhaps cause the person to stop calling you at 5:00 a.m. "for support." Inside the note, secrete the relic. Chances are he'll keep it; he never throws anything away, including expired coupons and balled up tissues, which will alert St. Jude to his needs. Remember to pray for this person as often as you can stand thinking of him without getting depressed. Meanwhile, the relic will sit there like a heavenly Webcam, keeping the saint's watchful eye on the person's PC monitor, liquor cabinet, or collection of German Lugers. When the next crisis arises, the saint will take care of the rest.

October 31

All Hallows' Eve: The Seven Deadly Courses

This holiday has a very long pedigree, reaching back into Celtic pagan days, when peasants believed that the times that marked transitions between the seasons—such as the autumn equinox, which happens around this date—opened the door between our world and the unseen realm of the spirits. For a few days every year, the dead could walk the earth again, and the eerie powers possessed by fairies, witches, demons, and other "resident aliens" were greater than ever. They could kidnap children, blight crops, poison wells, and bring on plagues with impunity on this night, which the Celts called "Samhain." In part to fool the spirits by passing as one of their own, country folk would dress up as these creatures themselves. They might also have hoped to placate these enemies of humankind—or even to make fun of them. It was this last meaning that Christian missionaries decided to give the holiday as they spread the new faith through old Europe. With few exceptions, monks and preachers gave their new converts permission to keep up their old traditions—provided they were willing to instill them with new meaning.

To help the newbies along, the Church created feasts of its own to fit the season. The Feast of All Saints (All Hallows) marks the special activity of friendly spirits from the Other Side—serving as a kind of Tomb of the Unknown Saints. The Feast of All Souls gives people the chance to pray for their dead friends and family and help them climb into heaven. Even today, it's much easier on this feast than at any time throughout the year, through a few simple prayers, to help your dead relatives escape the sufferings of purgatory—assuming you *want* to help them.

In America, the eve of All Hallows (Hallowe'en) has been commercialized and lurched backward quite a ways toward its pagan roots. It's hard to see how homosexuals marching through Greenwich Village dressed as Britney Spears have much to do with the Communion of Saints. But in other lands and certain regions the day is still marked with celebrations that carry a religious punch. For instance, Mexicans revive the gorier elements of their country's heartrending[7] Aztec past, celebrating their "Day of the Dead" by dressing up as skeletons, making cookies they call "Dead Man's Bread," and decorating their homes with *luminarias,* candles inside paper bags marked with skulls and other uplifting insignia that flicker, dangerously, all through the night.

Some Catholics in America have reacted against the paganizing trend by abandoning Halloween altogether. Influenced by their Evangelical neighbors, they're giving up on the hard work their ancestors did to harness the coolest parts of paganism and put them to work, and we think that's a shame. Others try to sanitize the day by dressing their kids up as saints and angels. This works pretty well for some of the girls, and the boys under five, but after that it gets old mighty quick. Instead make your All Hallows spooky, meaningful, and unforgettably delicious by throwing a Purgatory Soiree.

In case you've forgotten, purgatory is that awkward transitional phase most of us (we hope) go through en route from earth to heaven. Call it "metaphysical puberty," since it's marked by all the discomfort, awkwardness, and growing pains we associate with early teenagers and the newly dead. (One of our favorite religious films, *Beetlejuice,* depicts this nicely.) Like a teen, you're entering a strange new world—and you're not too happy about what's happening to your skin.

The doctrine of purgatory is pretty simple: When most of us die, our souls are like SUVs caked in mud. So God set up a kind of spiritual car wash for us to clean off all the crud we've accumulated over seventy mediocre (or twenty-seven really sexy and eventful) years. Dante, in his *Purgatorio,* saw the realm of purification as a mountain, around which sinners march in a spiraling path upward to heaven. Around and around the sinners would trudge, on a different level according to their favorite sin, hearing endlessly rehearsed everything they had ever done wrong, and

---

7. Literally. It's said that the Aztecs would rip out and eat some ten thousand human hearts a month from defeated enemies and helpless neighboring tribes, offering blood to the Sun God to keep him getting up in the morning.

what they should have done instead. (It's like slogging your way to the top of a sixth-floor walk-up—to have dinner with your parents.)

We can take this sobering reality and have some fun with it by turning the home into "Purgatory for a Day" and filling it with our very favorite sinners.

CELEBRATE: Make your front door the gateway to the spooky realm of purgative suffering by hanging the entrance, inside and out, with thick black velvet curtains. Keep the lighting dim and improvise a fog machine with dry ice and a fan—or clouds from your favorite hookah pipe.[8] Cover all the windows with black crepe paper, and rope off whole sections of the house with crime scene tape. If you have wooden floors, play a game with the kids, where you sketch the outlines of their little "corpses" on the floor. The atmosphere you want is something like a funeral parlor—run by the Addams Family. Drape all the mirrors with black or purple paper, and pull out the red candles you have left over from Pentecost.

You should announce that tonight costumes are mandatory—and they really should be thematic. If you want to be true to Dante, dress up the hostess as an angel and the host as the poet Virgil (a toga will do, with some bay leaves stapled—no, taped—to his head).

Of course, you won't want to be "true to Dante"—what kind of a geek are you? Instead, you'll probably dress as some great sinner of history, preferably one whose costume is easy to make. Attire the lady of the house as glamorously as a queen, with a homemade tiara—and a blood line of lipstick around her neck, to suggest Marie Antoinette, or Mary Queen of Scots. Gussy up the host as some famous megalomaniac, like General Patton or Jim Morrison. Attire the kids as the tiny devils who punish sinners. (Depending on your kids, this may strike too close to home.) Or have fun costuming each child as the deadly sin you know all too well he likes to indulge. Your sadistic son can carry some implement of torture, such as the TV remote. Your slutty daughter can wear whatever she would to a first date. And so on.

Tell your guests to come as their favorite dead sinner, without telling you who it is. And here's the key to the fun: everyone should show some sign of suffering—grimace lines painted on the face, some ashes smeared on the clothes to suggest burning, or a T-shirt from a Bible camp. Purgatory isn't like Woody Allen's sex-addict daydream of hell in *Deconstructing Harry*—an S&M club full of buxom, sweaty women, with Billy Crystal telling jokes. It's more like one of those Caribbean reform schools where suburban parents send their unmanageable kids. But tonight is their Senior Prom!

If your guests actually do play along and show up as historical sinners, don't ask their "identity" when they arrive. That's the key to the game you're going to play as you nibble on dinner—a cocktail spread of seven courses, one for each Deadly Sin. It's a guessing game, in which the guests in turn must answer questions about what they did, what their vices were, etc. The object is to figure out who each of the guests is supposed to be and what crimes they are "in for." Call it "prison interrogation" to get the boys interested.

---

8. It's like a bong, only for Arabs.

THE SEVEN DEADLY COURSES

Pride: Black Caviar, arrayed with chopped red onions, sour cream, toast points, and lemon wedges on your finest silver tray

Envy: Roasted Asparagus with Lemon and Garlic (something thin and green)

Gluttony: Dates Stuffed with Cheese, Wrapped in Bacon (See recipe)

Anger: Shrimp and Mussels Fra Diavolo

Lust: Figs, Coated with Belgian chocolate (the medieval symbol of sexuality)

Greed: Peanut Butter Cookies (something irresistible)

Sloth: Haagen-Daz Ice Cream, self-service, straight out of the container

---

Flaming Purgatory Punch

1 bottle red wine	Peel of one orange, white pith removed
1 bottle port	
2 cups brandy	Peel of one lemon, white pith removed
1-3/4 ounce cone piloncillo sugar	
3 cinnamon sticks	1 cup raisins
1 clove	1 cup whole roasted almonds
3 green cardamom pods	

Warm brandy in a large nonreactive pan. Add sugar, spices, and citrus peel. Stir till sugar dissolves; then light mixture. When flame goes out, add wine and cook just below a simmer for an hour; then add raisins. Turn off heat and add almonds; allow to steep another 15 minutes. Good served immediately or allowed to age for several days.

Makes 10–12 servings

Gluttony: Stuffed Dates

1 pound good quality dates	8 ounces Gorgonzola	1/2 pound bacon

Fry bacon to chewy stage. Drain on paper towels and set aside.

Remove pits from dates. Stuff the cavity of each with cheese. Wrap each date with 1/2 slice bacon. Pass under broiler momentarily and serve.

Important note: To illustrate the theme of Gluttony, do not make enough of these treats to satisfy all your guests; then watch them fight over scraps.

Makes 8 servings

Bonus Celebration: Sell Indulgences

One of the richest scandals in the history of the Church concerns the Renaissance practice of selling indulgences. The whole indulgence thing began innocently enough: the Church teaches that confessing your sins—provided you're sorry and at least vaguely intend to stop committing them—is enough to keep you out of hell. One confession will detoxify the soul of anyone: a tobacco executive, a Mafia don, or a modernist architect. God forgives the sins themselves—but He doesn't instantly wipe out the damage they have done to your soul, your lungs, or the New York City skyline. That part is up to you. In the early days, the Church used to assign elaborate, embarrassing penances that had to be performed in public—such as sitting in

front of your parish church every Sunday for a year, dumping ashes on your head, and holding a sign that said "masturbator." As the Church grew larger and her front steps filled up, a new approach became imperative. The Italians, who were running things by this point—having ousted the Israeli firm that founded the organization—came up with a more streamlined approach. The Church would assign easier, symbolic penances such as working among the poor, visiting old people, fixing the windows in the rectory, and so on. Performing such simple but vital acts of charity would serve to undo the damage sin had done to the soul (if not to the liver). These acts would reduce or even eliminate the need for purgatory, and they were dubbed "indulgences."

Because the Church's first penances were counted in "days" or "years" spent sitting on the church steps, these later, saner penances were reckoned in the same way. Prelates would assign to a particular act of charity the value of "One Hundred Days" or "One Year." That doesn't mean you're released from purgatory that many days or years earlier—for all we know, purgatory happens all at once, in a timeless psycho-spiritual thrill ride, like one of those drug trips that feel like they last a hundred years. It does mean you get credit for a hundred days or a year sitting outside the church with the scarlet "M" and ashes on your head.

Of course, the ordinary people didn't make these fine distinctions. They probably thought that purgatory worked like prison, with longer sentences for more serious crimes and pardons reckoned in years cut off a sentence. So misconceptions about indulgences became widespread. At the start of the Renaissance, when churchmen decided to get in on the fun everyone else was having and construct enormous churches with walls full of naked people, the Vatican used indulgences to raise the money. While popes never gave permission for indulgences to be sold outright, when faced with cartloads of gold coming in from Germany, they tended not to ask too many questions.

All this had something to do with the Reformation. The story goes—and it might not be true in every particular—that one Dominican friar named Johan Tetzel was the indulgences king of Germany. He sold them like the Church was going out of business (and thanks to him, it almost did). It seems he used to wander from town to town like a flying circus, imploring people to free their suffering friends and relatives from the terrible pains of purgatory, which he described as a "lake of fire." To make the point more vividly, he used to throw live cats and dogs into a little furnace, so customers could get an earful of what their parents were going through. Needless to say, Tetzel was extremely popular. People loved the little torture show and happily threw him some coins to spring their family members from the furnace.

Then Tetzel met up with a rather humorless German monk named Martin Luther. Outraged at the crass commercialism of the enterprise, Luther promptly declared the pope the Antichrist, his own interpretation of the Bible infallible, and his vows of celibacy void. He married a German nun and set up his own, competing church. Within a century, there were dozens of Protestant churches, and embarrassed popes were painting loincloths over the Vatican's naked paintings. Thus the tragic divisions that still afflict the Christian world began with the unhappy meeting of P. T. Barnum and Ingmar Bergman.

Studying this history makes us nostalgic for the "good old days" when you could pay for your sins in cash—which would then be spent creating great works of art. But the Church cracked down on the sale of indulgences, so our only choice is to do it at home.

It's true that you as an individual Catholic have absolutely no right to remit sins or lift the burden of penance, as indulgences are meant to do. But your dinner guests don't know that. You can help your kids earn some spending money by photocopying the handy "Indulgence Certificate" provided below onto parchment paper, for quick sale to your tipsy friends. Set your own price for the indulgences— say, $1 for a year, $20 for a complete or "plenary" indulgence. Once everyone is thoroughly lubricated by a few servings of Flaming Purgatory Punch, send the cutest of your kids around with these handy forms and black velvet bags and doleful looks. Equip them in advance with classic funeral industry sales scripts such as "Did you stop loving them, just because they're dead?" "Your parents need you— more than ever" and "When the coin falls in the box, the soul from purgatory flies." This exercise makes a great opportunity to teach your kids about Church history, the theology of penance, and good old-fashioned American salesmanship. Of course, if you really do have departed relatives for whom you'd like to do a good turn, the day after tomorrow (All Souls' Day) is the time. Assuming you've been to Confession recently, you can actually obtain a complete ("plenary") indulgence for any dead person by visiting a church and saying a prayer for that person. No money involved. The Vatican already has all the art it needs.

Certificate of Indulgence

In recognition of his/her pilgrimage in *pietatis causa* to the domestic shrine of the _____ family, and pious attendance on the Eve of All Hallows at the services honoring the Feast of All Saints, the penitent sinner _____ is hereby granted, by our full and solemn authority, an indulgence of _____ years/plenary indulgence (circle one) in satisfaction of temporal punishment for earthly misdeeds.

This indulgence granted by _____ , master/mistress of the domicile, this 31st of October, *anno Domini* _____.

November

November 1

All Saints' Day: Tomb of the Unknown Saint

This feast fulfills in the life of the Church the same role as such phrases in Academy Award thank-you speeches as "and all the other people, the *little people*[1] who pitched in to help me over the years, too many to name." All Saints' Day marks all those people who aren't named in this book, but who show up in the Book of Life.

True, when we hear the word "saint" we usually think of a famous mystic who learned to bilocate, a martyr who died with exceeding slowness in a picturesque way that inspired Renaissance painters, or an Irish abbot who taught small, furry animals to distribute Holy Communion. These are all important spiritual gifts. But they're not strictly required for sanctity. A saint is not necessarily someone we've heard of, complete with high school football teams named for him, tin medals that bear her face, or a glow-in-the-dark plastic dashboard statue all his own. A saint is anyone who got out of purgatory and into heaven. Period. So we're talking about a lot of people here—we hope.

This feast day reinforces the corporate nature of the Church, the fact that we aren't saved individually, by depositing our prayers and good works in an "Infinite Retirement Account" that pays off when we expire. No, salvation is much more like the Social Security system, with Christ as the great Franklin Roosevelt in the sky, collecting graces and virtues from one set of people and redistributing them where needed. This is what we mean by the Communion of Saints. We can only hope that the whole pyramid doesn't come crashing down when the Baby Boomers finally (*finally!*) meet their maker.

This feast is a Holy Day of Obligation, which means you are obliged to go to Mass. Yes, skipping church today is in fact a mortal sin—and one of the dullest in

---

1. We're assuming that award-winning actresses aren't attributing their success to leprechauns—although Fairies may have played a part. . . .

the book. Can you imagine being damned for blowing off the twenty-six-minute liturgy at your parish? You'd be the laughing stock of hell. Personally, we believe in making each of our mortal sins *count*; each one had better be *worth* the risk to our souls, the trip to Confession, the time spent purging our sins by reliving Groundhog Day over and over again. You get the idea.

So as Pope John XXIII said in his homily for this feast in 1961, "Haul your lazy ass to Mass" and commune with the millions of anonymous souls who dwell in perpetual beatitude with Christ and his angels, whom you treasure some (faint) hope of joining one day.

> **CELEBRATE:** Many Catholic peoples mark this feast by visiting the cemetery where family members are buried. The Cajuns of Louisiana and the French will clean and decorate the tombs of the departed and have a picnic on top of the graves. Irish Catholics also visit the places where their parents and siblings are buried—to say a solemn prayer, exchange a rueful memory or two, and make sure that the folks to whom they weren't speaking for decades while alive have in fact stayed dead.

November 2

The Feast of All Souls: A Black-Letter Day

In the traditional Catholic liturgy this feast was marked with a solemn funeral Mass for the "suffering souls" in purgatory. It marks the flip side of All Saints' Day, reminding us of the people who still need our prayers. For the liturgy, the priest would don a stark black chasuble and stole, and the choir would chant the *Dies Irae,* a chilling medieval meditation upon the wrath and the mercy of God. This is the feast to pray for the dead, particularly those of whom you were gladdest to be rid: that sibling who ruined all your holiday gatherings before she OD'd on crystal meth, your power-mad, butt-groping boss who fell off Mt. Rushmore, that slap-happy ex-husband who "just plain needed killing." At this Mass, we recall the souls who are neediest and most abandoned—often for very good reason.

Sacramental Executive Summary #7
Sacrament of the Sick

This Church rite used to be called Extreme Unction, because it was administered only to the dying, by a priest who consequently behaved with extreme unctuousness. After Vatican II, the sacrament was modified, restoring it to its function in the early Church as a means of healing— more comforting than morphine, if not quite as effective as Zithromax.

St. James himself, Jesus's cousin, recommended this practice highly: "Are any among you sick? They should call for the elders of the church and have them pray over them, anointing them with oil in the name of the Lord. The prayer of faith will save the sick, and the Lord will raise them up; and anyone who has committed sins will be forgiven" (James 5:14–15).

Please don't find this scripture verse (as so many seem) discouraging. Just because your aging uncle got the sacrament and didn't recover, it doesn't mean he didn't receive the grace that comes from it, or that his sins aren't forgiven. (Though the latter is perfectly possible, come to think of it.) At the moment of our births, theologians speculate, God stamps upon our soul the moment when he will call us back, a supernatural "Sell By" date, after which our souls are likely to turn sour—or, if you leave them out long enough, into yogurt. And no one wants that to happen.

upon the promise of Resurrection, the time at the end of time when every tomb around the world will explode like a plate of frying popcorn, as souls are clothed once again with their physical bodies, restored and purged of disease and defect. As for souls whose associated bodies share the same molecules, well, they're just going to have to duke it out to see who gets to keep that femur.

And when you go to that protracted wake for your friend or family member, that two- or three-day vigil of sitting in a funeral home staring at that embalmed and made-up body in an open casket, remember to kneel occasionally before that $8,000 bronze box and say a Rosary for the dead. (You want all the dead souls you can get on your side; they're much less likely to haunt your house, and they might even pray for you.) Then go back to greet all those relatives you haven't seen since the Vietnam War.

To keep the occasion special, we suggest you bring tasty, palm-sized snacks you can enjoy while covering your face and pretending to weep. These peanut butter Rice Krispies treats should do the trick:

Lengthy Wake Rice Krispies Treats

6 cups crisped rice
1/4 cup walnut oil
1-1/2 10 ounce bags
 marshmallows

1 cup natural peanut butter,
 crunchy style
1 cup dried apricots, chopped
1 cup roasted almonds
1/4 cup cocoa nibs

Grease a 13 × 9 inch pan. In a large pan over low heat, melt the marshmallows and butter, stirring. Remove from heat and stir in remaining ingredients; mix well. Press mixture into the pan, cool, and cut.

Makes 36 bars

November 3

Hubert (656–728): Bring Out Your Beagles

This saint's tale recalls for us fond memories—principally because Hubert's emblem, a cross between the horns of a stag, appears on the Jägermeister bottle. How many evenings, begun timidly with vermouth and quiet conversation, have ended with that velvety black liqueur and a raucous, howling hitchhike ride to Tijuana? More than we care to mention.

But there's much more to Hubert than that. This saint started out life as a rich Belgian nobleman, the heir to the powerful Duchy of Aquitaine. His favorite sport was hunting, and he pursued it obsessively—to the point where he attracted attention, eventually even God's. What brought poor Hubert up on the divine radar was the fact that he wouldn't skip chasing stags for Lent. Instead, he skipped his devotions and went hunting on Good Friday. Big mistake.

That holy day, as Hubert and his delighted dogs cornered a giant stag, he raised his spear to snag the beast, when it turned around to face him. A huge crucifix appeared in the creature's antlers, and the animal spoke to him: "Hubert, unless you turn to the Lord and lead a holy life, you shall quickly go down to hell."

Needless to say, this made an impression. Hubert fell into a funk—greatly disappointing his companions, and especially the dogs. His wife was none too happy with the "new Hubert," and she soon sickened and died. Hubert could take a hint: God had got hold of him and wasn't likely to loosen His jaws. So Hubert renounced his title, his wealth, and his beagles and entered a monastery—soon becoming a bishop famed for holiness and courage.

His story impressed the hunters of Europe, who soon adopted him as their patron saint. Since his feast day falls conveniently in the autumn, they made it the starting date for hunting season. Even today, a special Mass is held on his feast in churches across Europe to mark the start of the season. At the liturgy the organ is replaced by hunting horns, and the church is flooded with packs of hounds, who receive a special blessing from the priest. Hubert is the patron of hunters and dogs, and animal hospitals around the world still bear his name—as does a famous French hunting dog, the St. Hubert hound.

CELEBRATE: Take your dogs to church for a blessing today—which is said to help avert rabies—then spend the day chasing squirrels in the park. Remember to bring the dogs.

Bonus Saint: Martin de Porres (1579–1639): A Friend to Vermin

This saintly friar was born of a mixed-race unmarried couple in Peru and suffered discrimination throughout his life for his dark skin. But his spiritual greatness—concealed by a deep humility—has made him one of the most beloved figures in the Church. He also had a real way with rats.

At age fifteen, Martin joined the Dominicans as a Third Order friar, choosing for himself the humblest duties—mainly sweeping up and working in the kitchen. (He's usually pictured with a broom.) Because he'd trained as a barber—the equivalent of medical school in those days—Martin was also put in charge of the priests' infirmary. Unlike most doctors of the day, he actually healed some people, and he soon won a reputation in the region. He willingly treated plague victims, founded an orphanage and hospital for the neglected Indians and African slaves of Lima, and organized soup kitchens. The legend grew up that whenever he gave out food to the poor, it would miraculously multiply. (We think he was using Hamburger Helper, but we've no proof of that.)

His fervent prayer life granted Martin mysterious powers—including the ability to bilocate. People reported seeing him in Mexico, Guatemala, and Japan—although he never left Peru.

Best of all, Martin rid his rectory of rats—without harming them. He loved all God's creatures and could not bear to poison the little pests. But his superior was getting tired of all the squealing, so he ordered Martin to purge the place of vermin. So after a prayer, Martin summoned all the rats—who arrived in twos and three, until they made up a quorum. He then preached a sermon about their bad habits and bade them never to return. They never did.

Martin is the patron of social justice, interracial marriage, hairdressers, and exterminators.

··

November 5

Guy Fawkes Day: Go Out with a Bang

English-speaking Catholics who study history have a tendency to grow a little bitter.[2] Throughout the sixteenth and much of the seventeenth centuries, Catholic priests in Britain were hunted down by secret police and tortured to death, while layperson were executed, imprisoned, or bankrupted by a viciously intolerant Protestant government.

---

2. Particularly galling is the fact that all the most beautiful nineteenth-century churches in our home town, New York City, are Episcopalian. If Henry VIII had produced a few more Y chromosomes in his first marriage, those tasteful Gothic structures would be ours, damn it. So would Westminster Abbey.

With the death of Queen Elizabeth I, and the accession of James I, English Catholics had reason to hope that the repression they suffered might be eased. After all, his wife was a Catholic, and he was the son of Mary Queen of Scots, who lost her throne and her life in large part because of her faith. James made ambiguous noises about suspending the slaughter of priests and persecution of laymen.

They were quickly disappointed. Once James had consolidated his hold on the throne, he courted popularity among Protestants by continuing to hunt Catholics—excepting only a few royal favorites.

This marks the day that some of those English Catholics decided to try biting back. On this date in 1605, the bold conspirators Guy Fawkes and Robert Catesby, along with a dozen or so of their friends planned to blow up the English houses of Parliament, wiping out the entire political elite of the country, including the royal family, at one fell swoop. They then planned an uprising of Catholics across the country, intending to install a friendlier monarch on the throne.

The plan came achingly close to success, but was foiled at the last minute when one of the "friendly" lords (whose life they tried to save by warning him) snitched to the authorities. The conspirators were captured, tortured, and executed—and thousands of innocent, patriotic Catholics were persecuted in the ensuing terror.

To mark the occasion, English Protestants began to hold bonfires on the anniversary of the plot's discovery, creating stuffed effigies of Fawkes and burning them festively this night, accompanying the flames with fireworks, drinking, and general celebration. Sometimes instead of Fawkes they would burn the pope in effigy—a custom still popular in Northern Ireland.

CELEBRATE: While this day is not part of the Church's liturgical calendar, there's no reason we can't enjoy it—albeit giving the holiday a bit of a twist. Why not get the baking enthusiasts in your family (i.e., the girls) to make a House of Parliament out of gingerbread? Find pictures of these exquisite Gothic buildings on the Internet and make the best copy you can, lovingly adding details with icing, perhaps even forming a tiny King James I out of marzipan. Unveil it at the outset of tonight's family dinner—or at a gathering of friends. As dinner unfolds, tell the story of Guy Fawkes and his friends. Then for dessert take the gingerbread parliament outside, stuff it with M-80 fireworks, and blow it to hell.

November 11

Viennese Carnival: Pretzel Crowns and Explosives

The Carnival season in German-speaking lands begins for some reason on November 11, at 11:11 A.M., or *elften elften elf Uhr elf,* and continues for what must seem like 11 months. In fact, it goes right on up to Ash Wednesday, meaning that Carnival smooshes right up into Advent and Christmas, threatening to reduce the Church's ancient calendar of alternating feasts and fasts to a meaningless jumble.

Throughout this time, Teutons throw fancy dress parties and costume balls, dress a fat mustachioed man in skirts as a *Jungfrau,* designate the village idiot as "King," paint their faces blue, don pretzel crowns, send women out to hack off men's ties with scissors, march through the streets with banners, and generally act as happy as if there were a war on that they were about to win. Import some of that relentless joviality into your home by throwing an Austrian-themed *Fasching* (carnival) party.

Fireworks and noisemakers are an essential component of the evening; the Germans used them to drive out devils before starting Lent. Don't worry if these are illegal in your state; chances are you live within driving distance of a place where they're sold by the side of the Interstate. Put them in your trunk under several boxes of *fastnachts,* traditional German Carnival pastries, and your stash will be cop-proof.

To give this party the appropriately Austrian feeling, remake your home to resemble the Habsburg palace of Schönbrunn (for architectural plans, see *www.schoenbrunn.at*). This entails constructing an elaborate Hall of Mirrors, painting the ceilings with detailed *trompe l'oeil* murals of the open sky in a baroque or rococo style (according to your taste), and laying out elaborate formal gardens centered on fountains with ornamental statuary and carefully shaped topiary bushes in the shapes of fantastic animals such as unicorns, gryphons, and satyrs. Construct an Imperial greenhouse at least four stories high, so you'll never have to want for out-of-season fruits. To help with these tasks, first obtain control of a large central European empire, encompassing a wide variety of ethnic groups, each of whom will make vital cultural contributions to the rich, variegated cosmopolitan life of your ruling class. It is best, in our experience, to found a dynasty that will govern this empire for several hundred years before the celebration, to allow all the ingredients to marinate. Employ private music tutors to teach each of your children one of the parts from *The Magic Flute*, costume them appropriately, and surprise your guests with an impromptu performance of the opera!

Fastnachts[3]

These addictive potato-flour doughnuts appear throughout all German-speaking countries this time of year.

1 cup sieved cooked potatoes
1 cup potato liquid
3/4 cup canola oil
1/2 cup sugar
1 tablespoon salt

1 package yeast
3/4 cup warm water
2 large eggs, beaten
5 to 6 cups flour
Canola oil for frying

GLAZE:

6 cups powdered sugar   1 cup boiling water   Zest of 2 lemons

Dissolve yeast in warm water and let sit 5 minutes. Mix together potatoes, potato liquid, vegetable oil, sugar and salt. Stir into potato mixture.

Stir in eggs and enough flour to make dough easy to handle. Turn onto lightly floured surface. Knead for about 10 minutes until smooth and elastic. Place in greased bowl; turn greased side up. Cover. Let rise until doubled in volume, 1 to 1-1/2 hours. Do not punch down.

Pat out dough on lightly floured surface to 3/4 inch thickness.

Cut doughnuts with floured 2-1/2 inch cutter. Cover and allow to rise doubled in volume, about 1 hour.

Heat oil 4 inches deep 375 degrees, using a candy thermometer, in heavy pan. Fry doughnuts until golden, 2–3 minutes on each side. Drain on paper towels.

Mix glaze ingredients until smooth. Glaze doughnuts while warm. Store doughnuts at room temperature covered. Best eaten the same day.

Tip: Dough can be stored in refrigerator up to 3 days before using. Refrigerate in greased bowl immediately after kneading. Grease top of dough generously and cover with damp towel. If dough rises, punch down and cover with damp towel. Heat oil 4 inches deep 375 degrees, using a candy thermometer, in heavy pan. Fry doughnuts until golden, 2–3 minutes on each side. Drain on paper towels.

Makes 25–30 doughnuts

3. Courtesy of Mrs. Abigail Richard, Lafayette, Louisiana.

Bonus Saint: Martin of Tours (316–397): Goose-Strangling in the Suburbs

This military saint was made famous by his singular act of generosity. A convert to Christianity, he became a member of the Roman emperor's elite Pretorian Guard. One day, not long after his baptism, Martin encountered a pitiful, half-naked beggar. Inspired by Jesus's own words in the Gospel, Martin sliced his ceremonial cloak in half and gave a piece to the poor man. That very night, Christ appeared and informed Martin that He Himself had been that unclothed beggar. Martin hastily offered Christ the other half of the cloak.

Having ruined his uniform, Martin soon found himself posted to the front lines in Gaul. Ever the brilliant careerist, Martin announced on the eve of battle that as a Christian—the Faith was still illegal—he could not fight in this unjust war. His superiors denounced him as a coward and locked him in jail. However, once Martin was safely incarcerated and praying, the enemy melted away from the battlefield. In fact, they marched right back out of Gaul. Martin's superiors were so alarmed that they expelled him from the army before he could ruin any more perfectly good wars. He later became the bishop of Tours and enthusiastically led the destruction of pagan temples. Outraged ancient preservationists retaliated by dressing as Roman gods and haunting Martin by night. But Martin dismissed these visions as the side-effects of rich French cooking.

CELEBRATE: In most of Europe, this is the day that serves as Thanksgiving. New wine is sampled, fattened animals and birds are killed and salted away for winter, and a large goose is roasted to feed the gathered family. The bird's breast bone is plucked out after dinner, and its color used to predict what kind of winter will follow. Since this custom is most popular in Germany and England the answer is usually "a nasty one."

In Catholic Germany, children gather on this day with homemade paper lanterns to march at sunset behind a heavily cloaked soldier on a horse ("St. Martin"). He leads them through the town until they encounter a "beggar," whom they surround and regale with gifts. Then the children gather around a bonfire and sing into the night.

Why cook a goose? Most likely just because they're delicious, but ingenious medievals discovered a legend to explain the saint's connection with the roasted bird. According to the informative *Wilsonsalmanac.com*: "One day Martin was lecturing the folks in a village about their sinful ways, and a goose started honking so loudly that it interfered with his speech. Not to be outdone, the good priest ordered the goose slaughtered and then finished his sermon. Afterward the goose was cooked and served to him. St. Martin choked to death eating the goose." Share this story with your kids as you serve up the bird; they'll leave more behind for you.

Roast Goose

Not all butchers and supermarkets keep fresh goose on hand. If you live in the suburbs, your best bet is to take the kids along on a little jaunt to the nearest public pond. Chances are, you'll find these pudgy birds roosting by the hundreds, covering the benches and cars with smelly poop and chasing toddlers with snapping beaks. Offer a prize to the child who's first to subdue, strangle, and come back with one of the birds. If anyone (such as a nosy policeman) comes over to complain, adopt some sort of indeterminate foreign accent and explain, "To this great country I am coming new. It is in Old Country the custom to do this. Is not true here? Is true back home in Esperanto." Then offer the strangled bird to the cop. He'll let you off with a warning—and the goose.

Garlic Soup

This tasty treat from Austria will warm friends and family alike—though you might not be on speaking terms for a couple of days.

6 cups rich, full-bodied chicken or
   turkey stock
1-1/2 heads garlic, cloves peeled,
   stems removed, thinly sliced
2 sprigs fresh thyme
Sea salt and freshly ground black pepper

4 egg yolks, lightly beaten
Croutons brushed with olive oil and
   toasted
3 tablespoons freshly grated
   Parmigiano-Reggiano

In a medium saucepan combine stock, garlic, and thyme. Bring to a boil. Reduce heat and allow to simmer slowly, covered, for 40–60 minutes.

Remove thyme after 40 minutes. If reduced too much, add up to 1/2 cup water. Remove soup from heat. Whisk a few ladles of the soup into egg yolks and add mixture to the soup. Place a crouton in the bottom of each serving bowl. Pour soup over and sprinkle with cheese as you serve.

Makes 2–4 servings

November 12

Livinus (+633): Speaking in Tongue

The most decisive gift God can grant a soul is "final perse-verance," which means that if you're in a state of grace toward the end of your life, He'll help you stick it out to the bitter end, preserving you from falling into sin at *just* the wrong moment. The term also applies to the grace given mar-tyrs not to chicken out at the end. St. Livinus had more such perseverance than most. This Scottish monk traveled to Flanders in the really Dark Ages to spread the Gospel among the sullen, pagan Flegms. He converted many, and served as bishop of the Flegmatic city of Ghent, before some resentful unbe-lievers roused the energy to martyr him. They took their time killing the saint, pausing to cut out the tongue that had so eloquently preached. Through all the tor-ture, he never complained or flinched. But legend tells that the severed tongue went on talking a blue streak once Livinus was dead. It preached interminably about the Gospel, and its sheer, babbling enthusiasm soon won over the puzzled pagans.

November 22

Cecilia (+117): Cleaning Out the Choir Stalls

Here's yet another saint whose importance for Catholic tradition stems from a happy mistake. There was, indeed, a second-century martyr named Cecilia; her tomb was found in 1599, marked with her name and complete with a body that hadn't decayed in almost fifteen hundred years. We call that "forensic evidence."

Apart from that, what we know about Cecilia is confined to legend. But her story is one of the most poetic of all the martyr chronicles, and it has inspired countless artists to create important devotional works, from Raphael's portrait to John Dryden's "Ode on St. Cecilia's Day."

According to the tale, Cecilia was a young Christian woman in the wrong place at the wrong time: in Rome, during a pagan persecution. She took a vow of virginity at a young age—even though her parents had already promised her in marriage to a powerful aristocrat. It's written that Cecilia won her husband over to Christianity through a clever ruse. On their wedding night, she whispered to him that she had a secret: a glorious angelic spirit that only she could see accompanied her everywhere. Her husband demanded that this rival for her affections manifest himself. Cecilia said that he had to undergo a little ritual purification first. He agreed to the rite—which turned out to be baptism. As he left the font, the newlywed was amazed to see that Cecilia was telling the truth: he could now see her angel, plain as day. After producing a celestial spirit, Cecilia had little trouble convincing her groom to join the Church and respect her vow of virginity. He joined her as a fervent apostle of Christ—and like her, would die as a martyr.

So far, so good. But Cecilia's story doesn't end here. It's said that during her unwilling wedding, "at the sounding organs, the virgin Cecilia sang to her Lord, declaring in her heart (*cantantibus organis*): 'O Lord, let my heart and my body be immaculate, that I not be confounded.' "

In other words, she was ignoring the pagan music, and intoning a silent psalm to Christ. Pious souls whose grasp of Latin was even shakier than ours decided that the words *cantantibus organis* meant Cecilia was singing along to the organ. As a result, she began to be pictured in front of an organ, even playing one—and was adopted as the patroness of musicians. Another artistic tradition, sticking closer to the correct text, depicted Cecilia discarding musical instruments—rejecting the outer, pagan music of her wedding for the psalm of virginity in her heart.

CELEBRATE: This feast, which marks one saint's decision to abandon earthly music for the greater glory of God, offers a fine occasion for improving the music at your local parish. Chances are that there's at least one member of your choir who should have hung up his vocal chords years ago. We remember fondly a church we used to attend where this was true of all the singers, and the organist besides. Intoning every week a single Victorian operatic setting of the Mass that could be properly sung only by a team of highly trained castrati, these amateur golden throats formed what we liked to call the "St. Agnes Tridentine Latin Mass Alley Cat Choir."

Muster the courage and charity to have a little talk with those very "special" members of your choir. Tell them St. Cecilia's story. Will they take the hint? Perhaps if you described her lengthy, painful martyrdom.

Thanksgiving: Thank God for Mediocrity

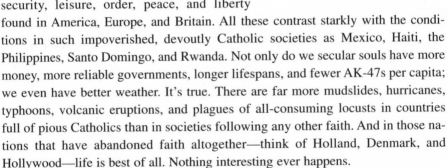

This feast day is the modern descendant of medieval Catholic harvest festivals, such as the grand goose feast that used to mark St. Martin's Day (Martinmas). There is much for which we in the "developed world" ought to be grateful— for instance, the comparative wealth, security, leisure, order, peace, and liberty found in America, Europe, and Britain. All these contrast starkly with the conditions in such impoverished, devoutly Catholic societies as Mexico, Haiti, the Philippines, Santo Domingo, and Rwanda. Not only do we secular souls have more money, more reliable governments, longer lifespans, and fewer AK-47s per capita; we even have better weather. It's true. There are far more mudslides, hurricanes, typhoons, volcanic eruptions, and plagues of all-consuming locusts in countries full of pious Catholics than in societies following any other faith. And in those nations that have abandoned faith altogether—think of Holland, Denmark, and Hollywood—life is best of all. Nothing interesting ever happens.

But why is this true? Is it simply that people in countries where life is nasty, brutish, and short are driven to prayer? If that were true, then we should expect a religious revival among post-Communist Russians, jobless English miners, and American adjunct professors. Does the Rosary stir up tropical storms, does the Eucharist crash tectonic plates together? Well, not directly.

There's a deep and disquieting mystery at work here. In his letter, St. Paul warned the Hebrews, "Whom the Lord loves he chastens, and every son he scourges." The Hebrews took the hint—how many have you seen in your parish recently? But the Lord has millions of sons and daughters, all over the world, and everywhere you find them you can count on also encountering poverty, oppression, chaotic politics, and periodic rains of meteorites that destroy the vital banana harvest.

It seems that God regards suffering in this world as a vital tool for perfecting human souls, and He pours it out generously on those whom He loves the most. Think of Job. Look how God's chosen people, the Jews, have suffered over millennia—leading Tevye in *Fiddler on the Roof* to implore God, "Could you please choose somebody else?" Remember the lives of those God loved the best: Jesus and Mary. They were full of suffering, persecution, scourging, and "swords through the heart." Compare this to the dull, prosperous retirement enjoyed by Pontius Pilate, the prosperity of corrupt Renaissance popes, the ever-improving golf handicap of O. J. Simpson. When God gives up on a person or a country, He pretty much leaves them alone.

So this is the day when we recall all the *spiritual* blessings that Divine Providence has spared us, thank God. Let's say a prayer of gratitude—but not too loud. We don't want to attract His attention.

....

The First Sunday of Advent: Scrooge You

In ancient Rome, the year began on the first of January, the month named for Janus, the god of transitions. Medieval Englishmen transferred New Year's Day to March 25, the Annunciation, since for them new life began with the Incarnation of Christ in the Virgin Mary's womb. After the Reformation, the English-speaking world gradually reverted to the old, pagan practice. But none of this has ever mattered to the Church, which begins its calendar today, with the first intimations of the coming of Christ.

This is also the beginning of the serious shopping season, as people begin to celebrate Christmas earlier and earlier each year. By the time the Christmas season actually does begin—on December 25—most of us are sick to death of it, and ready to move on.

Some pious, dour Catholics have started a countermovement, attempting to revive the original significance of Advent as a season of penance and prayer. Noting that in the early Church people fasted three times a week throughout this season and treated it as a little Lent, these people refuse to throw holiday dinners before December 24, skip office parties, and hold off on shopping and decorating their homes.

This suits us curmudgeons just fine: we usually forget to decorate until it's too late—when trees and wreaths just happen to be half price.

We've always gone Christmas shopping on Christmas Eve, usually in one stop at Barnes and Noble, which stays open till midnight and gift wraps for free.

We don't attend office parties. The combination of free liquor, forced good cheer, randy co-workers, and thinly suppressed office politics made such events a great occasion for getting in a foolish fling or a fist-fight—and then fired.

By insisting pedantically on the true meaning of Advent, you acquire a righteous excuse for skipping all this blather and playing Scrooge right up through December 24—after which you can enjoy the holiday season all to yourself. Open a bottle of wine and unwrap those presents you bought yourself.

December

Francis Xavier (1506–1552): A Piece of the Saint

This Spanish priest has been called a second St. Paul, for the vast distances he traveled and amazing success he achieved in spreading the Gospel. It all began, like so many stories, in college. Francis had planned for an ordinary academic career in philosophy, back when you could still get tenure teaching the humanities. He enrolled in grad school at the Sorbonne in Paris in 1525 and had already begun his dissertation when he was introduced to a mysterious traveler—an alum who was visiting campus to recruit men for a classified mission behind enemy lines.

No, he wasn't from the CIA—which wouldn't be founded for decades to come (though it would be run partly by Jesuits). This was Ignatius Loyola, the fiery Spanish soldier who was organizing a militia of priests, whom he'd arm with his sleek, ultramodern holiness technology—the Spiritual Exercises.

The first mission Ignatius proposed was a crusade to the Holy Land, where with any luck, they all would die as martyrs, taking the kingdom of heaven by violence. Francis signed up immediately. Together, the newly professed Society of Jesus (Jesuits) went to Rome to get papal permission to go and get themselves killed.

But Pope Paul III had other ideas. With Protestant bloggers churning out a new heresy seemingly every week, the pope couldn't see the sense in wasting so many perfectly good young Spaniards on a kamikaze mission. Instead, he ordered them to form themselves as intellectual warriors for the faith—a mission they accepted with fiery enthusiasm. Within thirty years, the Jesuits would be dominating the intellectual life of the Church and much of the world, gaining a sinister reputation for conspiratorial cleverness from Geneva to Tokyo. (The word "Jesuitical" still appears in dictionaries as a synonym for "sneaky"—which just goes to show you that history is written by the Protestants.)

Francis set out on a campaign of travel and propaganda fidei that made the great Christopher Columbus seem like an agoraphobic. In his forty-six years, the priest journeyed through India and Japan and (it's rumored) the Philippines, making thousands of converts along the way and planting churches that would endure through centuries of persecution. He healed the sick, spoke in tongues, raised the dead, and won over dozens of intellectuals and courtiers—faithful disciples who tried and nearly succeeded in converting the emperors of both China and Japan. When he died, Francis's body remained miraculously incorrupt and on public display for decades. But pious admirers kept nibbling away at it for sacred souvenirs (or "relics"), taking now a finger or two, an organ here, a shoulder blade there, until at last the Jesuits felt compelled to lock Francis away for safekeeping, sending only a golden arm to the Gesu church in Rome, where it still resides. You just can't make this stuff up.

CELEBRATE: Learn more about the method of prayer that made Francis great, Ignatius's Spiritual Exercises. Its secret was that it taught believers to visualize themselves at all the crucial moments of Jesus's life, using each of the senses and all the emotions to identify one's own experience with His. The Jesuit method suggests you close your eyes, compose yourself in prayer, and try to evoke the sights, sounds, tastes, smells, and feelings that Jesus must have gone through.

Of course, Ignatius recommends that we cover the really important, joyous, and stressful episodes in Jesus's existence. But since the Exercises help you get on the road to perfection—and we're more interested in gazing at it from the local watering hole, we recommend starting small, imagining Jesus:

- While he sat, bored, in the Temple, listening to the rabbis explain the Old Testament (which He'd written) or the universe (which He'd created).
- As He quaffed the good wine at Cana.
- As He laced into the Pharisees.
- As He blighted the unfruitful fig tree.
- As he stunned an entire village by raising Lazarus from the dead. Dig deep into the rotting stuff at the back of your refrigerator to evoke the scent; "Lord, by this time he stinketh" (John 11:39).
- As He descended into Limbo, and sprang Adam, Eve, all devout Jews, and virtuous pagans.
- As He chased the moneychangers out of the Temple. The next time you spot a really upsetting liturgical abuse, treat it as an opportunity to imitate Christ. If you lack knotted cords, a bicycle chain should do.

December 4

Barbara (+235): Death from Above!

This possibly legendary lady's tale[1] is one of our favorites. According to medieval accounts, Barbara lived in third-century Asia Minor, the daughter of a rich pagan, Dioscorus, who found her a trifle rebellious. Since there weren't any boarding schools available, he locked her in a tower with a troupe of tutors, poets, and philosophers. Instead of learning dutiful obedience, she picked up the Christian faith—perhaps from the great theologian Origen.

Her father was outraged, and he washed his hands of her. Okay, he went a step further and handed her over to the Romans to be executed. She escaped their custody, but Dioscorus tracked her down, dragged the poor girl home by her hair, and murdered her. (A father had the right to do this to any of his children in pre-Christian Rome.) He was rewarded almost immediately by a bolt of either lightning or fire raining down from heaven.

Inspired by this story, medieval cannoneers adopted Barbara as patron saint of their trade—raining death from the sky—and she still watches over artillerymen today. The American Artillery Marines based in Okinawa hold their annual "St. Barbara's Day Ball" in her honor. According to the United States Field Artillery Association (USFAA), "The Order of Saint Barbara is an honorary military society of the United States Field Artillery. Both U.S. Marine and Army field artillery along with their military and civilian supporters are eligible for membership. . . . The order links field artillerymen of the past and present in a brotherhood of professionalism, selfless service and sacrifice symbolized by Saint Barbara." To learn more, write the USFAA at P.O. Box 33027, Fort Sill, OK 73503.

••

December 6

Nicholas (+346): Kids in a Barrel

We may be going out on a limb here, but we think most readers have probably heard of this saint. Ever since he signed that endorsement contract for Coca-Cola, he and his army of pygmy toymakers and genetically modified reindeer have

---

1. Like many of our favorite saints with the coolest stories, Barbara was booted from the calendar after Vatican II.

maintained a high profile—sometimes to the point of distracting us from, you know, that kid in the manger.

Of course, the real story of St. Nicholas of Myra involves a few, carefully chosen gifts, and only rare visits to the North Pole. He really didn't have the time, since he spent long sentences in prison for the faith, served as bishop of a diocese in Asia Minor, and helped lead the Council of Nicaea, which reaffirmed the fact that Jesus was God as well as man.

But the association of Nicholas with gift-giving isn't entirely arbitrary. Some of the earliest accounts of his life include the charming suggestion that he would throw money through the windows of impoverished girls so their fathers could afford dowries and they could be married—instead of lapsing into lives of prostitution. It's said that in one household he tossed three bags of gold, one for each endangered daughter. This inspired pawnbrokers ever after to hang three golden balls outside their windows. So the next time you swing by a pawn shop to pick up, say, an engagement ring or a .38, remember to say a little prayer to St. Nicholas for success in marriage or marksmanship.

Another legend of St. Nicholas tells that three young boys had been killed by a local maniac in Myra, and their bodies preserved in a pickle barrel. (We're surprised this scene hasn't yet appeared in a movie with Nicholas Cage.) The bishop opened the barrel, discovered the corpses, and promptly raised them from the dead—winning acclaim ever after as the patron saint of children, pickles, and barrels.

CELEBRATE: It's traditional in Catholic Europe to celebrate St. Nicholas not on Christmas, but on his feast day (go figure!). Parents remind children the night before to leave their shoes outside the door, for St. Nicholas to fill with candy during the night. It's probably best *not* to stuff your kids into a barrel half-full of brine and then return in a Santa Claus costume announcing that St. Nicholas has raised them from the dead. Just trust us on this one.

December 8

Feast of the Immaculate Conception: The Addams Family Chapel

Most Catholics know this as the feast day that marks the fact that Jesus was born of a Virgin, without an earthly father. If you asked them why we had a separate feast for the Annunciation, they'd probably shrug and say, "I don't know. Why does the Church do a lot of things? Why is bingo always on Wednesdays?"

And they have a point. The Catholic faith is built on profound mysteries, salted throughout with little paradoxes and puzzles that keep the whole thing interesting.

But this feast isn't one of those puzzles. It has nothing to do with the birth of Jesus—commemorating instead an event that happened some fifteen years before: the Virgin Mary's conception in the womb of St. Anne. The fact that Mary, alone of all human beings except her son, was born without Original Sin, was infallibly declared a dogma of the faith by Pius IX in 1854. By virtue of Jesus's redemption, which applied to her retroactively (okay, so there is a puzzle here, but if you think God is bound by time you've got bigger intellectual fish to fry than this), Mary was granted the same innocence with which Adam and Eve were created. Theologians speculate that her freedom from original and personal sin meant she was spared the corruption of the grave—being instead assumed into heaven at her death (see the Vatican Space Program, August 15). Her free decision to bear a suffering Savior, which theologians call her *fiat,* is the cosmic reply to Satan's rebellion (*non serviam*) and Adam and Eve's desire to be "as gods."

So this feast marks more than a long-ago event in a first-century Jewish mother's uterus; it holds the key to mortality and immortality alike. *That's* why you have to go to Mass today, okay?

If the Immaculate Conception is all about the liberation from death and decay, no one told that to the Capuchin friars of the parish in Rome named for this feast, Santa Maria della Concezione. This chapel attracts only discerning visitors because—hold onto your lunch—it is *furnished entirely with human skeletons and skulls.* That's right, the friars who man this parish are disassembled when they die to be made into furniture. Tibia and fibia form the chandeliers, vertebrae line the ceilings, fleshless fingers poke from the walls, skulls are lined up like decorative tiles along the sides, and a complete human skeleton stands on the ceiling, waving a scythe made up of still more bones. As you walk through the crypt that holds the bones of four thousand friars, you pass a few skeletal Capuchins still wearing their robes—one bearing the message: "What you are now, I once was; what I am now, you will be."

This church isn't Gothic—it's Goth! We give it two thumbs up. Rated R.

CELEBRATE: Make this feast special, and honor the peculiar humility of the friars of this chapel, by fixing a specialty from their native land, the Italian treat "Dead Men's Bones."

Dead Men's Bones

1 cup cake flour
1/2 cup sugar
1 cup ground almonds
1/4 cup pine nuts, roughly
   chopped

Zest of 1 lemon
1 tablespoon butter
1 egg plus 1 yolk
1 egg white for glaze

Preheat oven to 325. Combine flour, sugar, nuts, lemon, butter, and eggs in stand mixer and mix until smooth. Add up to a tablespoon of water if needed. Roll dough into logs and cut into 1-1/2 inch pieces. Brush cookies with egg white. Bake on parchment-lined pans 20–25 minutes. Cool on racks.

Makes 3 dozen cookies

....

December 12

Our Lady of Guadalupe (1531): Bleeding Hearts, Liberated

If you think Mexican politics are raucous now, you should have been there in the sixteenth century. Before the Spanish arrived, the warlike Aztec empire based in Tenochtitlán held the neighboring nations in brutal slavery. The religious dogmas of the Aztecs were so dark and pessimistic, they make the *Left Behind* books seem appealing: These pagans believed that their gods were fragile and fading, and that if they weren't fed a steady diet of freshly spilled human blood and beating hearts, they'd die and the sun would go out. And as hot as it gets in Mexico, nobody really wants that to happen.

So the Aztec kings sent warriors to conquer nearby tribes and bring back prisoners to sacrifice on their vast pyramid-shaped temples. Their priests slaughtered some twenty thousand prisoners each year, whose bodies were cooked and served to the Aztec nobility. It's said that their favorite snacks were hands and thighs—which the last king, Moctezuma, liked stewed with tomatoes and chipotle peppers.

This regime was so popular with the non-Aztecs in the neighborhood, that when Hernando Cortés arrived in Mexico in 1519, he was swamped with volunteers to help him overthrow Moctezuma. Which he proceeded to do, exhibiting astonishing courage and ruthlessness; within five years he'd subjugated most of the country. At first, some thought the Spanish were benevolent gods returning to set them free. As the conquistadors enslaved the Indians and seized every shiny object in the country to send home to Spain, well, the truth sank in.

This stealing frenzy didn't win as many Catholic converts as one might have hoped. Despite an influx of Franciscan, Jesuit, and Dominican missionaries, the sullen, subjugated Indians showed no interest in Christianity, as somber letters Bishop Juan Zumárraga sent home to Spain make clear. It seemed to him that Mexico was liable to remain an entirely pagan country, ruled by an elite of kleptomaniacs in big tin hats. (Nice work if you can get it.)

But in 1531, something happened that changed everything. On December 9, an impoverished Aztec of noble lineage who'd taken the Christian name Juan Diego saw a woman on top of Tepeyac Hill, the former shrine of the Snake Goddess. She explained that she was there to hear the cries of her suffering people. She soon revealed herself as the Blessed Virgin. But she didn't resemble the pasty-faced holy pictures posted by the Spaniards. This lovely lady looked like an Indian.

She sent Juan Diego to Bishop Zumárraga with orders to build a church on the spot. The bishop was skeptical of this alien construction account and asked for some proof. On Juan Diego's next visit, the mysterious lady sent him to gather roses. He must have thought she was pulling his leg—it was a cold December.

But Juan Diego went where Mary sent him. And there he found a garden blooming despite the frost. He collected a tilma-full of fresh Castilian roses, carried them for miles, and spilled them on the floor of the bishop's palace. Then Juan Diego noticed they'd left a stain on his cloak. Since it came in the shape of an exquisite, miraculous portrait of the Blessed Virgin Mary standing atop the moon wearing native Aztec dress, he decided not to have it dry-cleaned.

The bishop nearly passed out. He picked up the roses—which grew in his home province, but not in Mexico—and examined the miraculous tilma. Then he fell to his knees. He ordered the first shrine of Our Lady of Guadalupe built on the site she'd indicated. He enshrined the tilma, which was made of cheap materials that usually decay within a decade, for public display. Natives flocked to see this Lady, who was not just the mother-goddess of the Spaniards, but their own patroness in heaven—and within ten years they had by the millions abandoned their pagan shrines and joined the Church.

You can still see the image of Our Lady today, in perfect condition after almost five hundred years on that flimsy tilma—and in ten thousand other places: painted on the walls of churches and barrios, fluttering on banners at soccer games, on bumper stickers and children's lunch boxes, and tattooed on the arm of that hard-working guy who's probably outside right now—remodeling your house.

CELEBRATE: Mark this magnificent, home-grown Mexican feast by serving a tasty native treat. No, we don't mean "Leg of a Tlaxcalan War Prisoner Who's Been Sacrificed to the War God Huitzilopochtli" over rice. We were kidding about that. More modestly, we suggest the delicacy called "Aztec truffle" *(huitlacoche)*, made from corn that has blossomed into giant, purple kernels that taste like the very best kind of mushrooms. You can pick it up canned at any ethnic food store or bodega. It makes a delicious filling for an enchilada or burrito, but our favorite way to serve it is in a fondue, the way they prepare it in Monterrey, Mexico.

Aztec Truffle Fondue

8 ounces Emmentaler cheese, cut
   into small cubes
12 ounces Gruyère, cubed
1 tablespoon flour
2 cloves garlic, peeled, crushed
2 cups Fendant or Neuchâtel white
   wine
1 tablespoon lemon juice

2 tablespoons cognac
Salt and freshly ground pepper (to
   taste)
5 ounces huitlacoche
Plenty of dippers: bread cubes,
   cornichons, boiled potatoes,
   and crudité

Toss cheese with flour and set aside.

Add garlic, wine, and lemon juice to heavy saucepan, enamel or stainless steel. Bring to a slow simmer and begin adding cheese, a handful at a time. Stir constantly with a wooden spoon in a figure-eight motion. Let each batch of cheese melt almost completely before adding more. The fondue will bubble but should never boil, becoming creamy and smooth.

Add huitlacoche, cognac, salt, and pepper, stirring constantly.

Transfer to fondue pot or place saucepan over a table burner. Moderate heat to keep fondue warm but not boiling.

Serve immediately. The action of your guests swirling their forks in the cheese will keep it well-stirred and creamy.

Makes 10 servings

Lucy of Syracuse (+269): Blind Man's Buffet

This saint, legend tells, had dedicated her life to a virginal marriage with Christ. But her pagan parents had other ideas and promised her in marriage to a nobleman. She procrastinated about the wedding, coming up with a multitude of excuses and dithering about a caterer, until at last her fiancée insisted. When she finally leveled with him, he didn't handle rejection in the most creative way: he denounced her to the Romans. She was arrested and sentenced to live as a prostitute. But when the guards showed up she simply would not be moved—not even by a team of oxen, which exhausted itself trying to drag the saint away. So the Roman judge decided to have her killed. She was tortured horribly first; the thugs in charge even pulled out her eyes. But an angel appeared to Lucy returning her eyes, so she could see clearly for her few remaining days. The soldiers surrounded her with wood and threw a torch, but the logs wouldn't light. At last, exasperated, the Romans slew her with a sword.

Because she lost and regained her sight, Lucy was given a feast on one of the shortest days of the year (before the Gregorian calendar it fell on the winter solstice, the very darkest day) and made the patroness of sight. Her story has inspired great works of art, such as John Donne's poem "A Nocturnal upon Saint Lucy's Day" and paintings by Veronese and Caravaggio, and the charming Swedish folk custom of making a crown out of pine boughs and candles for young girls to wear on her feast. (To see this custom in action, with Judy Davis and Kevin Spacey done up in St. Lucy crowns, rent the delightful satirical Christmas film *The Ref*).

The Church has maintained a wide array of services for the visually impaired that it names for St. Lucy, from schools for blind children to centers for Braille and audio books.

But our favorite fruit of Lucy's legend appears in those gruesome holy cards and statues that appear throughout the Mediterranean world featuring Lucy looking mournfully up to heaven as she holds her eyeballs out before her on a plate. These four-eyed Lucies are surpassed only by the St. Lucy eyeball rings complete with pupil and little red veins that superstitious Catholics wear against the Evil Eye. You can find them by the bucketful at thrift stores in New York City. Be sure to buy a matching pair and wear them on adjacent fingers. They make quite an impression at job interviews.

December 14

John of the Cross (1542–1591): The Saint of OCD

Here's one of those saints who both inspires and scares us. On the one hand, he was an immensely creative personality who wrote some of the greatest poetry in Spanish, began an important religious reform, and was named a Doctor of Mystical Theology for his profound insights into the union of the soul with God. But then there are all those penances and all the terrifying things John writes about the spiritual life to warn the orthodox but casual Catholic (i.e., us) in bright red letters: Do Not Enter.

John doesn't even address the soul steeped in

worldiness and struggling with ordinary sins; he assumes that his readers are already pious, devout, and perfectly orthodox. Having narrowed his audience down to a sliver, he proceeds to warn them of all the further dangers they'll face on the road to God: the spiritual gluttony that can result from taking too much pleasure in prayer, sacred music, and devotional arts; the subtle attachment a half-starved monk or nun might derive in having his or her prayers answered; the danger of taking pride in praise. In short, he strips away any satisfaction one could imagine taking from anything short of God Himself. All of this in preparation for the really *tough* part of mystical life—the Dark Night of the Soul, in which one gives up the sense that God is present, loves us, or even necessarily *exists*. He promises that after all this is done one will be suffused with the glory of union with the Godhead. We're in no position to argue with him. But we don't aim to find out.

At age twenty-one, John joined the Carmelites, which had begun as one of the most austere orders in the Church, but whose practices had mellowed over the centuries with encouragement from a number of accommodating, sensible popes. Like his spiritual consort, Teresa of Avila, John was appalled by these compromises, and he joined her in a movement to restore the order to its primitive severity. They symbolized this by adopting harsh penances and extreme poverty and by refusing to wear shoes—even naming their group the Order of Carmelites, Discalced (barefoot). The order's initials are O.C.D. That's Providence, not a coincidence.

....

December 24

Adam and Eve: Schmucks!

These two Old Testament bumblers got us into the mess we're in today. We've them to thank for migraines, labor pains (in every sense), cellulite, wrinkles, warfare, mortality, and Hawaiian Shirt Fridays at the office: Every aspect of life that would seem out of place in Paradise stems from the original disobedience of our first parents. In his *Confessions,* St. Augustine describes how the Fall lies at the root of both impotence and embarrassing, unwanted arousals, an insight he gained while splashing around at Carthage's public baths.

The Church teaches that when our first parents were created (however that happened[2]) these two were in a state akin to Christ's after the Resurrection: Their bodies were impervious to physical injury, they had perfect control over their desires,

---

2. Since Pope Pius XII's document *Humani Generis* (1950), Catholics are perfectly free to theorize that man's body developed from earlier forms of life. We just can't assert that it was an accident or that different races of men derived from a variety of first parents who "just happened" to all evolve in the same way—a favorite theory of the Nazis, which Pius was quick to condemn. We also must believe that our first parents committed some grave sin that lost them divine favor, requiring a redemption. The rest is up for grabs.

and they naturally wanted to do the will of God. Some theologians have daringly speculated that Adam and Eve could walk through walls, bilocate, and fly. If that is true, then before our first parents sinned, human beings were empowered to live like Spider-Man.

And these two geniuses blew it all. We know, we know, "*O felix culpa,* O Happy Fall of Adam that brought such a Redeemer" and all that. But tell that to a cancer patient, a woman in labor, or somebody in need of a root canal who has run out of Vicodin.

It's tempting to mark the day given to these Old Testament patriarchs by serving twin turkeys surrounded by garden vegetables, each stuffed with an apple.

But truthfully, Adam and Eve have suffered enough. They lost their awesome, rent-controlled place in the country. Then they had to eat sweaty bread and give birth in anguish while serpents nipped at their heels. And on top of all that, one of their kids murdered his brother and then went out to live "on the road" with a tattoo on his face. When they finally died, our first parents had to spent hundreds of thousands of years in Limbo, as the place gradually filled up with judges, kings, Levites, patriarchs, matriarchs, and a rabble of virtuous pagans and prophetic Hebrews, until finally Christ broke into the place and rescued the hostages.

In fact, since we know that they were redeemed and brought to heaven, the Church honors Adam and Eve as saints. So let's go ahead and invoke them. But maybe not ask their guidance in practical matters.

The Twelve Days of Christmas: One Fibber Fibbing

In the mid-1990s we began to hear about a hidden meaning that underlay the charmingly nonsensical song "The Twelve Days of Christmas." According to Fr. Hal Stockert of the Catholic Information Network, the song was a coded catechism, used by persecuted English Catholics to pass on the faith to their children. Here's what he said the various gifts in the song really mean:

My true love = Christ

1 partridge in a pear tree = the One God
2 turtle doves = the Old and New Testaments
3 French hens = Faith, Hope, and Charity
4 calling birds = the Four Gospels/Evangelists
5 golden rings = the first five books of the Old Testament, the "Pentateuch"
6 geese a-laying = the six days of Creation
7 swans a-swimming = the seven sacraments
8 maids a-milking = the eight Beatitudes
9 ladies dancing = the nine fruits of the spirit
10 lords a-leaping = the Ten Commandments
11 pipers piping = the eleven faithful apostles
12 drummers drumming = the twelve doctrines in the Apostle's Creed

The author didn't provide his source for this information, and a number of critics have raised objections—for instance, the fact that Anglicans, too, believe in each of the things enumerated above (except for seven sacraments; they've slimmed down to three). A more obvious point: Would using such a song really help kids remember all those complex, sometimes abstruse theological points?

In the scientific spirit, we propose an experiment. Try out this handy mnemonic device on your or a neighbor's child. Better yet, try it on a group of several children of both sexes and various ages and temperaments. Remember what nuns and brothers always considered the secret to successful, lifetime rote learning: corporal punishment. Administer it liberally. It's Christmastime: brook no laxity.

Ruler in hand, teach the children the song and then "decode" it for them, carefully explaining the beatitudes, the points of doctrine in the Creed, the fruits of the spirit, and the notion of the Pentateuch. (That should take you a good six months of weekly CCD classes.) Once you're done, sing the song again and demand the kids recite back the symbolism encoded among the leaping lords, lactating cows, and menstruating geese. Remind them how important all this is, and how many English Catholics died horribly for these points of doctrine. (Go into detail. See October 25: The British Martyrs.) When they start to cry, your work is done.

December 25

The Nativity: Christmas on the West Bank

There's nothing more delightful than going to the home of a friend or family member who has really pulled out all the stops to provide an old-fashioned Christmas feast. Roast turkey or (better) goose with fresh cranberry sauce, roasted potatoes, festive veggies, and plum pudding—all presented on the very best china, with the scent of spiced candles, real pine boughs, and a roaring fire. All these Victorian English trappings have come to define Christmas celebrations for us, and we wouldn't have it any other way—so long as someone else is hosting.

Because, face it folks, providing all of the above is a heck of a lot of work. What's more, if you do it right, chances are you'll get stuck hosting Christmas every year—filling your home with long-lost family members, unmarried high school friends with hungry eyes, bawling children, and sticky pets. Do you really want that kind of "perfect storm" to engulf your overcrowded apartment every December until you finally succumb to Alzheimer's? (They might keep showing up even then, but at least you won't mind.)

CELEBRATE: We'd like to suggest a better way. If family members have been broadly hinting that it's "someone else's turn" to host the holiday, we suggest you leap to your feet this year and volunteer. That'll get you points for being proactive.

But when your guests arrive on Christmas Eve or Day, they're in for a big surprise. You'll be serving no turkey, no ham, no stuffing, and no eggnog. There won't be a trace of pine, poinsettia, holly, or mistletoe. And no Christmas carols either.

Because, as you will inform them upon arrival, you'll have decided to host an "authentic Middle Eastern Christmas," just like they have over in Bethlehem. That means you'll serve completely unfamiliar Arab and Israeli dishes, play Lebanese, Syrian, and Chaldean liturgical music (order some from *www.keyrouz.com*; they're exquisite but alien to Western ears), along with the funky Israeli singer Ofra Haza. Neglect all "holiday" programming in favor of documentaries on the sufferings of Christians in the Holy Land. Put up potted palms around the house, and somberly explain that "this is the real Christmas." Bone up on the impoverished lives of Christians stuck between two sides on the West Bank, and take up a collection to benefit them. Send what you can to the Franciscan Foundation for the Holy Land, 1400 Quincy St., N.E., Washington, DC 20017.

Remind any children who get all stoked about their gifts that "Jesus never had a GameBoy—all he got was some myrrh." We guarantee you that you'll never have to host Christmas again.

Lebanese Ice Tea

Feta Cheese Cigarettes (see recipe)

Green Salad with Yogurt Dressing

Leg of Lamb with Roast Eggplant and Potatoes

Chicken with Apricots (see recipe)

White Beans with Saffron and Parsley

Basmati Rice with Dates and Almonds

Baklava

Feta Cheese Cigarettes

The sour piquancy of the sumac combined with the spice of feta filling, wake up the palate.

Sumac, Za'atar, and Ajvar (a Balkan pepper mixture) can be found at Middle Eastern markets.

15 sheets phyllo dough
1/4 cup melted butter
3 tablespoons sumac
2 tablespoons Za'atar spice mix

1/2 pound feta cheese
2 tablespoons extra virgin olive oil
2–3 tablespoons hot ajvar
Coarse sea salt to taste

Preheat oven to 375. Line 2 baking sheets with parchment.

In a small bowl combine feta, oil, and Ajvar. Season to taste.

Working on a clean, hard surface lightly brush work area with butter. Lay one sheet of phyllo down and brush lightly with butter. Sprinkle with sumac. Place another sheet of phyllo on top and brush lightly with butter. Sprinkle with sumac. Place a third sheet on top of that and brush with butter. Sprinkle with za'atar.

Using a small spatula, spread a thin layer of cheese evenly on phyllo.

Using a sharp knife cut into thirds lengthwise and crosswise. You will have 9 pieces.

Roll each strip into tight cigarettes. Place on a parchment-covered baking sheet. Sprinkle with coarse sea salt.

Repeat process until all phyllo sheets are used.

Chill until firm. May be frozen and covered two days ahead.

Bake 9–11 minutes until golden brown.

Makes 45 pieces

Chicken with Apricots

This simple and shockingly good dish is inspired by Persian Chicken Polo from Claudia Roden's classic *A Book of Middle Eastern Food.*

3 tablespoons butter
1 onion, finely chopped
1 large chicken, cut into serving
   pieces
Salt and freshly ground pepper

2 tablespoons raisins
1 cup dried Turkish apricots,
   chopped
3 cinnamon sticks
1 teaspoon ground cinnamon

Heat butter in large heavy-bottomed saucepan. Add onions and sauté until golden. Season chicken on all sides and add piece by piece to pot in order to maintain constant heat. Brown on all sides. Add fruit and turn in fat for 2–3 minutes. Add cinnamon. Stir and cook 1 minute. Pour in water to cover; bring to a boil and reduce heat. Simmer gently, covered, stirring occasionally. Chicken will be falling-off-the-bone tender and sauce thick and rich.

Makes 6 servings

....

December 31

The Circumcision of Christ (Vigil): No Skin Off His Nose

On the old Church calendar, New Year's Day was the Feast of the Circumcision. This ancient feast was tucked neatly out of sight along with St. Christopher at Vatican II, but what do we care? It has centuries of tradition behind it, has inspired famous poems (we're not kidding; see the Milton lyric below), and provides a delightful theme for your New Year's Eve or Day celebration.

Since it falls on the eighth day after Christmas, this feast marks the day when Jesus's parents, like all devout Jews, took Him to be circumcised and receive His name. Ingenious Christian theologians noted that this was the first blood Christ shed on earth—foreshadowing all that would be spilled on the cross. This symbolic importance led Church authorities to mark January 1 as a Holy Day of Obligation—which it still is. That's right, you have to go to Mass on New Year's Day—

although now it's in honor of "the Solemnity of the Virgin Mary, Mother of God," whatever that means.

We prefer the older feast, whose point was more sharply drawn and imagery quite vivid, especially for those of us who've ever attended a genuine bris. (Bet you didn't know how *loud* a baby could cry.)

CELEBRATE: Since circumcision is the distinctive, sacred mark that Yahweh asked His people to adopt to set them apart from Gentiles, the day when this happened to Jesus is certainly worth making a big deal about. To mark this distinctly Jewish, masculine, sanguinary feast, start with a few easy, thematic touches:

- Stress the connection of this feast to the Hebrew Bible by doing up the kitchen with Jewish-themed paper plates, napkins, and favors (available from *www.mazaltovpages.com*).
- Reiterate the idea of redemptive blood shed for our sins by adding bright red streamers and napkins to the mix. For drinks, serve mimosas and champagne, and the Bloody Bris—a Bloody Mary, served with a steak knife instead of a spoon. For entrees, nothing will do but a sausage platter.
- When it comes to suitable music, the genre of circumcision songs is unfortunately a small and specialized one, so you won't find many CDs ready-made to suit this occasion. (However, the Catholic University of Leuven, Belgium, does offer a printed guide *Circumcision Songs of the Kikuyu*, available from *www.kuleuven.ac.be/upers/ics.htm*). Otherwise, just pick up something with klezmers.
- Show people what Jesus really went through by popping in *The Circumcision Video* ($49.95 from amazon.com). a detailed video portrait of the various methods used in this procedure. Start it up when you bring out the sausages; it will guarantee more leftovers for you to enjoy in days to come.

Upon the Circumcision John Milton (1634)

Ye flaming Powers, and wingèd Warriors bright,
That erst with music, and triumphant song,
First heard by happy watchful Shepherds' ear,
So sweetly sung your joy the clouds along,
Through the soft silence of the listening night,—
Now mourn; and if sad share with us to bear
Your fiery essence can distill no tear,
Burn in your sighs, and borrow
Seas wept from our deep sorrow,
He who with all Heaven's heraldry whilere
Entered the world, now bleeds to give us ease.
Alas! how soon our sin
Sore doth begin
His infancy to seize!
O more exceeding Love, or Law more just?
Just Law indeed, but more exceeding Love!
For we, by rightful doom remediless,
Were lost in death, till He, that dwelt above
High-throned in secret bliss, for us frail dust
Emptied his glory, even to nakedness;
And that great Covenant which we still transgress
Intirely satisfied,
And the full wrath beside
Of vengeful Justice bore for our excess,
And seals obedience first with wounding smart
This day; but oh! ere long,
Huge pangs and strong
Will pierce more near his heart.

About the Authors

John Zmirak's work has appeared in *USA Today, Investor's Business Daily, Commonweal, The Weekly Standard, The New Republic, The Atlantic, The American Conservative,* and *First Things*. He has served as senior editor at *Faith & Family* magazine and as a reporter at *The National Catholic Register*. He is currently a contributing editor at Godspy.com and editor of the annual guide *Choosing the Right College*. He used early drafts of this book as a litmus test, sending it to potential romantic matches on Catholic dating Web sites to expose them to his personality. He is still single.

Denise Matychowiak has worked as a cook and pastry chef at Louis XVI Restaurant in New Orleans and La Caravelle in New York City, and served as food editor at *Faith & Family* magazine. She now works as a private chef in Manhattan. But if the right man came along. . . .

Of Related Interest

Lorenzo Albacete
GOD AT THE RITZ
Attraction to Infinity

A Priest-Physicist Talks About Science, Sex, Politics and Religion

"*God at the Ritz* deals with the most awesome experiences of life. These experiences propel the human search for truth, beauty, justice, solidarity, and personal development. They confront us with the great Mystery that always lies beyond." — *From the Introduction*

"Lorenzo Albacete is one of a kind, and so is *God at the Ritz.* The book, like the monsignor, crackles with humor, warmth, and intellectual excitement. Reading it is like having a stay-up-all-night, jump-out-of-your-chair, have-another-double-espresso marathon conversation with one of the world's most swashbuckling talkers. Conversation, heck — this is a papal bull session!"
— Hendrik Hertzberg, *The New Yorker Magazine*

"Monsignor Albacete has a keen insight into the mystery of God and a wonderful sense of humor even when he is speaking about very heady subjects. Perhaps it is precisely this sense of humor — and wonder — that bring people of all faiths to Msgr. Albacete's writings to find there a source of goodness and strength."
— Theodore Cardinal McCarrick of Washington, D.C.

"Father Albacete, whose organization addresses what he calls 'not the need to believe but the need to begin to consider believing in a skeptical age,' likes to leaven his theology with flashes of humor. His book *God at the Ritz* looks at the spiritual struggles of postmodern people."
— Winifred Gallagher, *O Magazine*

0-8245-1951-5, $19.95 hardcover

crossroad

Of Related Interest

H. J. Fischer, Veteran Vatican Journalist
POPE BENEDICT XVI
A Personal Portrait

The All-New, Definitive Biography of
POPE BENEDICT XVI

Inspired by the author's thirty-year personal and professional
relationship with Joseph Ratzinger.

Dr. Fischer is the ideal biographer of the new Pope. As a theologically trained journalist, a friend of Joseph Ratzinger, and a twenty-five-year Vatican correspondent for Germany's leading daily newspaper, Dr. Fischer has observed and accompanied the professor and cardinal for three decades. He understands the life and work of this gifted church leader as well as the challenges and questions that confront Benedict XVI in his new role.

Includes more than sixty color and black-and-white photos.

ISBN 0-8245-2372-5, $19.95 hardcover

Please support your local bookstore,
or call 1-800-707-0670 for Customer Service.

For a free catalog, write us at

THE CROSSROAD PUBLISHING COMPANY
16 Penn Plaza, 481 Eighth Avenue
New York, NY 10001

Visit our website at
www.crossroadpublishing.com
All prices subject to change.

crossroad